Art and Socie[ty]
Three
WORSHIP

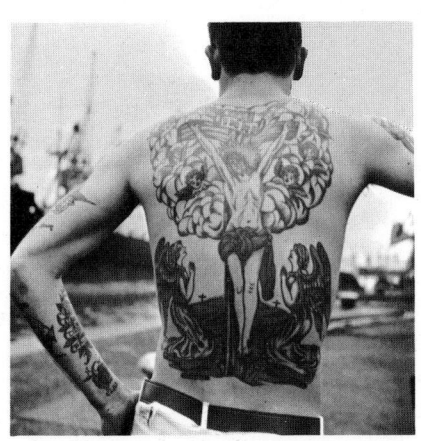

Ken and Kate Baynes

Welsh Arts Council/Lund Humphries

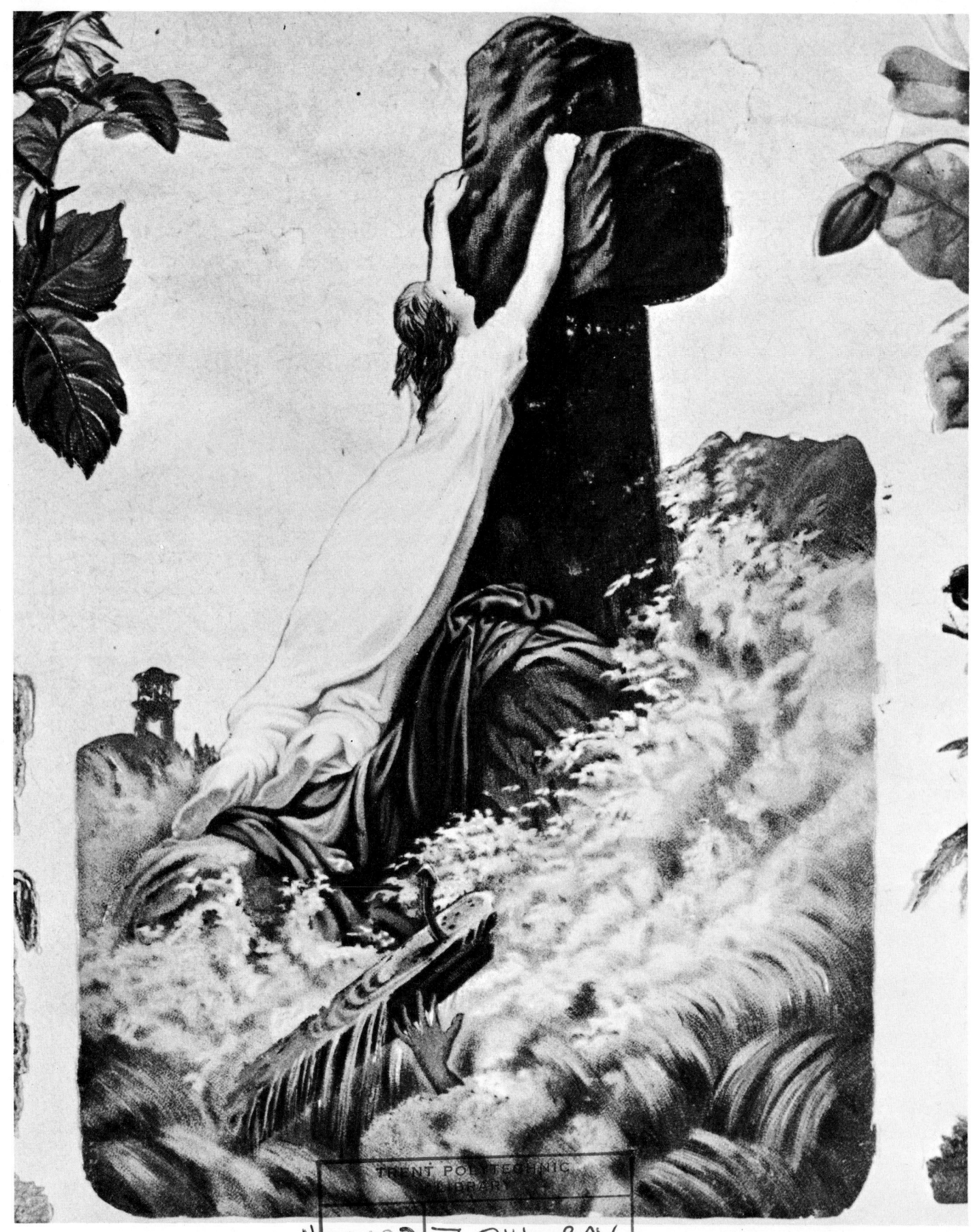

Cover and title page:
Tattoo:
CRUCIFIED CHRIST
by Les Skews
1966
Photographed by John Deakin
(John Deakin)

1 Scrapbook page:
FIGURE, SURROUNDED BY
STORMY SEAS, CLINGING TO
A ROCK IN THE SHAPE OF A
CROSS
(Museum of Childhood,
Edinburgh)

2 Embroidered text:
THE BIBLE: GOD'S GIFT TO MAN
Wales, nineteenth century
(John H Thomas)

3 overleaf
Photograph:
MUSLIMS AT PRAYER IN A
MOSQUE IN NAIROBI
Photographed by Günter R. Reitz
(Barnaby's Picture Library)

We are grateful to the Welsh Arts Council and to Lund Humphries for their continued enthusiasm for the Art and Society series. Peter Jones, John Taylor, and Charlotte Burri have all helped tremendously in developing the ideas which are presented here. In Cardiff, Mrs Joy Goodfellow gathered the material together and, in London, Steve Storr, Mrs Anne Porter, and Mrs Margaret Tully have all made valuable contributions to the day-to-day running of the project.

As always we owe a considerable debt to those who have allowed us to reproduce rare and important material from their collections. It would be invidious to single them out, but anyone looking at the captions (where each lender is credited) will see that we have been particularly helped by the Pitt Rivers Museum in Oxford, the Anthropological Museum in Aberdeen and the Mansell Collection in London. We are grateful to them all.

Ken and Kate Baynes
Battersea 1971

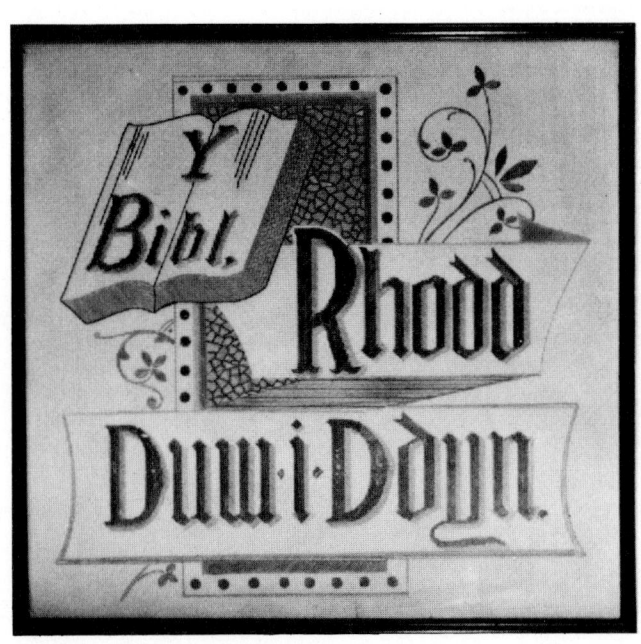

Copyright © 1971 Arts Council of Great Britain

First edition 1971

Published by Lund Humphries Publishers Ltd
12 Bedford Square London WC1

SBN 85331 307 5

Book designed by Steve Storr/Ken and Kate Baynes

Made and printed in Great Britain by
Lund Humphries, Bradford and London

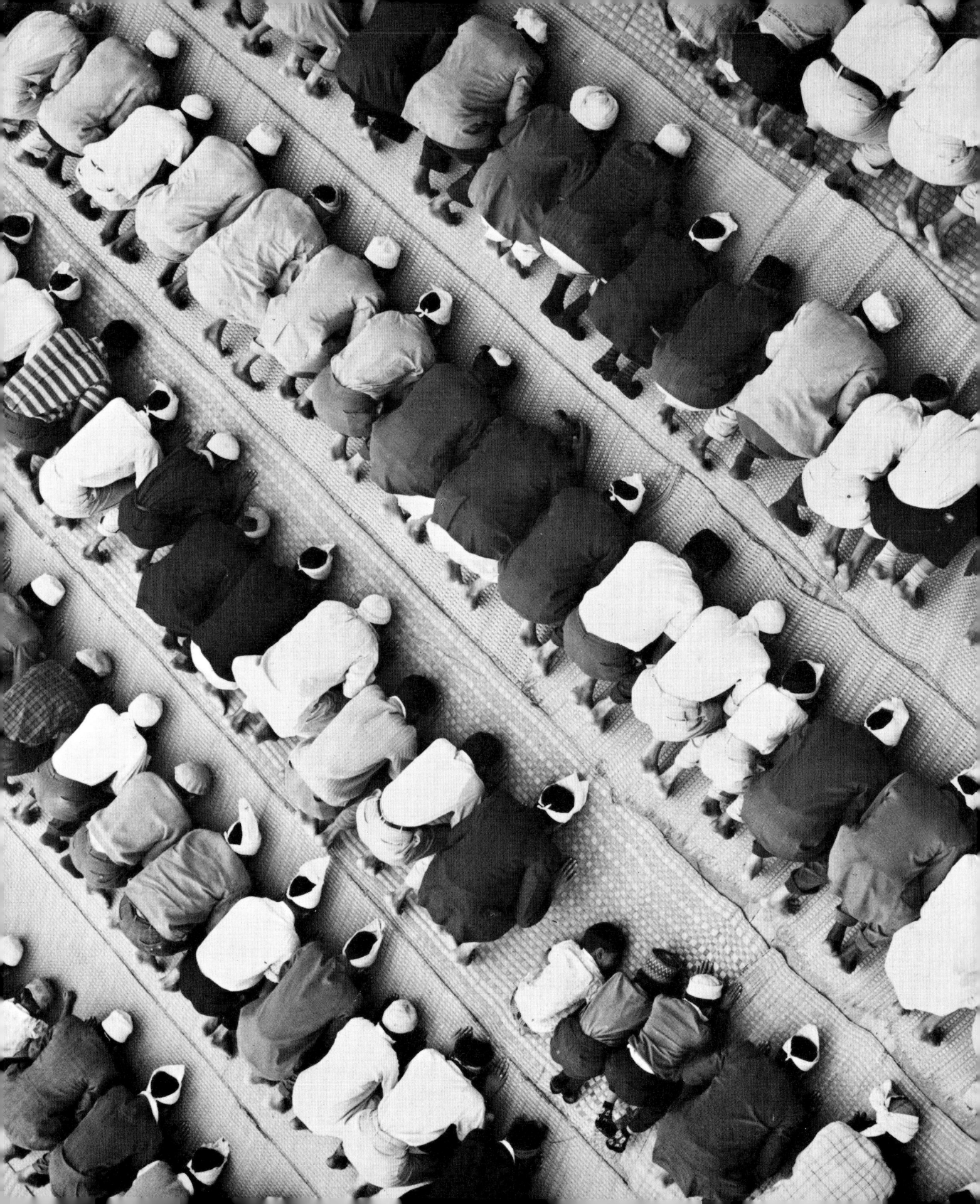

The Art and Society series is based on a very straightforward idea: that the majority of people will find art easier to understand if they have a greater insight into the relationship between art and life. It started as one of a number of projects in which the Welsh Arts Council set out to make art more accessible, either physically or intellectually. The particular form was proposed by Gordon Redfern in 1968 when he suggested a number of exhibitions 'concerned with the things in which people have intense and well-known interest – War, Work, Worship, Sex – and combining numerous art forms'.

In the event, the formula proved to contain ingredients that went far beyond a recipe for effective popularization though, as the success of each exhibition showed, it was that too. Working together, Ken Baynes, the organizer, and Peter Jones, assistant director of the Council, interpreted 'numerous art forms' so broadly as to challenge traditional categories. This approach came from the idea that the old categories were obsolete in an industrial society based on mass communications, and also from the conviction that the sources of culture had changed dramatically in the destruction of aristocratic values since the industrial revolution. The effect was to place seaside postcards next door to oil paintings; graphic design next to sculpture; film stills next to stained glass. If there was irreverence in this attitude, there was also a strong element of celebration, and a positive desire to look again at the cultural achievements of the past in a way that would focus on the experience offered by society to ordinary people.

Bertolt Brecht[1] wrote:

> Who built Thebes of the seven gates?
> The history books give the names of kings.
> Did kings carry the lumps of rock?

There was evident in the approach of the organizers a rather similar scepticism, about both the actual circumstances in which great art was created and about its cultural role. The questioning came first from the simple coming together of objects normally kept apart, and second from the need to construct a new framework which would allow them to be seen and discussed in a coherent way.

The themes of the exhibitions provide a classification by 'use' which is extended more systematically in the present book. It was not perhaps realized, at the start, just how radical this basis of classification could be. For example, the first book, WAR, preserved a discussion of visual styles as the key to organizing its material. What is evident now is that, in the long term, the attempt to understand art as a social activity will have to involve a great variety of analyses at many different levels. In that sense the present series is a pioneering one, attempting to map out areas for further investigation and to suggest possible methods.

All the same, the aim is to achieve a degree of completeness: to provide an effective introduction to the social function of art. The intention is to show how art reflects, interprets and supports man's concept of himself and the significance of his role in the world. In short, to show that art is an integral part of the mechanism of social existence, as well as being concerned with personal expression and aesthetic exploration. Or rather, to show that these aspects are, and always have been, totally interdependent.

[1]From *Questions of a Reading Worker*. Quoted here from **FISCHER, ERNST.** The Necessity of art: a Marxist approach. Harmondsworth, Penguin Books, 1963.

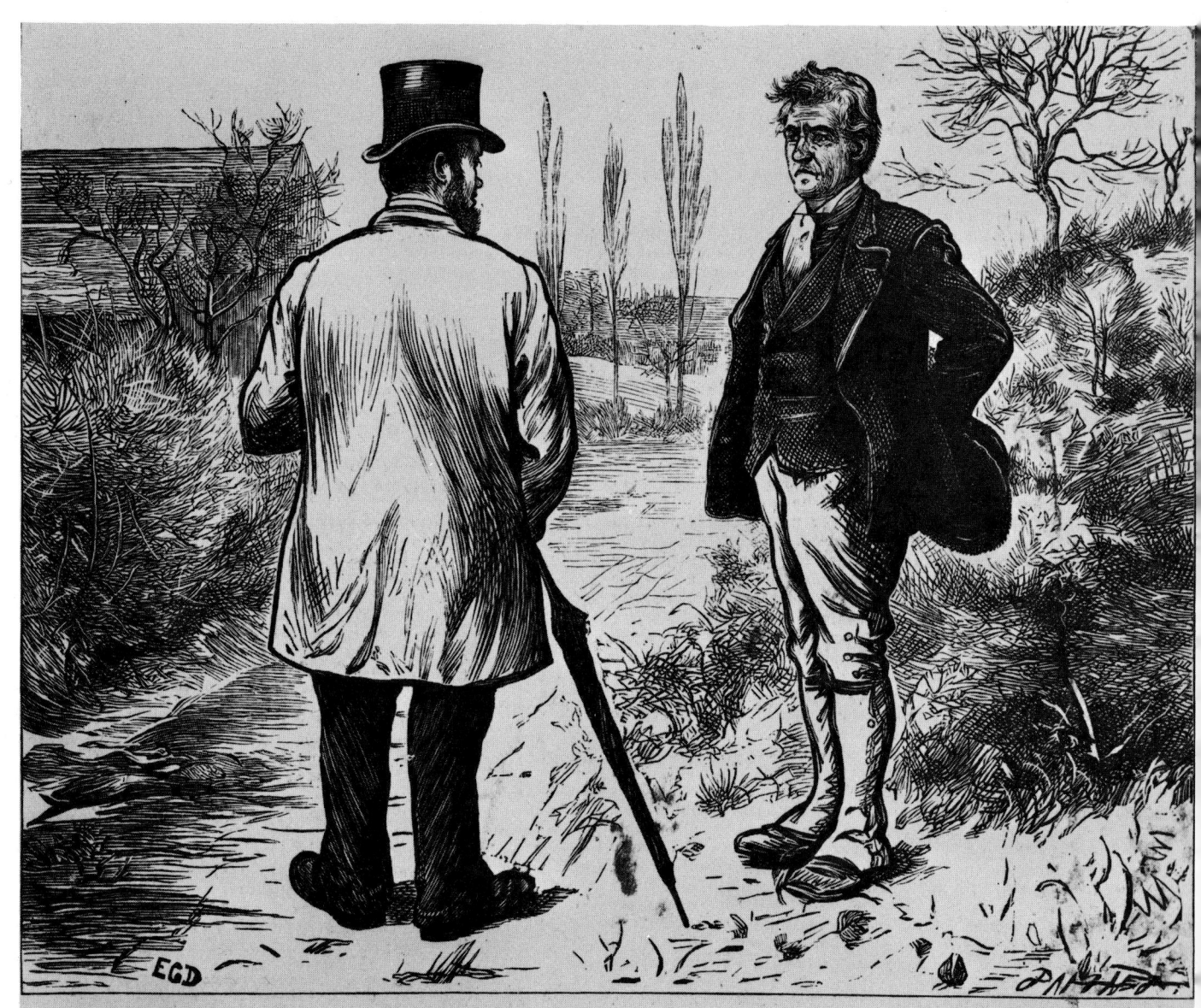

A COMPLIMENT?

Rector :—"WELL, THOMAS, AND WHAT DID YOU THINK OF THE BISHOP'S SERMON LAST SUNDAY ?"

Tummas :—"SORR, OI DIDN'T LOIKE IT A BIT; IT WAS BY FUR TOO PLAIN AND SIMPLE TO SUIT ME; OI LOIKES A SERMONT WHUT JOOMBLES THE JOODGEMENT, AND CONFOOZLES THE SENSES, AND OI NEVER COME ACROST ONE TO COME UP TO YERSELF FOR PREACHIN' THEY !'"

Art and Worship

The theme of this study is the relationship between art and religion, and the way in which that relationship operates in the setting of human society. No book of this size could possibly hope to do more than sketch in the enormous and fundamental richness of such a topic, and to suggest some particular methods of analysis that may yield useful insights. That is what we are setting out to do in this introductory essay, and in the three pictorial sections which follow it.

Religion provides one of the most challenging areas for art criticism. Not only did art and religion exist together in some form right from the very beginnings of organized communities, but they were also inextricably mixed so that it is sometimes impossible to tell them apart. At the start, they operated in a world which did not display the highly differentiated categories of our own society. Art, religion, politics and agriculture were all submerged – and latent – in a basically magical interpretation of the universe. The social function of art and the social function of religion were bound together in the charismatic power of image-making, dance and ritual.

At times one is tempted to think that art made religion possible. At others, that it was the opposite way round. It would be more accurate to say that they began together before any question of this kind had meaning. Such a complex interweaving makes it particularly rewarding to try to tease out the varying threads of art's social function. It also challenges the validity of much conventional thinking about art's role in the world, particularly where such thinking presents art as a category separate from the ordinary business of living. In fact, art is at the core of thought, action and feeling and this is nowhere more obvious than in relation to the act of worshipping.

In making all this more comprehensible, the first element we have to consider is the nature of art itself. Why and how does it exert any power at all?

It is important at the outset to recognize that art has its own terms of reference. It is not a mirror reflecting life. It is radically different in function, form and content from the world of sensations, though it becomes a part of that world. Art is not mainly a description of reality, but a parallel reality of its own, existing in a subtle symbiosis with experiences and activities of other kinds.

This quality of 'separateness' which art has can be described in philosophical terms, and the conditions affecting its existence can be outlined. But this is dry as dust and can make it hard rather than easy to understand why art should be so fascinating, or why it has found such a universal relevance in the affairs of men. The trouble is that the vitality of art's actuality vanishes when it is translated into theory. Even the greatest art criticism suffers from this disability. Any explanation must leave untouched the central core of art because it already exists in a form that cannot be recreated in another medium, and cannot be adequately described.

In one of his BBC Listening and Writing programmes,[2] the poet Ted Hughes tried to explain his perception of this separateness, as it occurs in a poem, by linking it with memories of his childhood activity of hunting animals:

> In a way, I suppose, I think of poems as a sort of animal. They have their own life, like animals, by which I mean that they seem quite separate from any person, even from their author, and nothing can be added to them or taken away without maiming and perhaps even killing them. And they have a certain wisdom. They know something special . . . something perhaps which we are very curious to learn. Maybe my concern has been to capture not animals particularly and not poems, but simply things which have a vivid life of their own, outside mine.

Art has a vivid life of its own: that is the condition of its existence. But this does not mean that art is unconcerned with, for example, truth or morality, transcendence or love. It is very much concerned with such things, just as it is with work or sex. Its separateness has nothing to do with its ostensible subject matter, but with the terms on which that subject matter can be organized, interpreted and understood. At the most fundamental level art accords with Alain Robbe-Grillet's statement that 'the function of art is never to illustrate a truth – or even

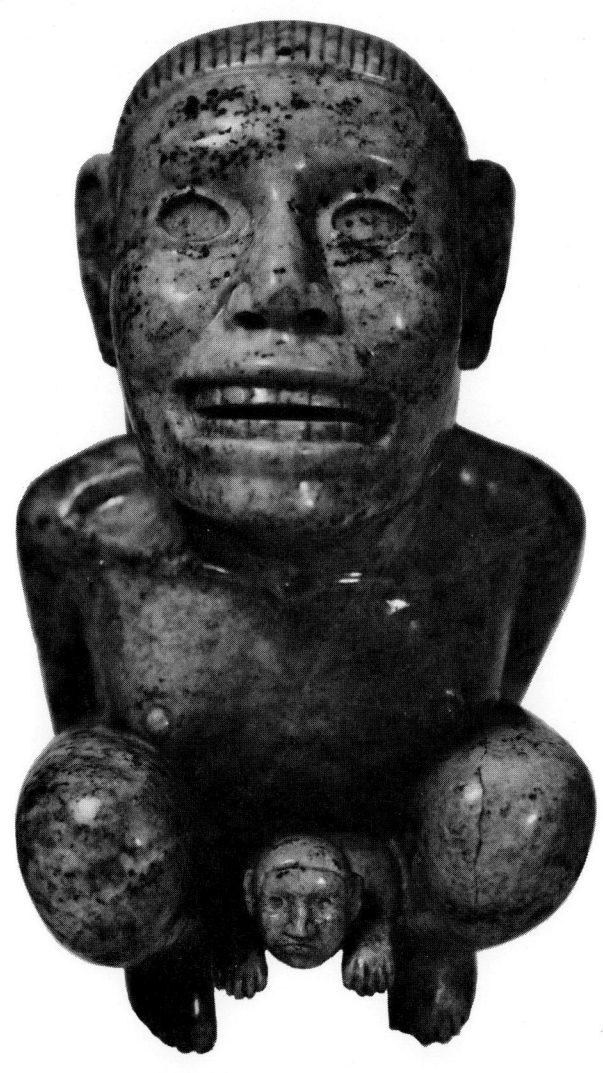

an interrogation – known in advance, but to bring into the world certain interrogations (and also perhaps in time certain answers) not yet known as such to themselves'.

In short, art is not so much a reorganization of reality, or a selection from it, as the creation of a new piece of reality. Herbert Read[3] writes that:

> art ... is an autonomous activity, influenced like all our activities by the material conditions of existence, but as a mode of knowledge at once its own reality and its own end. It has necessary relations with politics, with religion, and with all other modes reacting to our human destiny. But as a mode of reaction it is distinct and contributes in its own right to the process of integration which we call civilization or a culture.

However, the separateness of art, which we have been emphasizing and which it is important to understand, literally has no meaning without a social context. Here there are two vital aspects. The first is that all human perception, and not just art, is a creation. The second is that it is impossible to discuss individuals without reference to society or vice versa. The entanglement between people, art and society is complete.

'Art has a vivid life of its own: that is the condition of its existence. But this does not mean that art is unconcerned with, for example, truth or morality, transcendence or love. It is very much concerned with such things, just as it is with work or sex.'

5 Sculpture:
THE GODDESS [OF CHILD-BIRTH] TLAZOLTÉOTL
Aztec, Mexico
(Dumbarton Oaks Collections, Washington D.C.)

[2]HUGHES, TED. Poetry in the making: an anthology of poems and programmes from listening and writing. London, Faber and Faber, 1967.

[3]READ, HERBERT. Art and Society. London, Faber and Faber. Revised edition, 1945.

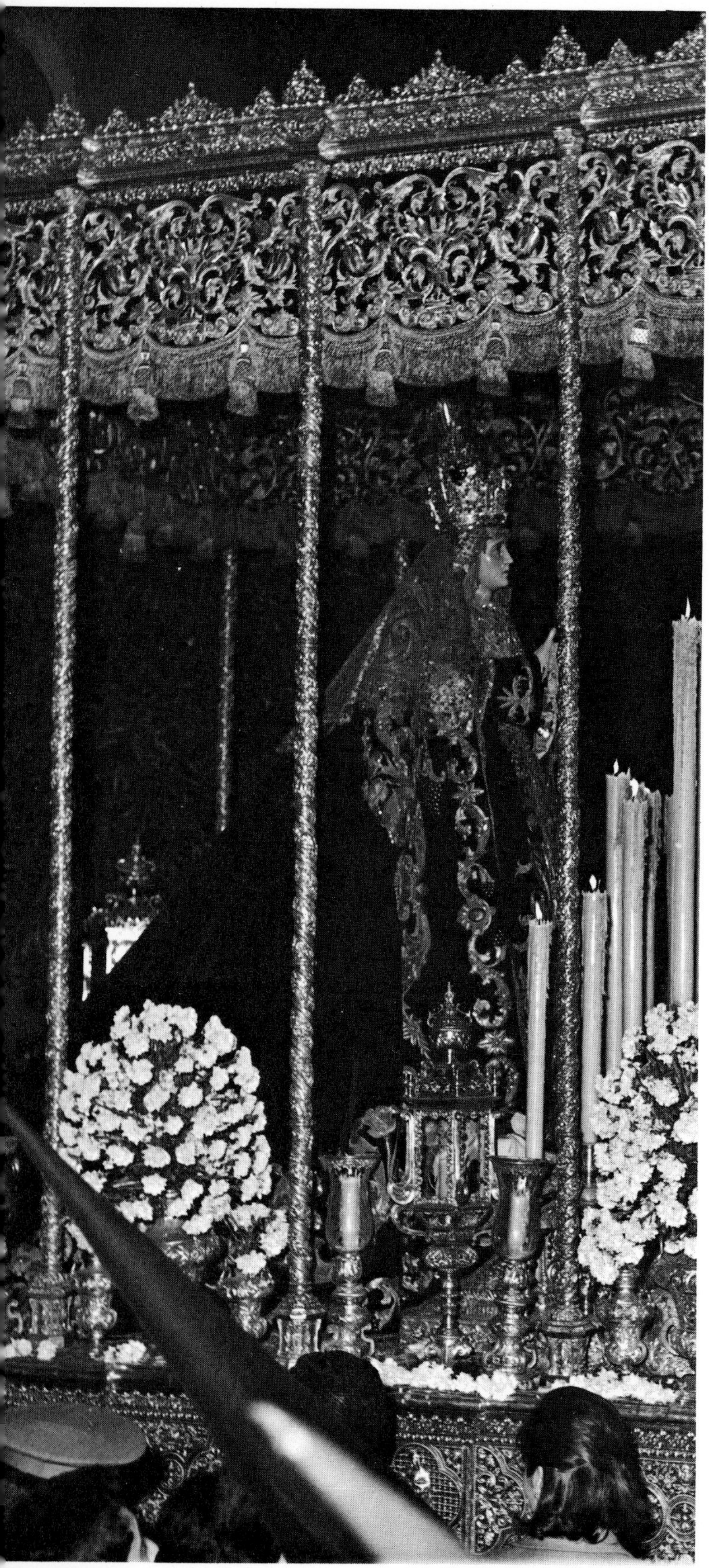

For example, Robbe-Grillet's reference to 'interrogations' being brought into the world is almost certainly meant to refer to what is generally thought of as innovative art. But his statement will effectively cover activities as diverse as the writing of a sermon or the dancing of an obscene dance, even if they are highly derivative or based on tradition, as is the case with the greater part of religious art. The sermon, however literal, exceeds by its particular form the truth it was originally intended to illustrate: the dance exceeds by its particular form the lust it was originally intended to arouse.

But it is possible to go much further than this: J Z Young[4] writes that:

> *in some sense we literally create the world we speak about . . . The point to grasp is that we cannot speak simply as if there is a world around us of which our senses give true information. In trying to speak about what the world is like we must remember all the time that what we see and what we say depends on what we have learned . . . . .*

The world of the individual is a world created by a process of learning. And the source of the learning is society to which, in his turn, the individual contributes. In her book Patterns of Culture,[5] Ruth Benedict puts the relationship like this:

> *Society in its full sense . . . is never an entity separable from the individuals who compose it. No individual can arrive at the threshold of his potentialities without a culture in which he participates. Conversely, no civilization has in it any element which in the last analysis is not the contribution of an individual.*

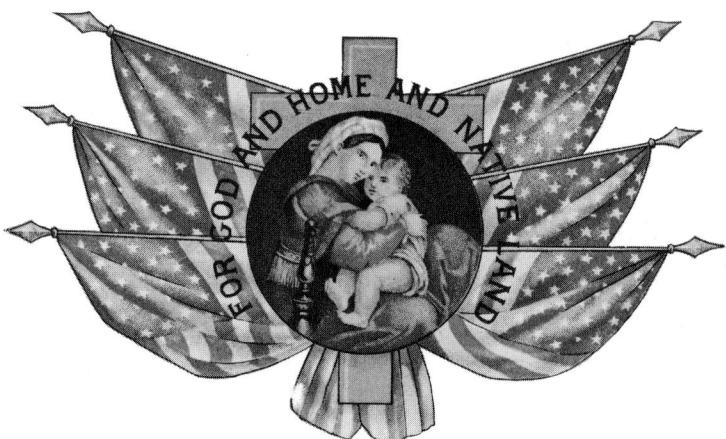

[4]**YOUNG, J Z.** Doubt and certainty in science: a biologist's reflections on the brain. Quoted here from WILLIAMS, RAYMOND. The long revolution. London, Chatto and Windus, 1961. Williams takes Young's discussion of how perception is learning as the cornerstone of the interpretation of creativity used in the present book.

[5]**BENEDICT, RUTH.** Patterns of culture. London, Routledge and Kegan Paul, 1935.

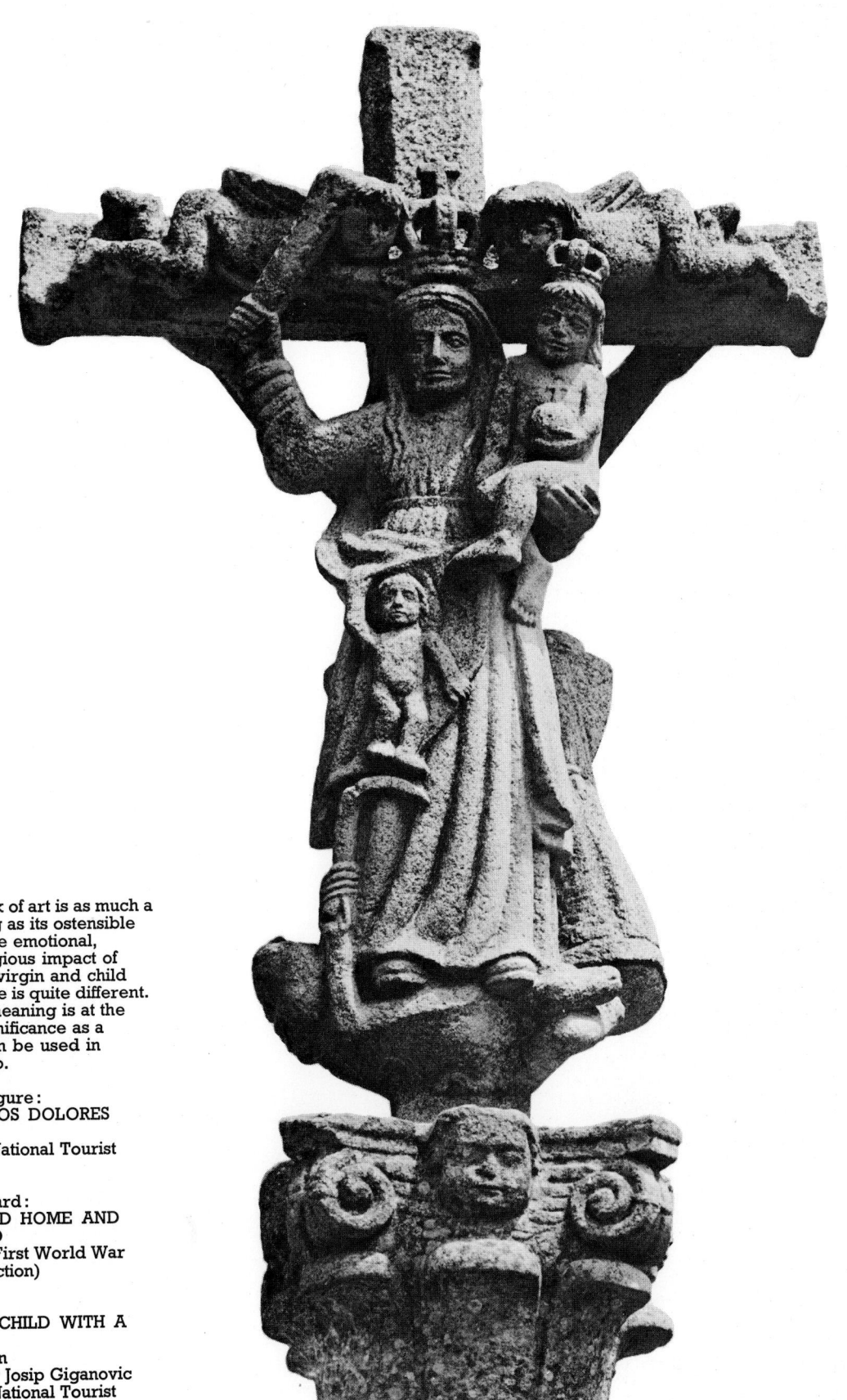

The form of a work of art is as much a part of its meaning as its ostensible subject matter. The emotional, aesthetic and religious impact of each of the three virgin and child images shown here is quite different. This variation of meaning is at the centre of art's significance as a 'language' that can be used in relation to worship.

6 Processional figure:
   VIRGEN DE LOS DOLORES
   Seville, Spain
   (The Spanish National Tourist
   Office)

7 Detail of postcard:
   FOR GOD AND HOME AND
   NATIVE LAND
   United States, First World War
   (Mansell Collection)

8 Sculpture:
   VIRGIN AND CHILD WITH A
   CROSS
   Sangenjo, Spain
   Photograph by Josip Giganovic
   (The Spanish National Tourist
   Office)

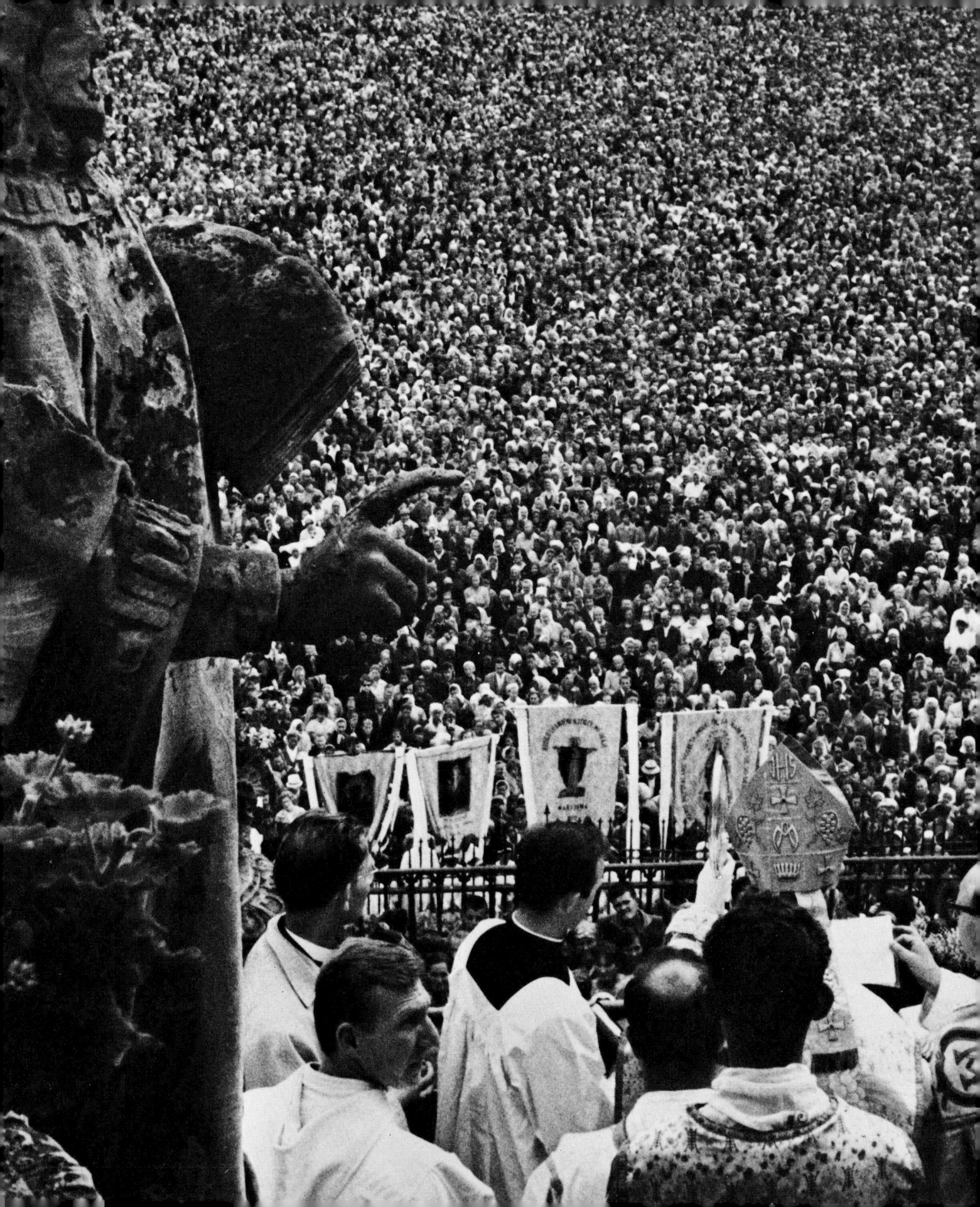

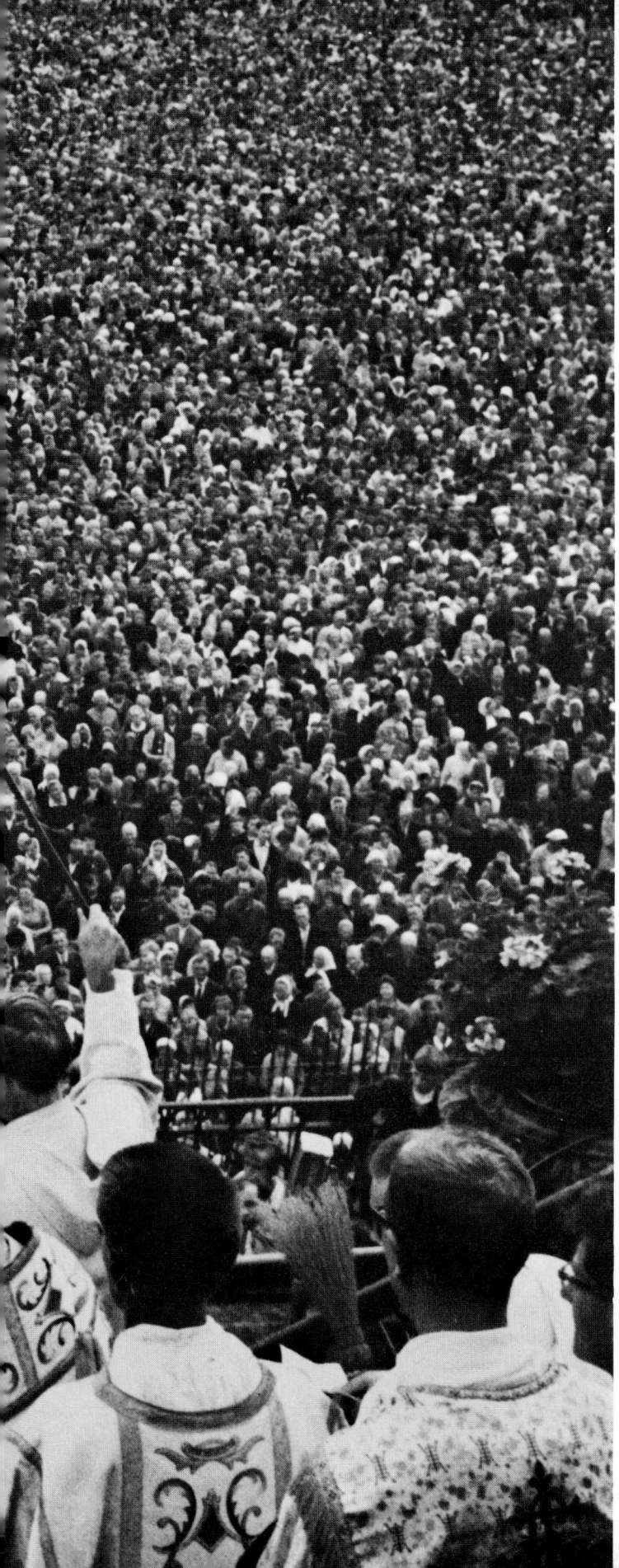

What we have to grasp is that the reality of art's involvement in life can only be truly seen through these three perspectives simultaneously: through its separate nature as a particular 'mode of knowledge'; through its significance as a process of creation or learning; and through its ability to create and to preserve social communications.

For art to be said to exist a 'work' must be produced. But, even although the work is the focus and can be studied and described as an artefact, its real significance is to be found in its making and in its use. In many important ways it is simply of a piece with all the other material things – cities, utensils, gardens – that men have made in an attempt to control the world and to understand it. They are all things exterior to man, but created by him, which symbolize, define and extend the meaning of his life.

What we have to penetrate, and try to grasp, is the nature of the relationships that can exist around an artefact that is a work of art. In order to do this we have to understand the limitations of the kind of artefact we are looking at, and the 'rules' of custom and definition that have allowed it to be made and through which we are ourselves viewing it. We have to appreciate that our own vision is very exactly the product of what we have seen in the course of our lives.

To understand and articulate this network of maker, observer and social context around any one artefact is hard. It is even harder to understand and articulate the human network while retaining a clear picture of the terms on which art exists at all – of the 'separateness' of art which is also the source of its power and magic. On the other hand, it is only in this way that it is possible to understand something of the circumstances of art's origin, its pervasive assimilation with religion and, later, with other quite different social forms. Art has not got a single function, but a rich variety of functions, each of which can be analysed in terms of: the 'rules' of art as expressed at a particular point of historical development; the creative or learning experience given

'What we have to grasp is that the reality of art's involvement in life can only be truly seen through these three perspectives simultaneously: through its separate nature as a particular "mode of knowledge"; through its significance as a process of creation or learning; and through its ability to create and to preserve social communications.'

9 Photograph:
   OPEN-AIR SERVICE IN POLAND
   by Elliott Erwitt
   (The John Hillelson Agency Ltd)

to individual makers and users; and the social purpose which is being articulated.

The second element we have to consider is the extreme difficulty of assigning priorities to these three perspectives and their related forms of analysis.

As an example, let us compare the way in which two important critics give alternative readings to the origins of art and religion. The critics are the Austrian Marxist Ernst Fischer and our own great educationist Herbert Read. Notice how their priorities drastically affect their interpretations. Both argue from their view of the present, and the needs of the present.

In The Necessity of Art, **Ernst Fischer** presents the history of art in terms of a journey from the time of primitive collectives, through the development of trade, industry, capitalism and the bourgeoisie, to a point where the definition of art lies in its awareness or unawareness of the class struggle. For him, religious art is simply an aspect of power: of man's attempt to control the material world through a belief in occult forces and, more subtly, to assure himself of the reality of the great collective of humanity.

In Art and Society, **Herbert Read** concentrates on the primacy of the individual and on the role of art in championing feeling as against reason. His interpretation is naturally related to his pioneering work in education. It represents a clear statement that art is an end after which society should strive. At base he argues from a conviction that the pursuit of art is the high point of civilization, and that the artist offers to the community individual insights that it desperately needs. He identifies art as having a philosophy of its own which can be described and contrasted with other aspects of a particular period. This is how he sets out the methodology of his book:

> Since it is necessary to treat the subject within a limited space, I shall confine myself to very broad types of society, and shall not attempt to trace the intricate counterplay of forces within such societies. Accepting the ideology of each period as 'ready-made', I shall try to ascertain the give and take between the ideology and the artist.

Herbert Read's emphasis is on the artist rather than the ideology. He says:

> The practice and appreciation of art is individual; art begins as a solitary activity, and only in so far as society recognizes and absorbs such units of experience does art become woven into the social fabric. The strands in the

'pattern of culture' represent the supernormal activity of a few individuals, however communal the pattern itself may be; and the value of the pattern will depend on the delicacy with which the relationship between the artist and society is adjusted.

Both Read and Fischer consider the significance of those early cave paintings that show vivid representations of animals. Here is what Fischer has to say:

> Clearly the decisive function of art was to exert power – power over nature, an enemy, a sexual partner, power over reality, power to strengthen the human collective. Art in the dawn of humanity had little to do with 'beauty' and nothing at all with aesthetic desire; it was a magic tool or weapon of the human collective in its struggle for survival.

> It would be very wrong to smile at the superstitions of early man or at his attempts to tame nature by imitation, identification, the power of images and language, witchcraft, collective rhythmic movement, and so on. Of course, because he had only just begun to observe the laws of nature, to discover causality, to construct a conscious world of social signs, words, concepts, and conventions, he arrived at innumerable false conclusions and, led astray by analogy, formed many fundamentally mistaken ideas (most of which are still preserved in one form or another in our language and philosophy). And yet, in creating art, he found for himself a real way of increasing his power and enriching his life. The frenzied tribal dances before a hunt really did increase the tribe's sense of power; war paint and war cries really did make the warrior more resolute and were apt to terrify the enemy. Cave paintings of animals really helped to build up the hunter's sense of security and superiority over his prey. Religious ceremonies with their strict conventions really helped to instill social experience in every member of a tribe and to make every individual part of the collective body.

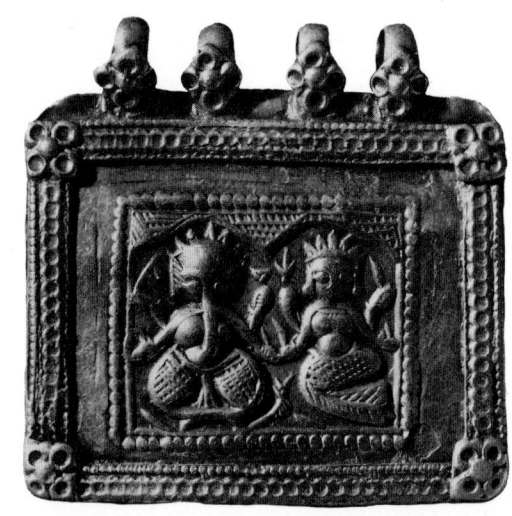

Herbert Read distinguishes between
the origins of art and the origins of
magic, though he recognizes a
powerful connexion between the
two. It is indeed hard to decide where
the formal values of a work end and
magical functions begin, and even
harder to know if such distinctions
would have had any meaning for the
original makers and users.

10–13 Sculpture:
AMULETS
(VIKRAM DALAL)

These Indian charms are intended to
bring the wearer good fortune and to
protect him against evil. However,
they are more than symbols. Haku
Shah, writing in **Graphis 127**, records
some comments by those who wear
them in India today. 'This is my
mother. You may call her Ambaji,
but I call her Chamunda. One day she
came to me in my dream and asked
me to keep her **thala** [amulet] on my
neck, and she assured me that every
job I do will be right, and there will be
no hindrance in my path.' 'These are
the footprints of the late wife of my
husband. Four years ago the former
wife of my husband died. If I don't
keep her footprints round my neck,
she may harass me.'

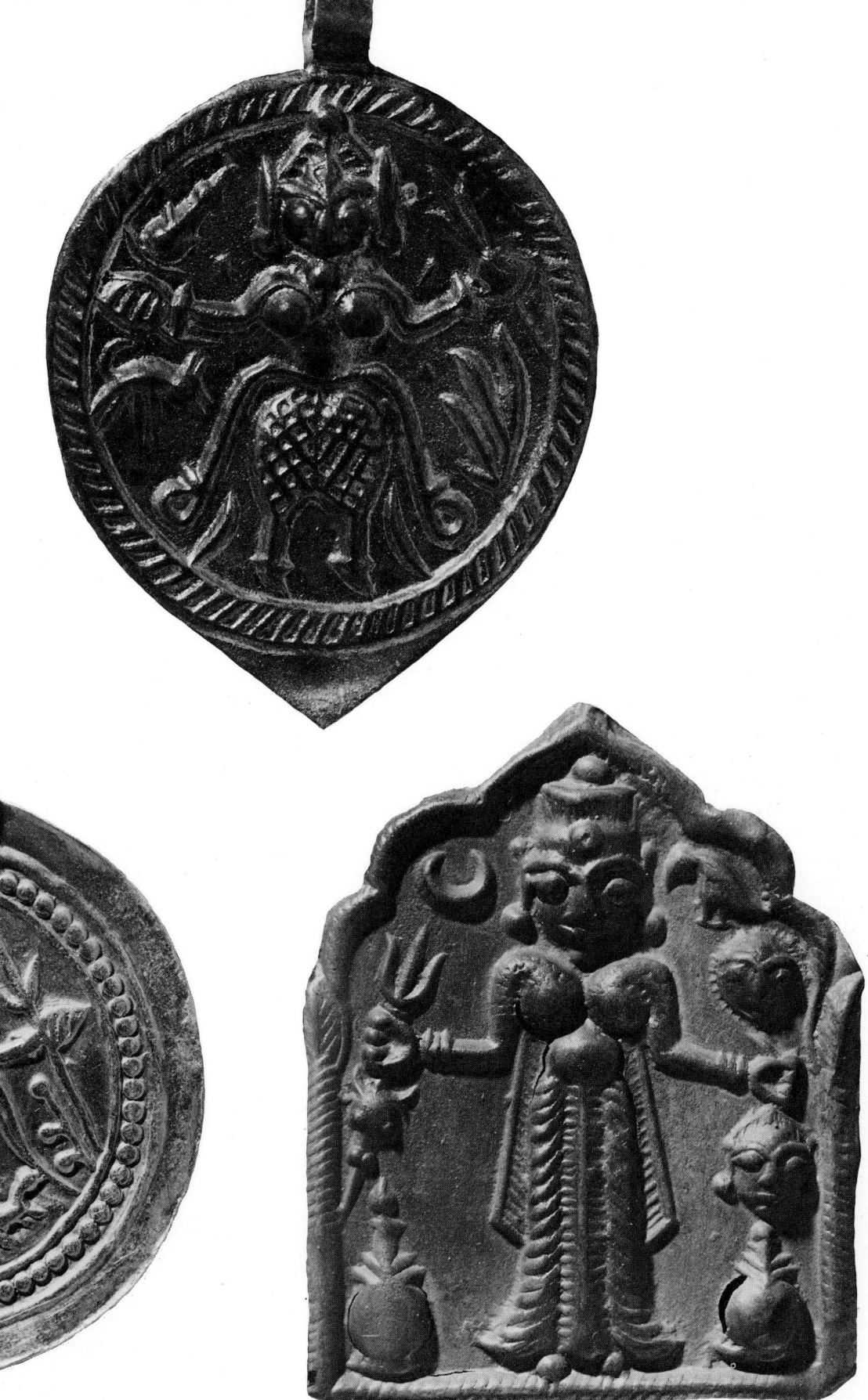

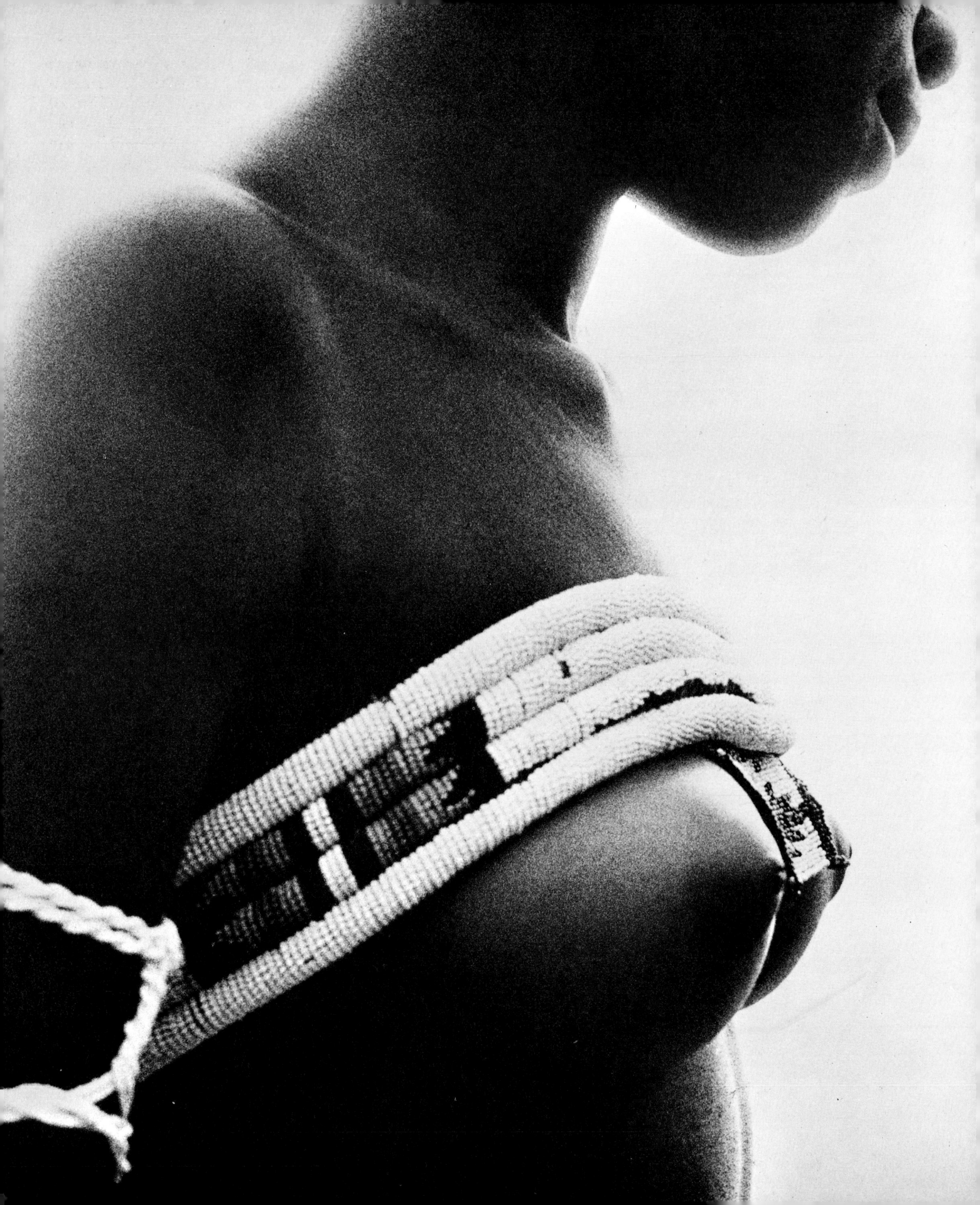

In this passage Fischer totally identifies the work of art that is the cave painting with its social and communicative functions. For him the sensibility and ability of the artist is clearly of less importance than his social role as a magician. This attitude unfolds logically into Fischer's contemporary interpretation which sees the artist as, above all, a political instrument.

Herbert Read's point of view is almost the opposite. Here is part of his discussion of the cave paintings:

> The paintings are, in fact, highly selective stylizations of the object – so vital that we cannot doubt that the man who painted them took a disinterested pleasure in the manner in which he did his job. An attempt has been made to explain this perfection as due entirely to the cave man's desire to make his representations magically effective – 'par le désir d'obtenir l'efficacité', as M. Schuwer expresses it. But when this critic used the word 'desire' I think he has given his case away. Primitive man has a desire to paint efficaciously. He has the desire to make one painting more effective than another. That is to say, he distinguishes between one painting and another, but surely not by the magical results obtained from it. It is quite fantastic to imagine that the stylistic mannerisms of the Altimara paintings were arrived at by a process of trial and error . . .

> Admitting the aesthetic nature of palaeolithic art, its interpretation . . . remains a vexed question. At the one extreme there are anthropologists who are unwilling to concede to man of the Old Stone Age any such degree of mental development as a system of magic would imply, and who therefore regard these cave-paintings as entirely aimless, the product of the enforced leisure of hunters. They explain the vividness and aesthetic value of all the drawings as due to the intense images which must have haunted the minds of primitive men, dependent for their lives on their animal prey. At the other extreme are anthropologists who read a magical significance into every stroke they can discover in the gloomy bowels of a cave. The position I take up is an intermediate one: the magical significance of some of the drawings is beyond question; but there is no reason to assume that every drawing had this kind of significance. Primitive man was already human, and must surely have enjoyed the creative activity he was endowed with, and pursued it for its own sake. In other words, the art existed independently of the magic; had its separate origin and only in the course of time came to be associated with magical practices . . .

In its turn, Read's attitude unfolds logically into his contemporary interpretation which places art and the artist at the centre of society, but on their own terms.

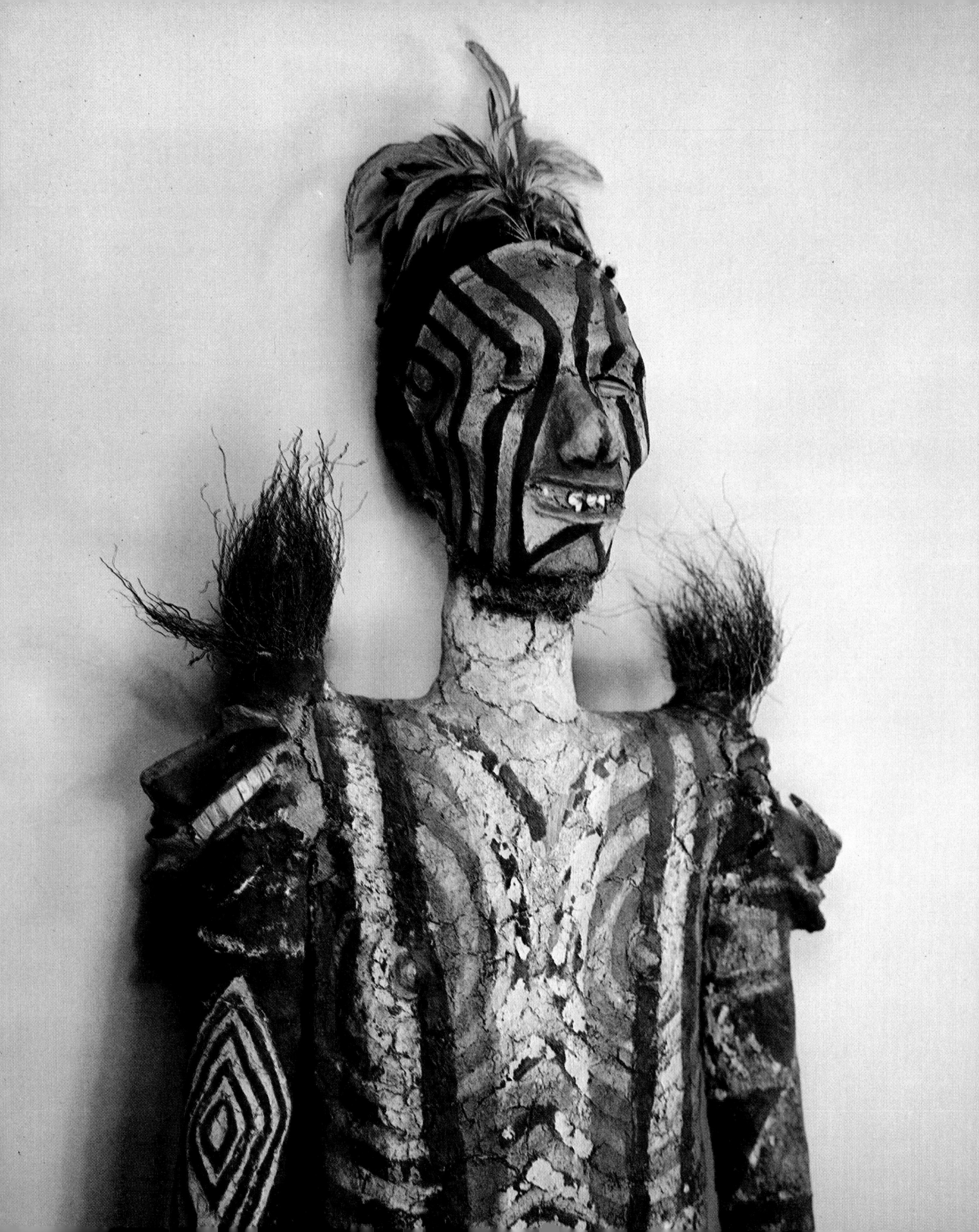

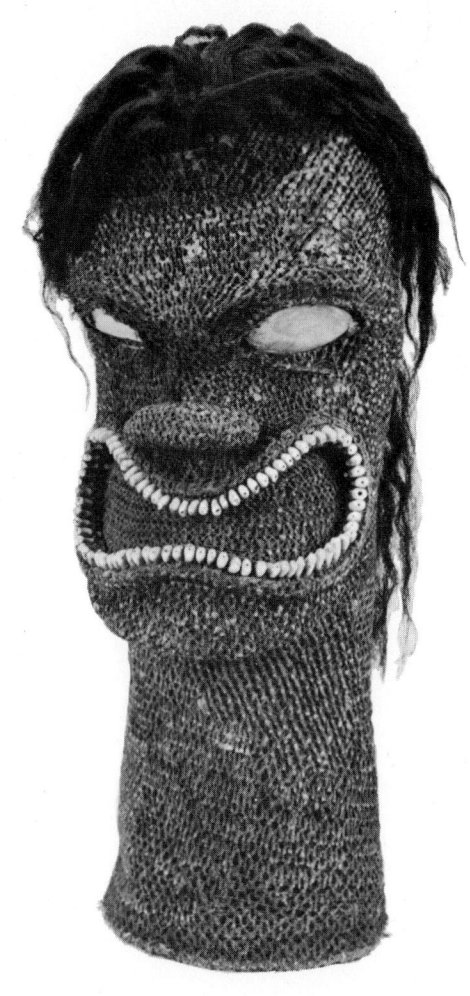

'The records of explorers are full of a disdainful, fascinated incomprehension of what they found . . . marvelling at the exotic crudity of what were actually figures of gods and goddesses, or high occult symbols intended to bring the dead and the living nearer together.'

15   Sculpture:
     AN EFFIGY OF A DEAD MAN
     from Malekula, New Hebrides
     (Pitt Rivers Museum, University
     of Oxford)

16   Sculpture:
     GOD IMAGE
     (Pitt Rivers Museum, University
     of Oxford)
Collected in the South Sea Islands by
Captain Lord Byron in 1825. It was
perhaps made specially to trade with
Europeans because the eyes are not
finished in the traditional manner.

We would be inclined to say, with Fischer, that art can well be described as a tool. Tools have limitations of their own, and produce recognizable characteristics in the resulting work. But art is a tool whose ends cannot be circumscribed qualitatively in Marxist terms. Its detailed application is constantly being redefined and altered to meet the changing needs of society. Art can be highly conservative, as it mostly is in relation to religion, or it can be directly revolutionary as in the case of some Communist art. Or it can be defiant and life-preserving as in the case of, for example, the steadfast continuation of day-to-day Jewish artistic, academic and cultural activities carried on by the doomed inhabitants of some European ghettos during the Second World War.

The point is that the priorities of the critic affect the interpretation: the meaning of a work of art changes as it ages and as society alters.

The records of explorers are full of a disdainful, fascinated incomprehension of what they found. Captain Cook's collector, Johann Reinhold Forster, uses the term 'curiosities' at the head of his inventory of items collected on the great voyage,[6] marvelling at the exotic crudity of what were actually figures of gods and goddesses, or high occult symbols intended to bring the dead and the living nearer together. Certainly, the scholars of the eighteenth and nineteenth centuries saw little aesthetic value in such pieces, and the sculptures had to wait over a hundred years before their imagery suddenly permeated modern painting like some kind of blood transfusion designed to frighten academism out of the veins of early twentieth-century Fine Art.

Yet this later concentration on aesthetic worth, rather than religious significance, was itself a distortion. It was projected onto the objects by the pioneers of modern painting who recognized in them qualities relevant to the twentieth century.

So far we have tried to suggest the significance of three perspectives in the understanding of art. These are a social perspective, a creative or learning perspective, and a perspective to do with the medium itself. We have also insisted that these are interdependent and that each is essential to any reasonable analysis. In addition, we have set out to show the inevitability of distortion in interpreting the work of the past when it is seen through the preoccupations of the present.

[6]PITT RIVERS MUSEUM. From the islands of the South Seas 1773–4. Oxford, Pitt Rivers Museum, 1970.

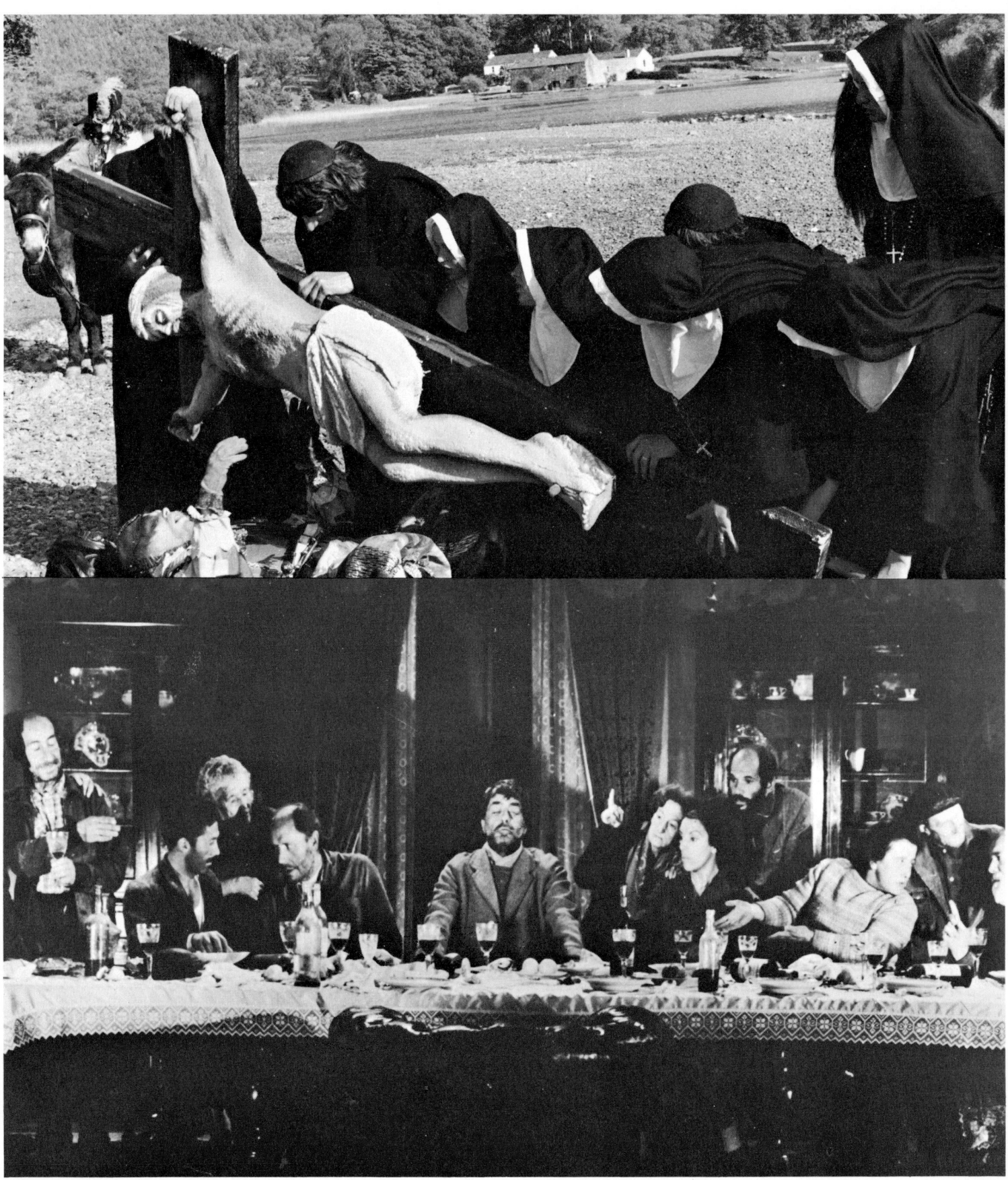

Renaissance imagery infuses our own culture, particularly where religion is concerned. The gestures, style, costumes and compositions of that period are immediately available as a source of reference and echo even in the mass media, or in works which are critical of traditional beliefs.

17 Television film still:
    from THE DANCE OF THE
    SEVEN VEILS
    directed by Ken Russell
    (BBC-TV)

18 Film still:
    from VIRIDIANA
    directed by Luis Buñuel, 1961
    (National Film Archive, Miracle
    Films)

The problem is indeed a severe one, particularly so in relation to the link between art and religion. The vast majority of religious art has been created to take its place in an existing system of shared understanding and belief. Step outside that system and something is lost from the work – a whole dimension of meaning – that was originally absolutely essential to it. Fail to step outside and the possibility of objective comparison between systems vanishes.

It is here that we can see our own highly differentiated culture, with its vivid awareness of historical time, as providing at once a tremendously rich breadth of vision and a terribly impoverished degree of involvement.

A particularly complex difficulty is provided by our identification of worth with innovation. A work intended to fit into an existing system of belief may well be original, but to emphasize and prize this element beyond others is to bring to bear critical machinery that is in a true sense irrelevant.

It is only since the Renaissance that the idea of the artist-as-innovator has been fully developed. The strands entwined in the concept are complex, involving first of all the possibility of change based on speculation, and then the notion of the artist as a Promethean hero set apart from the mundane society of ordinary men by the quality of his vision. It is a paradox that the Renaissance, which more than any other age depended on art for the articulation of its humanistic philosophy, should have been the starting point for separating Fine Art out into 'art for art's sake'. But the Renaissance was fired with Tasso's proposition 'there are two creators, God and the poet', and this contained the seeds which were to elevate art to the status of an independent religion, and its practitioners to the status of secular high priests. It also excluded by inference any work which did not aspire to such exalted ends.

Traditional criticism is not invalid, but it is most at home in approaching art produced in the context of those social and economic conditions which gave it birth. It is essentially relevant, coherent and articulate when discussing a situation in which individual artists are trying to innovate on the basis of a pre-existing body of work. It is from here that we derive the classic forms of criticism: close discussion of the minutiae of quality; categorization by groups, schools or styles; and an obsessive concern to identify and describe the 'finest' works of any one period.

But in what way is such a methodology relevant to 'folk' art or, for that matter, to the great religious

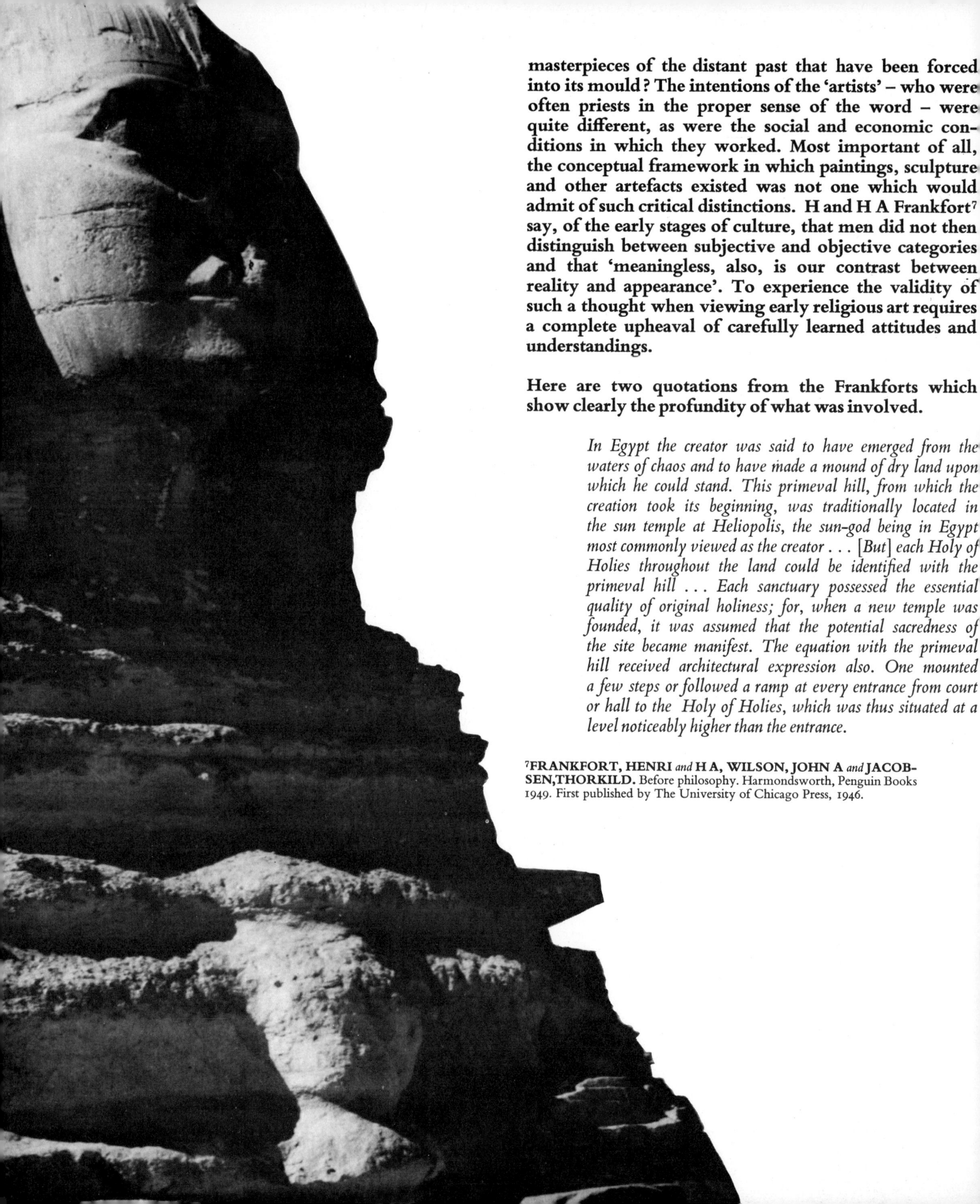

masterpieces of the distant past that have been forced into its mould? The intentions of the 'artists' – who were often priests in the proper sense of the word – were quite different, as were the social and economic conditions in which they worked. Most important of all, the conceptual framework in which paintings, sculpture and other artefacts existed was not one which would admit of such critical distinctions. H and H A Frankfort[7] say, of the early stages of culture, that men did not then distinguish between subjective and objective categories and that 'meaningless, also, is our contrast between reality and appearance'. To experience the validity of such a thought when viewing early religious art requires a complete upheaval of carefully learned attitudes and understandings.

Here are two quotations from the Frankforts which show clearly the profundity of what was involved.

> In Egypt the creator was said to have emerged from the waters of chaos and to have made a mound of dry land upon which he could stand. This primeval hill, from which the creation took its beginning, was traditionally located in the sun temple at Heliopolis, the sun-god being in Egypt most commonly viewed as the creator . . . [But] each Holy of Holies throughout the land could be identified with the primeval hill . . . Each sanctuary possessed the essential quality of original holiness; for, when a new temple was founded, it was assumed that the potential sacredness of the site became manifest. The equation with the primeval hill received architectural expression also. One mounted a few steps or followed a ramp at every entrance from court or hall to the Holy of Holies, which was thus situated at a level noticeably higher than the entrance.

[7]FRANKFORT, HENRI and H A, WILSON, JOHN A and JACOBSEN,THORKILD. Before philosophy. Harmondsworth, Penguin Books 1949. First published by The University of Chicago Press, 1946.

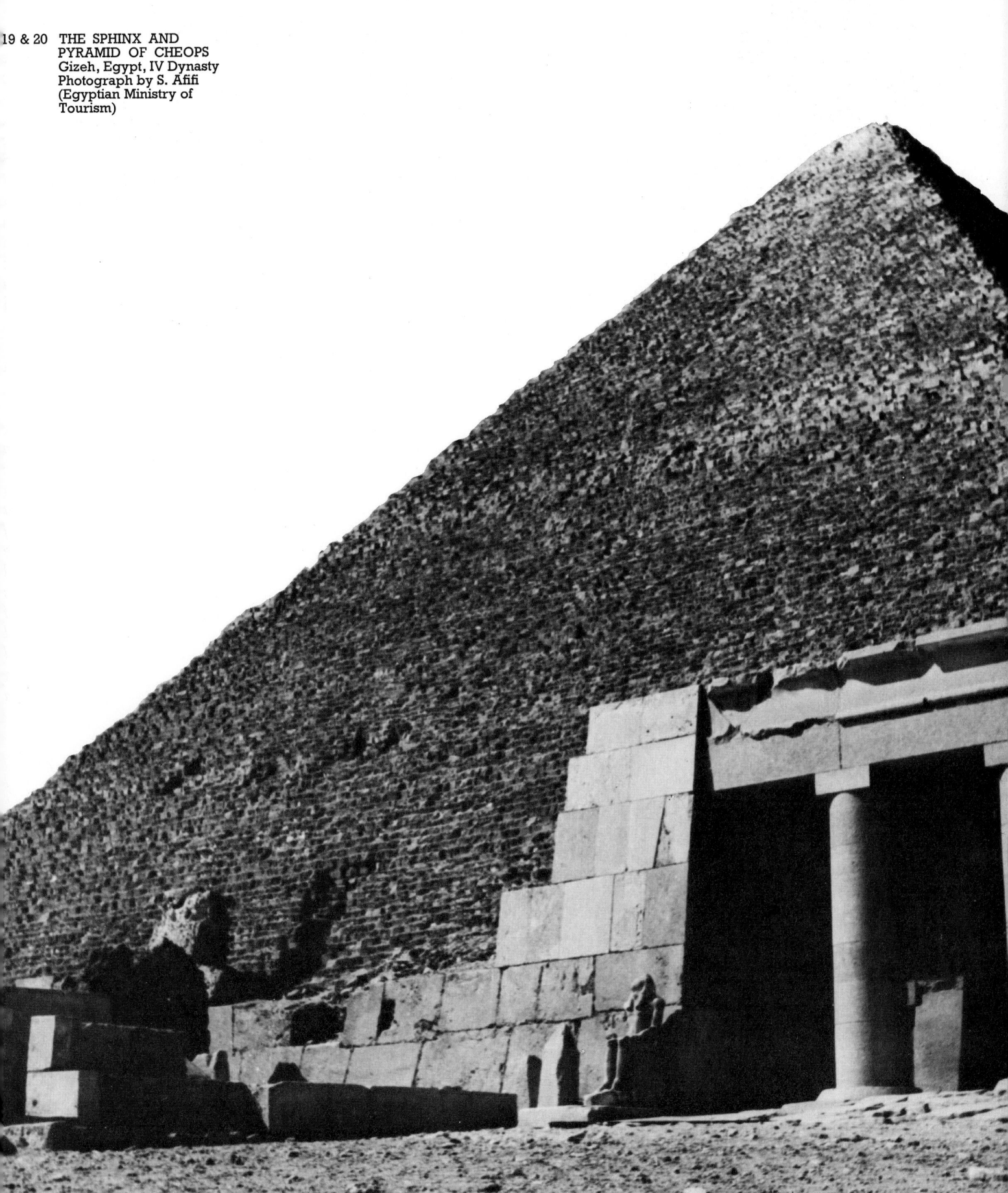

19 & 20 THE SPHINX AND
PYRAMID OF CHEOPS
Gizeh, Egypt, IV Dynasty
Photograph by S. Afifi
(Egyptian Ministry of
Tourism)

A myth seems to be a work of art or literature where spiritual meaning and formal reality are one and the same. It has been usual to understand a myth as being a story – often one with a secret meaning hidden from profane understanding. However, most great myths came into being in a climate of social acceptance and belief and were intended to be widely understood, and the mythological criterion can apply as much to visual art as to literature. The examples shown here embody different myths about the Sun god in two widely separated cultures.

21 Sculpture:
STELE
Guatemala, fifteenth or sixteenth century
(Museum für Völkerkunde, Berlin)
from a site at Cozumalhuapa, Guatemala. The Sun god is at the top: a sacrificial rite in his service is being performed at the bottom.

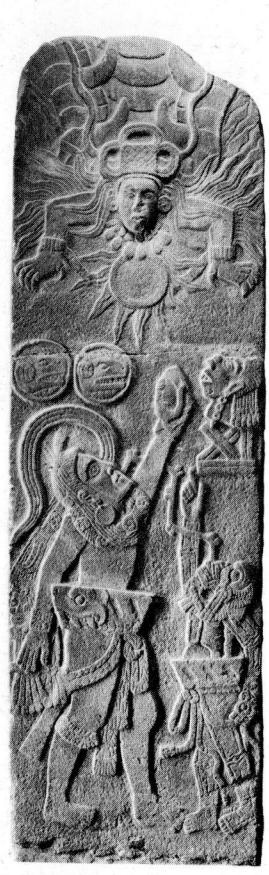

22 Sculpture:
SUN WHEEL
Konarak, India, thirteenth century
(Information Service of India, London)
from the Sun Temple at Konarak, India. The temple, with twelve great pairs of wheels, is said to be erected on the site of a healing miracle performed by Vishnu-Suraya, the Indian Sun god.

But this coalescence of temples with the primeval hill does not give us the full measure of the significance which the sacred locality had assumed for the ancient Egyptians. The royal tombs were also made to coincide with it. The dead, and, above all, the King, were reborn in the hereafter. No place was more propitious, no site promised greater chances for a victorious passage through the crisis of death, than the primeval hill, the centre of creative forces where the ordered life of the universe had begun. Hence the royal tomb was given the shape of a pyramid which is the Heliopolitan stylization of the primeval hill.

This was not symbolism in our sense of the word, nor in the sense used by Christianity in medieval Europe. It was symbolism enclosed in a concept of space and time which was qualitative and concrete, not quantitative and abstract. In other words, the pyramid was, by its qualities and its concrete reality, the actual primeval hill. The primeval hill could exist in more places than one, and the men who made a pyramid were making a spiritual mythological reality, not a sign for it.

The next quotation shows this kind of conceptual framework even more clearly.

Like Isis, the sky-goddess Nūt was considered to be a loving mother-goddess; but the Egyptians of the New Kingdom arranged for their ascent to heaven without [direct] reference to her will or acts. They painted a life-sized figure of the goddess inside their coffins; the dead body was laid in her arms; and the dead man's ascent into heaven was assured. For resemblance was a sharing of essentials, and Nūt's image coalesced with its prototype. The dead man in his coffin rested already in heaven.

Nūt's painted arms were also her actual arms. The art was a functional art, creating the presence of divinity and making it real in life.

In Passion and Society[8] Denis de Rougemont characterizes a myth as a sacred story which endures because of the power of the truth it conceals from, or half-reveals to, profane eyes and ears. He sees the meaning of a myth as always different from its apparent theme. In his careful analysis of the true significance of the story of Tristan and Iseult he brilliantly identifies the Manichean heresy which it conceals. The real passion of the lovers is for death, thus to escape the irredeemably corrupt world. But he is drawing general conclusions from a rather special case. Most myths exist in a climate of social acceptance, not of rejection. There have always been

[8]DE ROUGEMONT, DENIS. Passion and society. London, Faber and Faber. Revised edition 1956.

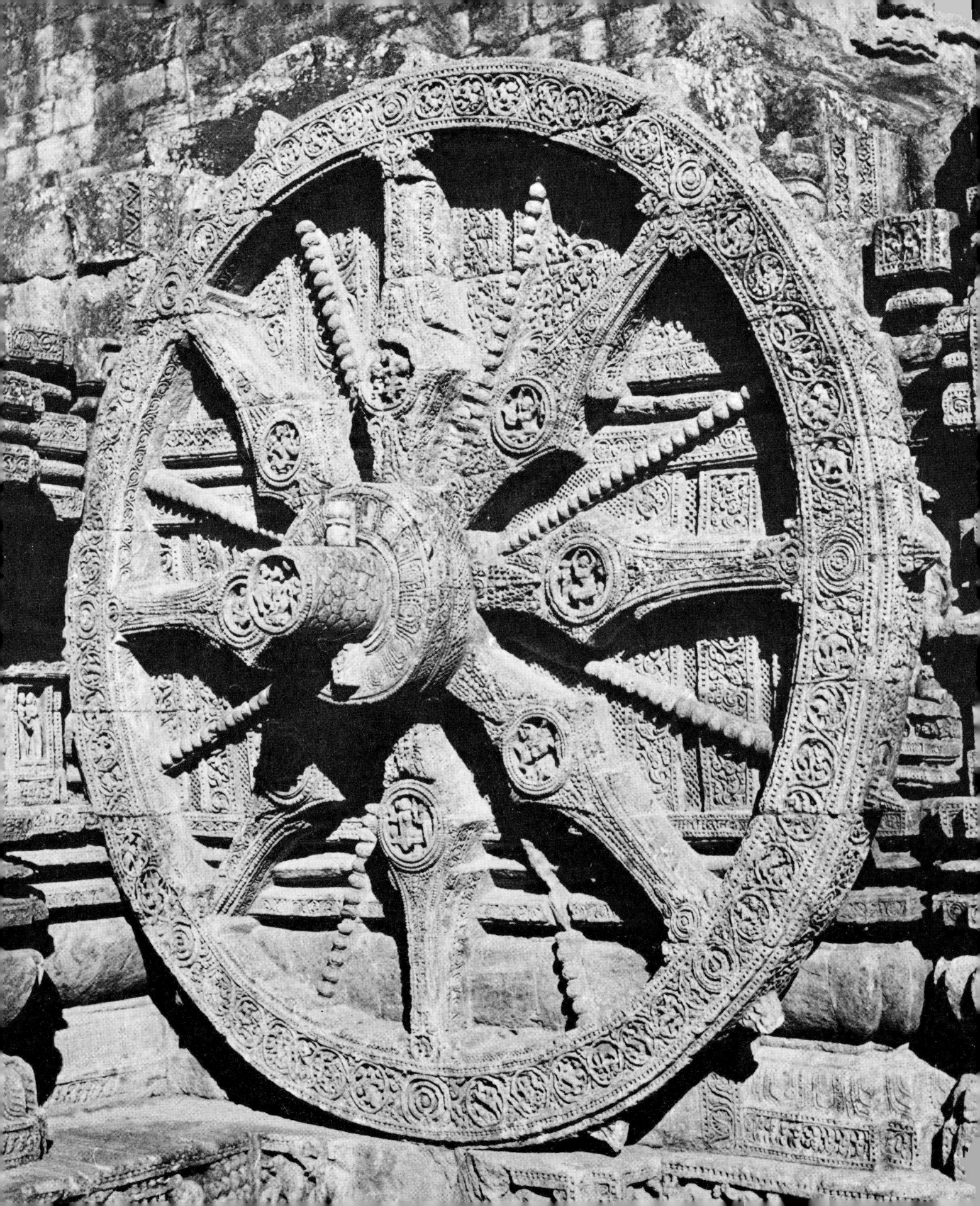

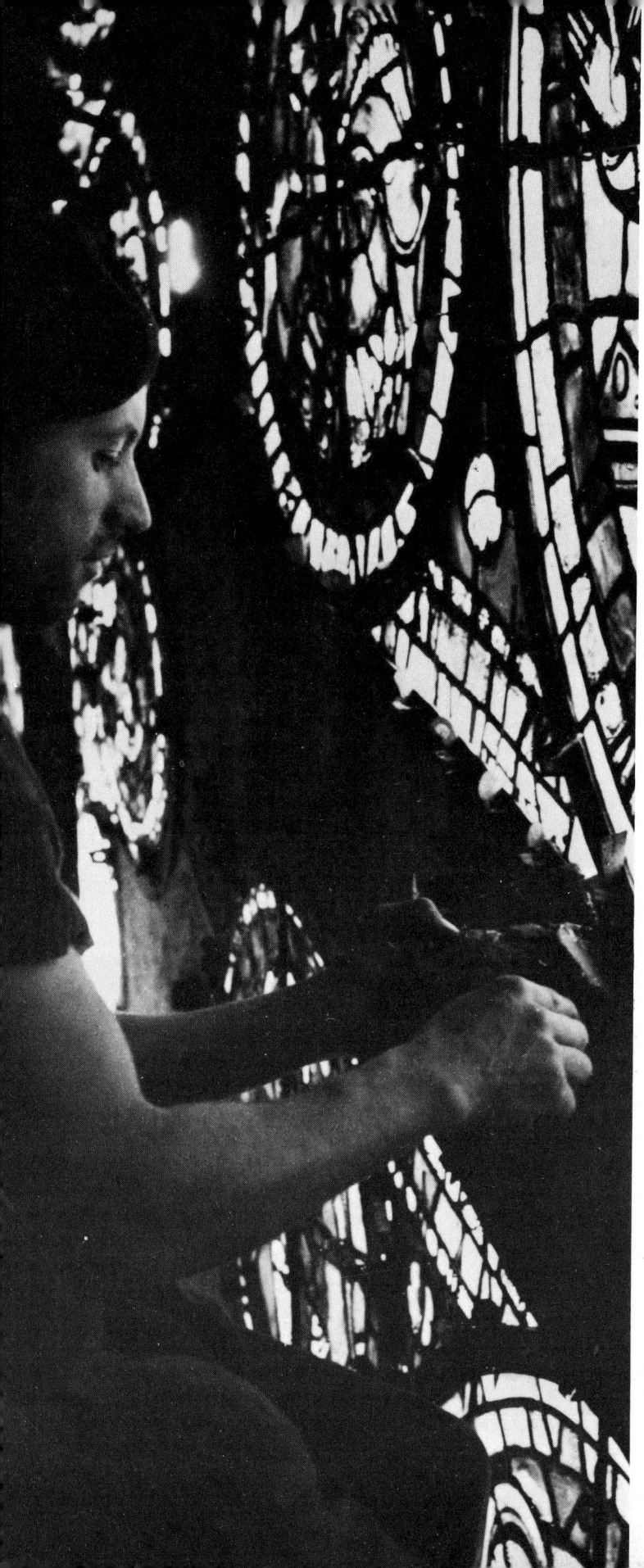

'mysteries' to protect the most holy truths, but a more reasonable, and simpler definition of a myth seems to us to be: a work of art or literature where spiritual meaning and formal reality are one and the same.

Whatever we call it, this was the condition of religious art in the first highly organized civilizations of the world. It is a condition which requires from us a difficult feat of imagination if we are to be able to grasp it at all. And one which calls for a drastic revaluation of the words 'art' and 'artist' as we commonly use them.

A similar reorientation is necessary in discussing the religious art of the European Middle Ages.

In medieval Europe, changes in styles and forms of art happened only very slowly: the whole pattern of working was more akin to craftsmanship than that which we now associate with painting and sculpture. The methods must have been very like those which George Sturt describes as still living on in the making of farm wagons in the late nineteenth century.

> *The waggon-builder was obliged to be always faithful, to know always what was imposed on him in wheels, shafts,*

'In medieval Europe, changes in styles and forms of art happened only very slowly: the whole pattern of working was more akin to craftsmanship than that which we now associate with painting and sculpture.'

23 Photograph:
REPAIRING STAINED GLASS
AT CHARTRES CATHEDRAL
Eleventh–thirteenth century
(French Government Tourist Office)

24 Photograph:
WEST FRONT OF RHEIMS
CATHEDRAL
Thirteenth century
(French Government Tourist Office: photograph by Jean Roubier)

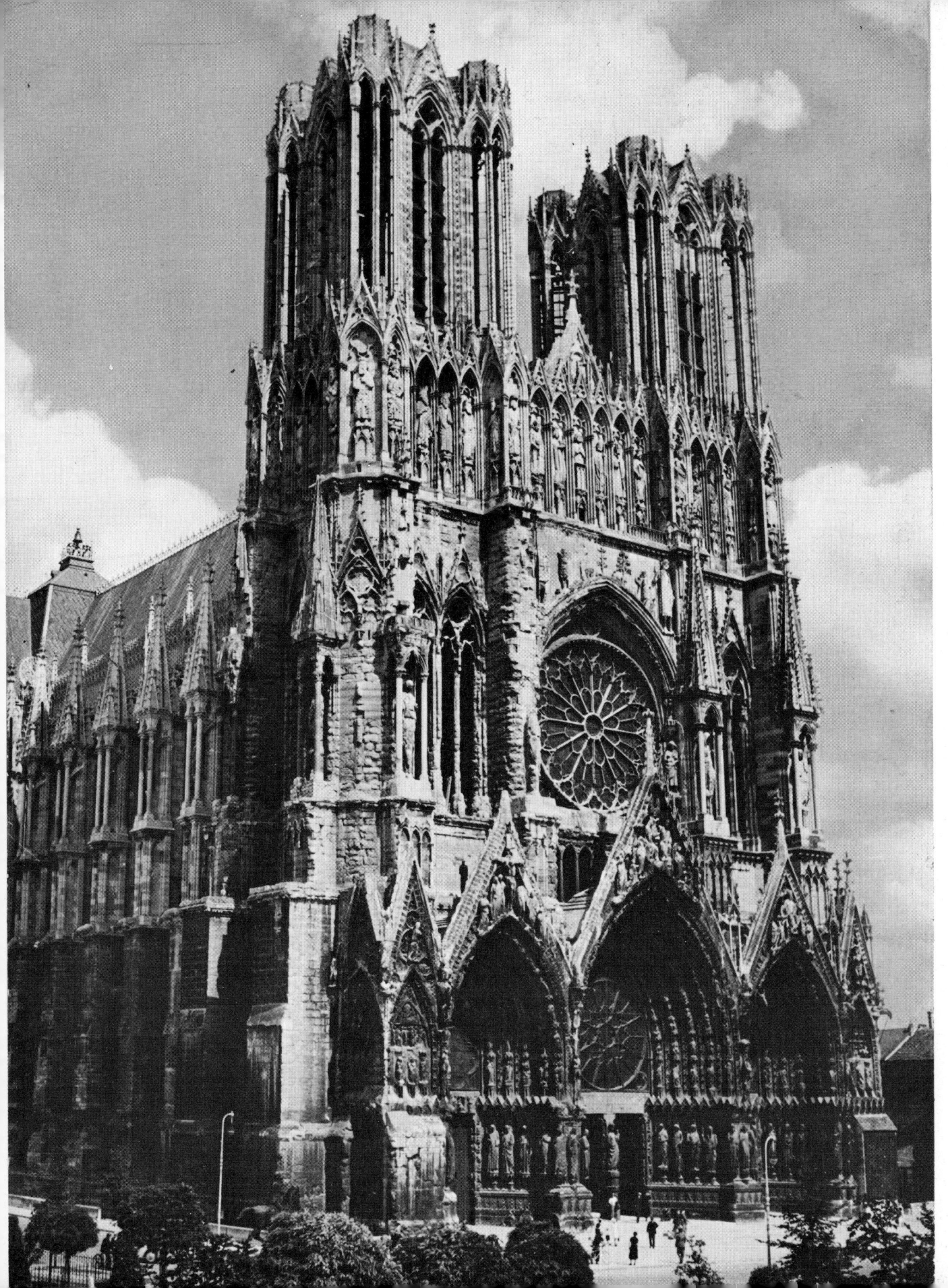

axles, carriages, everything. The nature of this knowledge should be noted. It was set out in no book. It was not scientific. I never met a man who professed any other than an empirical acquaintance with the waggon-builders' lore. My own case was typical. I knew that the hind-wheels had to be five feet two inches high and the fore-wheels four feet two; that the 'sides' must be cut from the best four-inch heart of oak, and so on. This sort of thing I knew, and in vast detail in course of time; but I seldom knew why. And that is how most men knew. The lore was a tangled network of country prejudices, whose reasons were known in some respects here, in others there, and so on. In farm-yard, in tap-room, at market, the details were discussed over and over again; they were gathered together for remembrance in village workshops; carters, smiths, farmers, wheel-makers, in thousands handed on each his little bit of understanding, passing it on to his son or to the wheelwright of the day, linking up the centuries.[9]

The means of transmission indicated by this sort of framework is much more like Fischer's view of art as a 'tool' than it is like Read's view of art as a collection of individually created works. Certainly, in medieval times, the producers thought of themselves more as artisans than as artists and the situation of the audience for their work was totally different from that of the Renaissance aristocracy or our own mass gallery-going public.

Here is G M Trevelyan's[10] account:

The peasant as he stood or knelt on the floor of the church each Sunday, could not follow the Latin words, but good thoughts found a way into his heart as he watched what he revered and heard the familiar yet still mysterious sounds. Around him blazed on the walls frescoes of scenes from the scriptures and lives of the saints; and over the rood-loft was the Last Judgement depicted in lively colours, paradise opening to receive the just, and on the other side flaming hell with devil executioners tormenting naked souls . . .

The peasant knew some of the sayings of Christ, and incidents from his life and those of the saints, beside many Bible stories . . . He never saw the Bible in English, and if he had he could not have read it. There was nothing in his own home analogous to family prayers and Bible reading. But religion and the language of religion surrounded his life.

There is here no separate concept of 'art' which we can recognize.

Finally, let us look at a description of the significance of sculpture and craft in the belief of Voodoo, which is a complex Haitian version of African religion affected by contact with Christianity and taken across the Atlantic by the slaves. It comes from Muntu[11] by Janheinz Jahn. The 'loas' he refers to are the Haitian gods, Bon Dieu, Legba, Damballah – and many others – personifications of natural forces or characters from the Voodoo underworld. Jahn takes the attitudes he describes as being typical of all Africa.

According to African philosophy, the metal, the stone, the clay, out of which the smith, the stone-cutter, the potter moulds a piece of sculpture is a kintu, a 'thing', and nothing more. Only the piece of wood that the wood-carver uses for his sculpture is something more than other 'things': it comes from the tree, from the 'road of the invisible ones', as they say in Haiti, from the vertical that unites the water – Nommo of the depths with the cosmos. As 'repository', as the seat of the loas, the wood of such trees is a privileged kintu; the Nommo of the ancestors has given it a certain consecration, a symbolic value – just as a flag is a privileged piece of cloth: the force of respect, a symbolic force has been invested in it. The respect, however, is never for the wood itself, but for the Muntu-beings who have chosen it as their 'seat'. Since it stands closer to the loas, the orisas, the ancestors, it is favoured as a material – for the materials one works with also have a hierarchy . . .

With the help of Nommo, the word . . . the goldsmith [like other artists or craftsmen], makes an ornament out of a piece of gold. He works magic. His manual skill is an addendum, an important addendum, but what is decisive is the word, the 'magic formula', which brings it about that the 'thing' is turned into something else, what it is destined to be: an image.

Once again, it requires from us a feat of imagination to put ourselves into a situation where the ceremonial activities around a sculpture, and even the particular material it is made from, may be more important in determining what it means than the form it takes. What we have here is not a conjunction of reality with appearance, but the insignificance of appearance as against a

[9]STURT, GEORGE. The wheelwright's shop. Cambridge, Cambridge University Press, 1963. Originally published 1923.

[10]TREVELYAN, G M. Illustrated English social history, Vol.1. Harmondsworth, Penguin Books, 1944. Originally published (without illustrations) 1942.

[11]JAHN, JANHEINZ. Muntu: an outline of neo-African culture. London, Faber and Faber, 1961.

25 Photograph:
CONTEMPORARY NALINDELE MASK MADE BY THE MAMBUNDA OF ZAMBIA
by Sam Haskins
(Sam Haskins)
from **African Image**, published by the Bodley Head Ltd

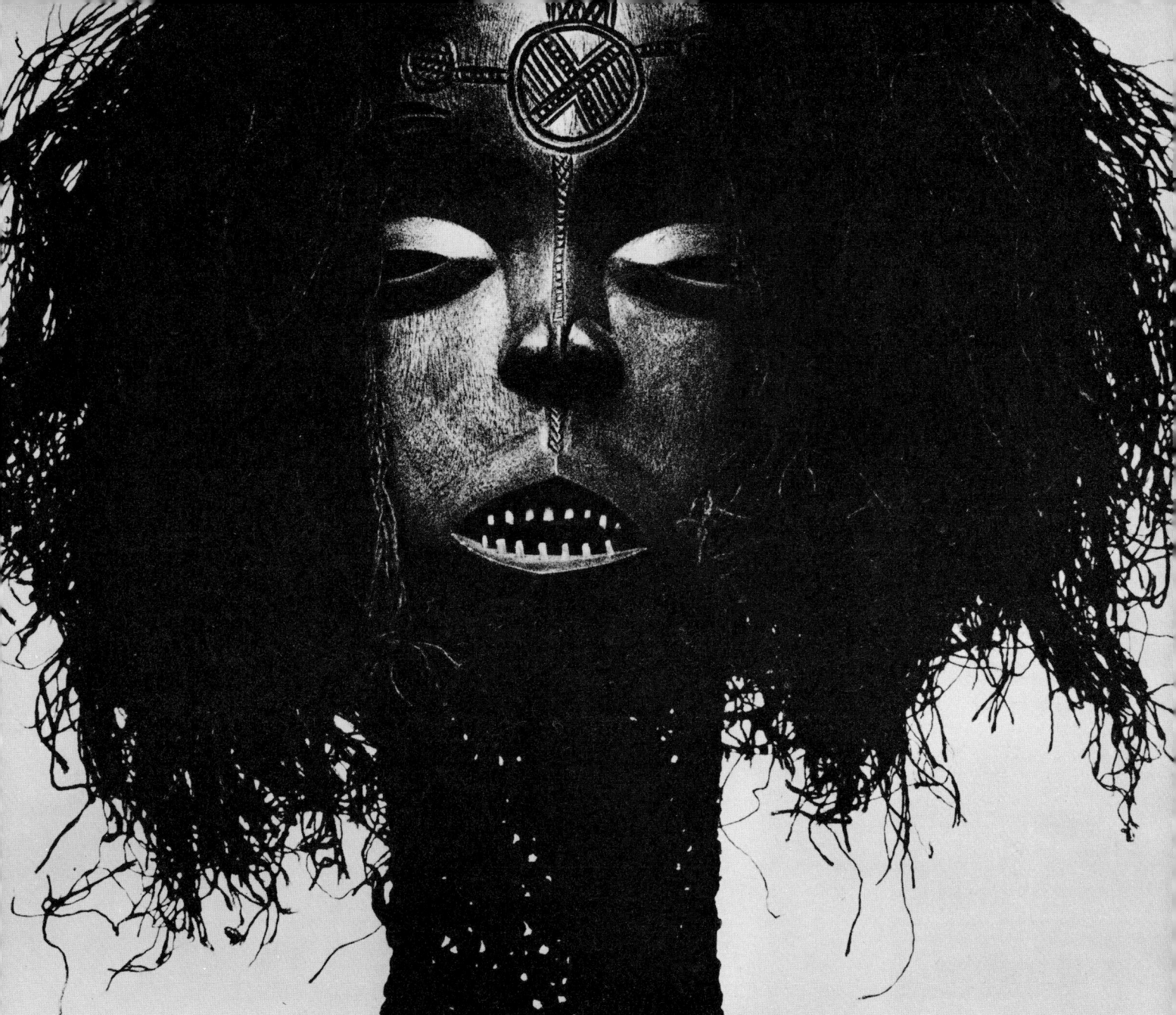

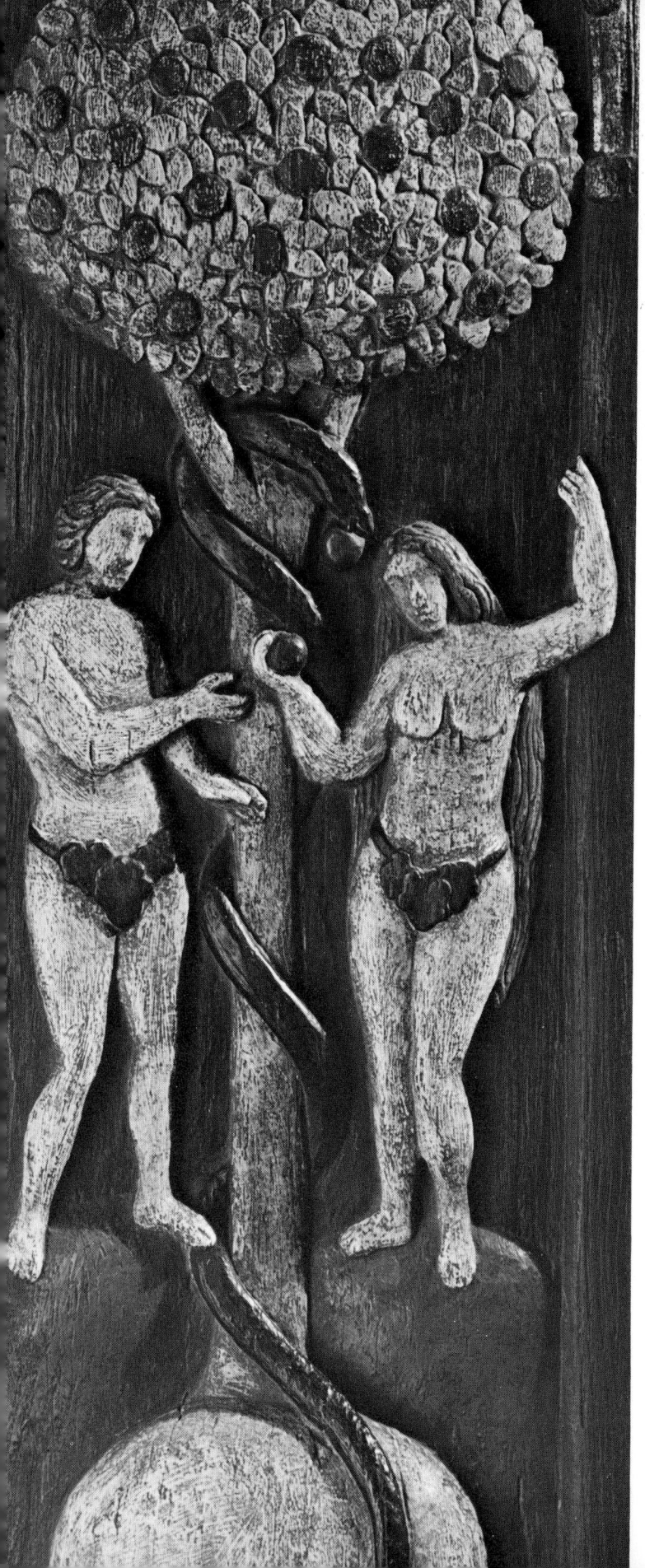

designated meaning. The art is still a functional art, but the mechanism of the function is exterior to the work not integrated with its formal imitation. All of which is an incredible distance from the attitude of Western Fine Art since the Renaissance, but quite fundamental to any real understanding of religious and ceremonial art from many different places and periods.

Of course, nothing can place the works of the distant past back into their original context, or make it possible for us to share fully in their charismatic power. It is easier with Christian imagery, but comparisons between, say, medieval France and nineteenth-century Wales reveal enormous social, economic and aesthetic differences as well as underlying continuities.

In medieval Europe the view of the world was one of stability. Even though there was, in fact, much chaos and war this existed inside a framework of Christianity which was thought to be changeless. Even heresy, a most disruptive force, was only perceived as such in the context of orthodoxy. The future was assured in its full complexity of redemption and salvation, and change, in the sense of a journey towards this known end, was really only seen in relation to the possibility for good or evil in each individual life. In this situation art restated and reinforced the changeless destiny of the world as a whole and ceaselessly reminded the individual of his responsibility in that future. Design was handcraftsmanship and the mode of affecting the future was by copying the time-honoured designs of the past.

In the nineteenth century, however, we can already take as our key theme the idea of 'progress', and the reinforcement of this ethic with the Protestant values of self-help and hard work: 'God helps those who help themselves'. Here art continued its moralizing not only in the context of a morality which was assumed to be eternal, but also in respect of material change on earth. Thus it is easy to understand the ectstatic visions opened up by the new technologies and the zeal in carrying God, capitalism, bourgeois art and industry throughout the world.

Naturally, medieval religious art, or nineteenth-century religious art, can be appreciated in purely aesthetic terms. But it is important to recognize that such an appreciation, by itself, misses out a large part of the most human aspect of what was made.

It seems to us that one of the best ways to give back some of the original meaning to religious art is to concentrate on its use rather than on its role in the history of art. There is a continuity of meaning in terms of function that is just as strong as the continuity in terms of time and style, and we have already seen how much religious art is primarily functional rather than formal. We are, if you like, deliberately taking the social and learning perspectives that we discussed earlier, and giving to them a higher priority than the perspective to do with art as an autonomous 'language'. And yet, our own conviction is that we are likely, in the end, to understand the nature of the 'language' best if we look at the way it has been used by men and women in their everyday lives. That, after all, is the touchstone of its existence.

But even this is too vague a programme to be effective in the small amount of space available. It has seemed necessary to go further, and to select one particular aspect of religion's social function, so as to give it more extended treatment by relating all our examples to it. As it is the nature of art's involvement with society that we are trying to explain, rather than the nature of religion, this has seemed a justified – and even prudent – method of presentation.

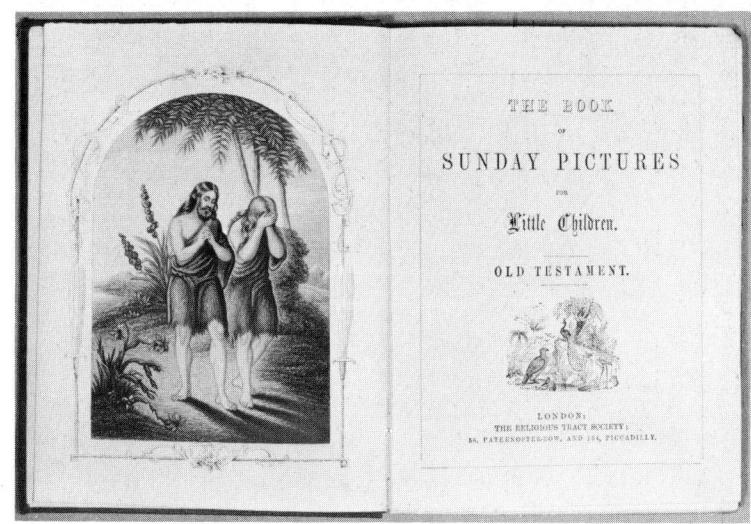

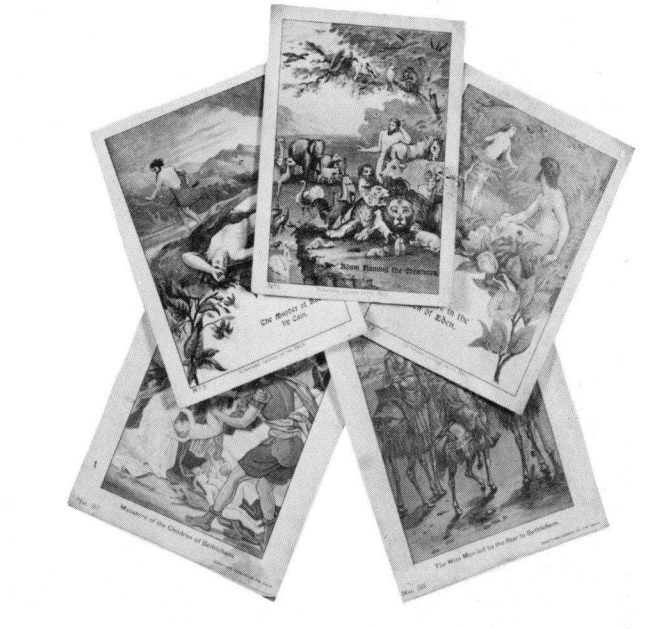

Social, economic and aesthetic differences affect religious art as much as underlying continuities of belief, imagery and subject matter.

26 Detail of carved wooden cross:
ADAM AND EVE
Czechoslovakia
(National Museum, Prague:
photograph by Alexandr Paul)

27 Illustration:
ADAM AND EVE
from **The Book of Sunday Pictures for Little Children**
late nineteenth century
(Museum of Childhood, Edinburgh)

28 Sunday School cards:
ADAM NAMING THE CREATURES
late nineteenth century
(Museum of Childhood, Edinburgh)

29 Sculpture:
EVE
by Gislebertus
Autun Cathedral, France
(Copyright Trianon Press, from
Gislebertus, Sculptor of Autun)

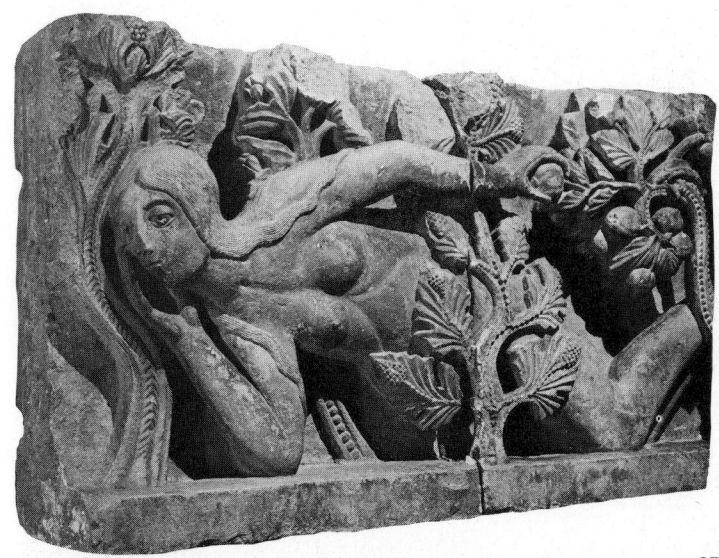

The aspect of religion that we have selected is its ability to make real the congruence of past, present and future.

Although in some ways this is a mystical idea, it is also a highly practical one that forms the basis of any durable social contract. Actually the concept is not totally dependent upon conventional religion, or even upon belief in God, but for the overwhelming majority of people in most periods it has been a supernatural authority which has provided the frame of reference. And, of all the social effects of religious belief, the stabilizing of society through an appeal to immortal custom is one of the most common, and one of the most powerful. It is also one in which art is much involved as a medium of communication.

The remainder of the book, then, consists of three pictorial chapters: one each for Past, Present and Future. In them, works with uses that are basically similar are brought together regardless of the culture or period from which they come. We believe that this is a helpful arrangement, and one which helps to reveal the intentions of the original makers and users.

30 Drawing:
THE FAMILY
by Polly Baynes
(Ken and Kate Baynes)
In this drawing members of the family ride in a train: dead as well as living people are included.

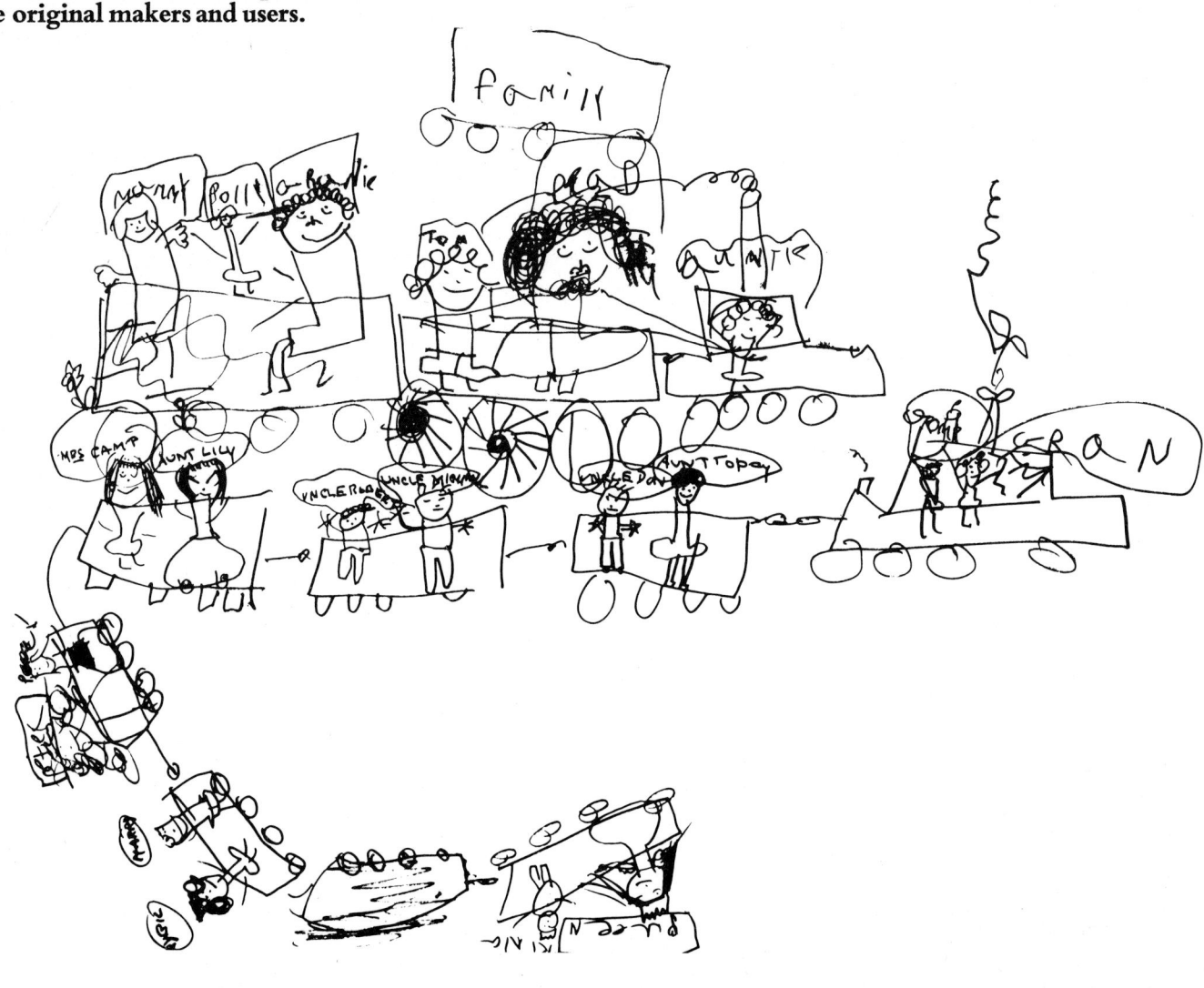

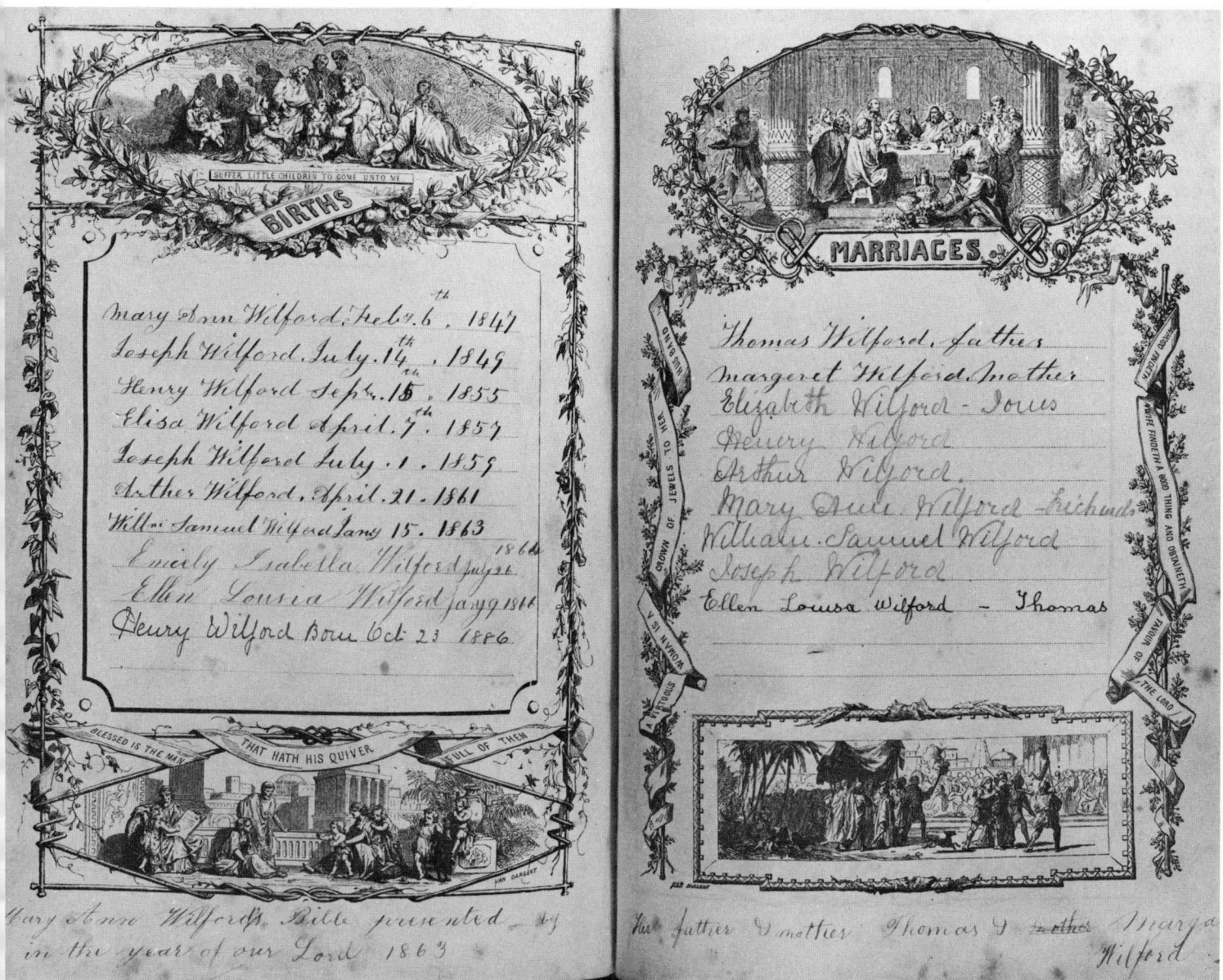

BIRTHS

SUFFER LITTLE CHILDREN TO COME UNTO ME

Mary Ann Wilford Feb. 6, 1847
Joseph Wilford July 14, 1849
Henry Wilford Sep. 15, 1855
Elisa Wilford April 7, 1857
Joseph Wilford July 1, 1859
Arthur Wilford April 21, 1861
Will. Samuel Wilford Jany 15, 1863
Emily Isabella Wilford July 26, 1864
Ellen Louisa Wilford Jany 9, 1866
Henry Wilford Born Oct 23, 1886

BLESSED IS THE MAN THAT HATH HIS QUIVER FULL OF THEM

Mary Ann Wilford's Bible presented by
in the year of our Lord 1863

MARRIAGES

Thomas Wilford father
Margaret Wilford mother
Elizabeth Wilford – Jones
Henry Wilford
Arthur Wilford
Mary Ann Wilford – Richards
William Samuel Wilford
Joseph Wilford
Ellen Louisa Wilford – Thomas

Her father & mother Thomas & mother Marya
Wilford

31 Pages from a family Bible:
BIRTHS, MARRIAGES
the Bible was presented to its
first owner in 1863
(Mrs Joy Goodfellow)

Family Bibles in the nineteenth
century always contained these pages,
and another for deaths, thus vividly
embodying the concept of past,
present and future which underlies
the organization of the present book.

Past, Present and Future

The concept of past, present and future around which the three pictorial sections of this book are organized is not an historical one. The category of past stands for custom, the category of present stands for ritual and ceremonial in life, and the category of future stands for immortality either for the individual or for humanity as a whole.

The perspective is that of a person within a particular cultural situation.

He looks back to stories of the Creation, to myths which explain the nature of the relationship between men and God, and to the wisdom and practices of his ancestors. In everyday life the reality and vividness of this background is made manifest in ritual and ceremonial, and spiritual forces are called upon for good or ill. He looks forward to his appointed fate: to becoming a spirit perhaps, or to being reunited with family and ancestors in the presence of God.

The process is circular, or spiral, because he, himself, one day becomes an ancestor or a part of the past.

In social terms the pattern is most often one of reassuring stability, linked to the continuation of accepted customs, institutions and behaviour. In such a situation art is not concerned so much with novelty as with reaffirming truths which are already accepted in essence. Only when the philosophical framework is destroyed by change or when proselytizing zeal takes up art as a weapon, does this alter.

What we see in this book as most typical are works created within a system of belief for people who shared that system, thought it entirely true, and who, unlike ourselves, had little enough knowledge of the relationship between their culture and others that were different.

Past, present and future were, as in medieval times, points between which an individual had to travel but which existed within a timeless scheme. Art described the terms of the person's journey and made it real.

32   Painting:
THROUGH THE TRINITY ON
EARTH WE HONOUR THE
TRINITY IN HEAVEN
by C F Brun
Switzerland, 1868
(from **Le Déserteur** by Jean
Giono published by Éditions de
Fontainemore, Lausanne)

C F Brun, 'Le Déserteur', was a
fugitive from French justice who lived
for twenty-one years in the woods of
the Valais in Switzerland. Here he was
protected by the local population
and earned his living by painting
religious pictures to order. This
particular painting beautifully
epitomizes one of the basic functions
of religious art: the symbolic
representation of heavenly order in
earthly form so that it can be
worshipped.

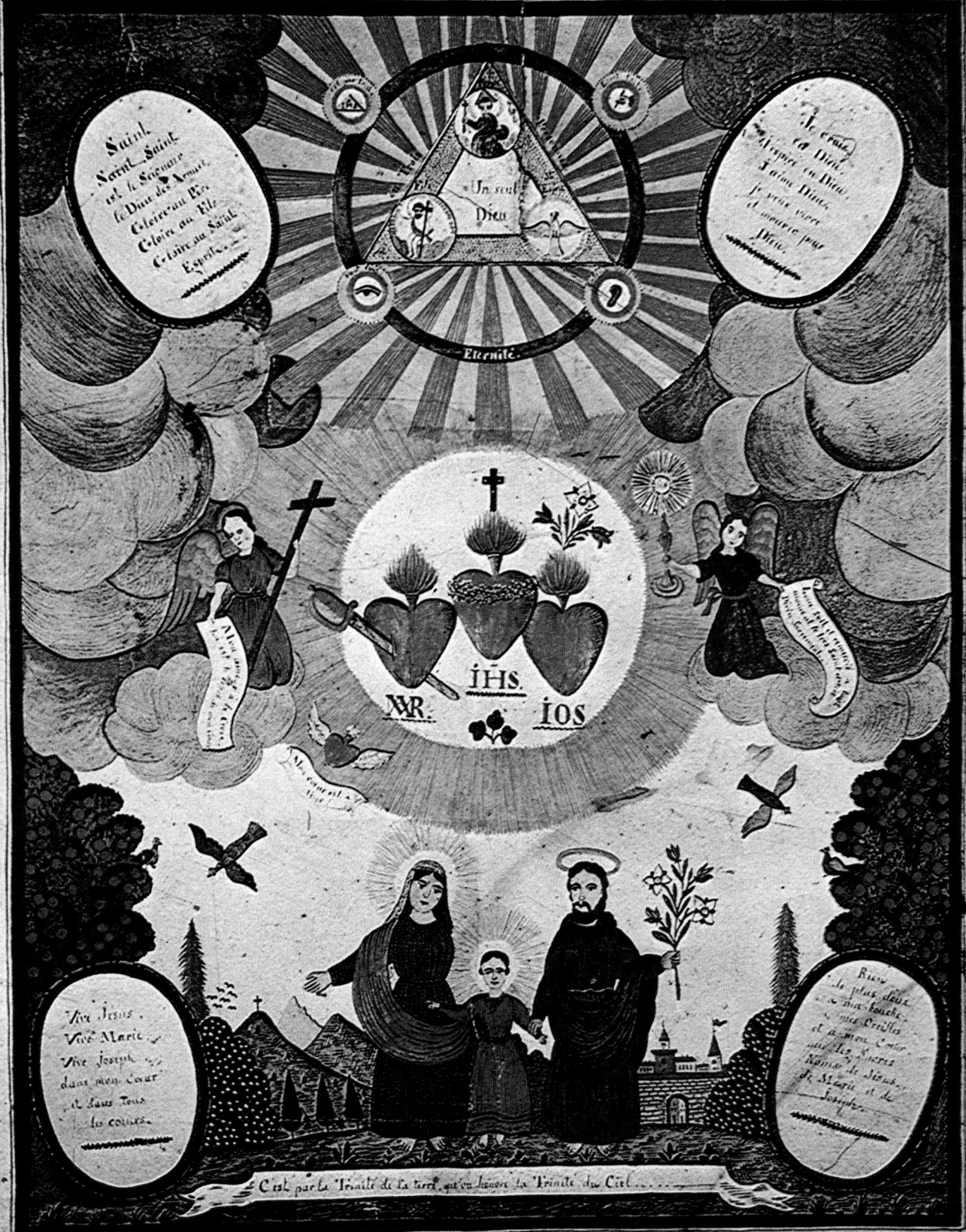

When heaven had not yet come into existence,
When men had not yet come into existence,
When gods had not yet been born,
When death had not yet come into existence.

from an ancient Egyptian pyramid text quoted by
H and H A Frankfort in Before Philosophy, 1949.

And God said, Let us make man in our image,
after our likeness: and let them have dominion
over the fish of the sea, and over the fowl of the
air, and over the cattle, and over all the earth, and
over every creeping thing that creepeth upon the
earth.

So God created man in his own image, in the
image of God created he him; male and female
created he them.

And God blessed them, and God said unto them,
Be fruitful, and multiply, and replenish the earth,
and subdue it: and have dominion over the fish of
the sea, and over the fowl of the air, and over every
living thing that moveth upon the earth.

And God said, Behold I have given you every
herb bearing seed, which is upon the face of all
the earth, and every tree, in the which is the fruit
of a tree yielding seed; to you it shall be for meat.

from Chapter 1, verses 26 to 29, of the First Book
of Moses, called Genesis.

Afterwards the gourds were boiled in animal fat
to make them more resilient and waterproof.
With her own delicate hands [the goddess] Marimba assembled the instrument, arranging the gourds
and planks in gradually diminishing sizes, while
vast crowds of Wakambi men and women watched in awe and astonishment.

Thus the xylophone – the marimba – was born.
Soon this melodious companion of the feast and
the dance was sending its notes through the festive
air, each note as gentle as a maiden's promise . . .
Indeed it is an instrument worthy of bearing the
name of the goddess of music.

from My People – writings of a Zulu witch-doctor
by Credo Mutwa. Published by Penguin Books,
1971.

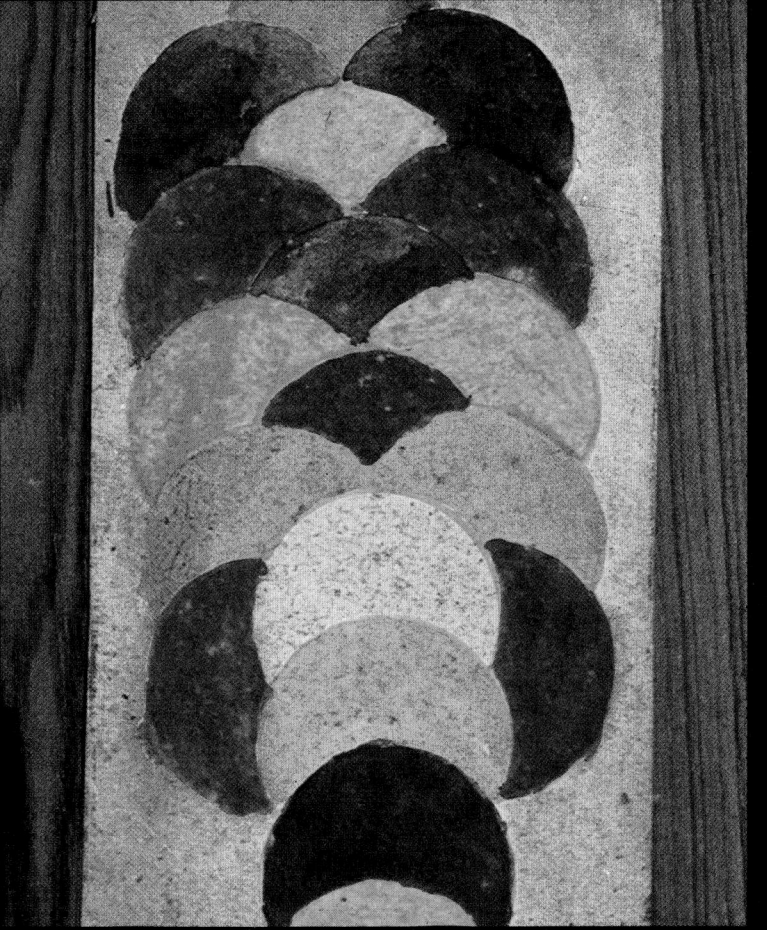

33 Painting:
   CREATION OF THE UNIVERSE
   Western India, eighteenth
   century
   (from **Tantra Art** by Ajit
   Mookerjee)

This Tantric painting is from a
manuscript called the **Suddha-
chittavani** or **Course of Correct
Understanding.** Visual art is
extremely important in Tantric
philosophy, taking its place with
sound as one of the fundamental
elements through which the universe
can be understood. It is said that the
creation of the universe involves
three co-existing forces: **sristi** –
creation – **kriya sakti**; **sthiti** –
maintenance – **maya sakti**; and
samhara – dissolution – **kala sakti**.
Yantras (diagrams of forces) are used
in Tantra: they are not abstractions,
but living images of cosmic forces or
graphs of processes. In the **Yantras**
a spheroid is looked upon as a sphere
in the process of breaking itself into
separate units each with its own
centre. A spheroid therefore stands
for the world-egg.

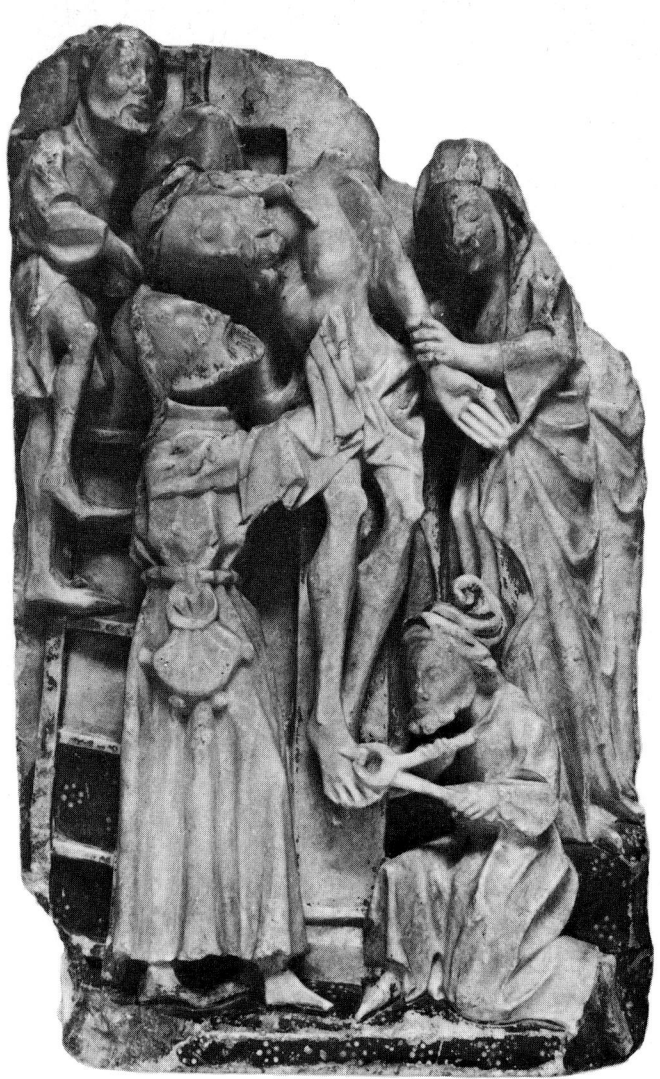

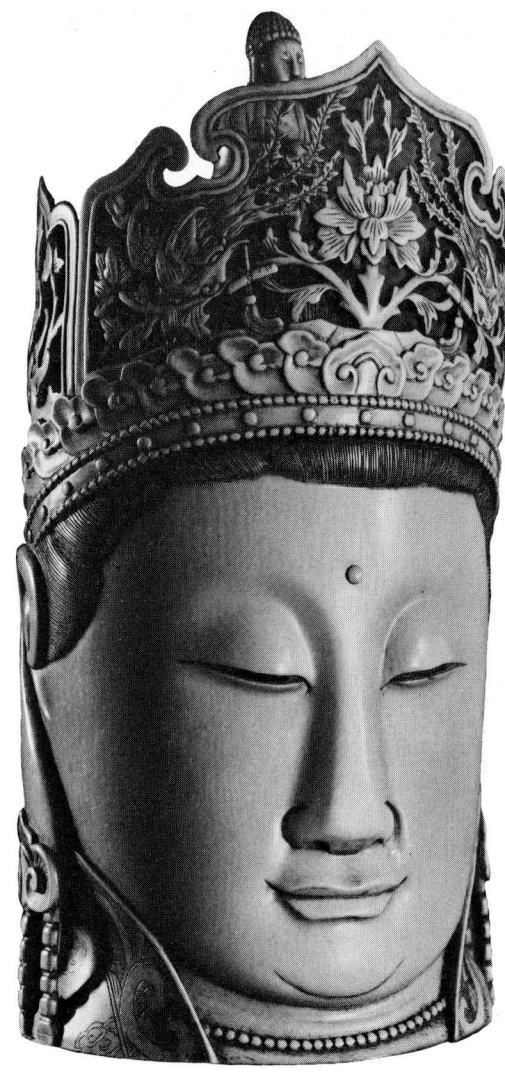

The representation of God, or gods, and stories about them has been one of the most common uses of art since the beginnings of religious thought. Scales and styles have varied enormously, as have the social and economic conditions in which the works existed, but there has always been the element of focusing emotion and understanding in an object more enduring and more authoritative than the imagination of an individual man.

34 Sculpture:
    CRUCIFIXION
    sixteenth century
    (City Museum, City of St Albans)

35 Sculpture:
    HEAD OF KUAN YIN
    China, eighteenth century
    (The Graves Art Gallery,
    Sheffield)

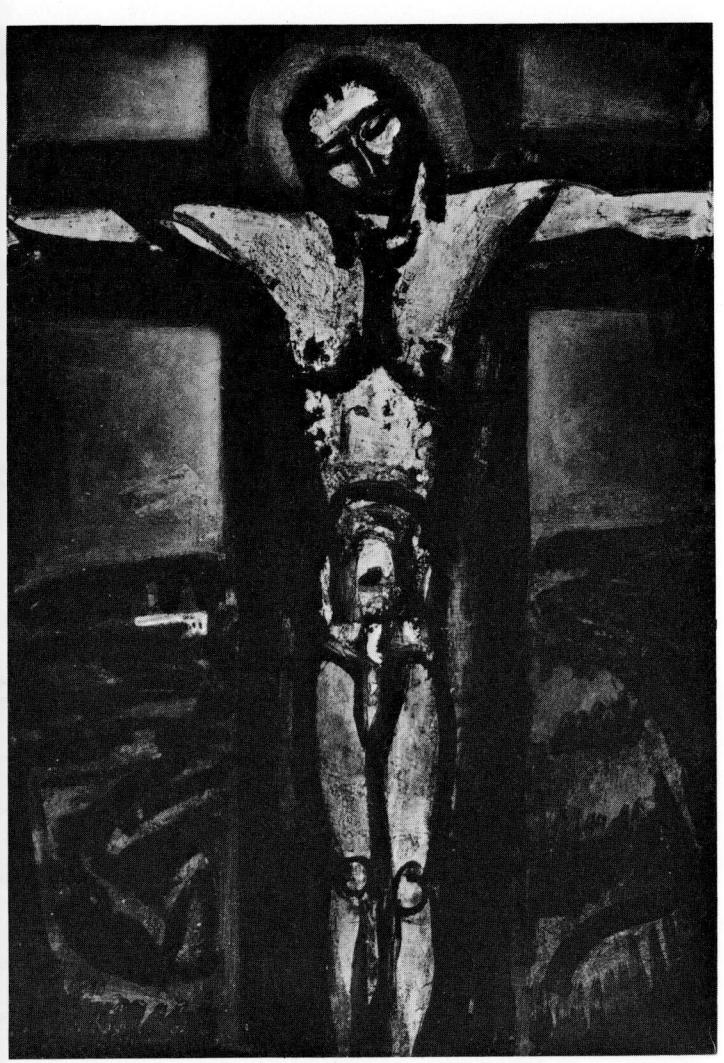

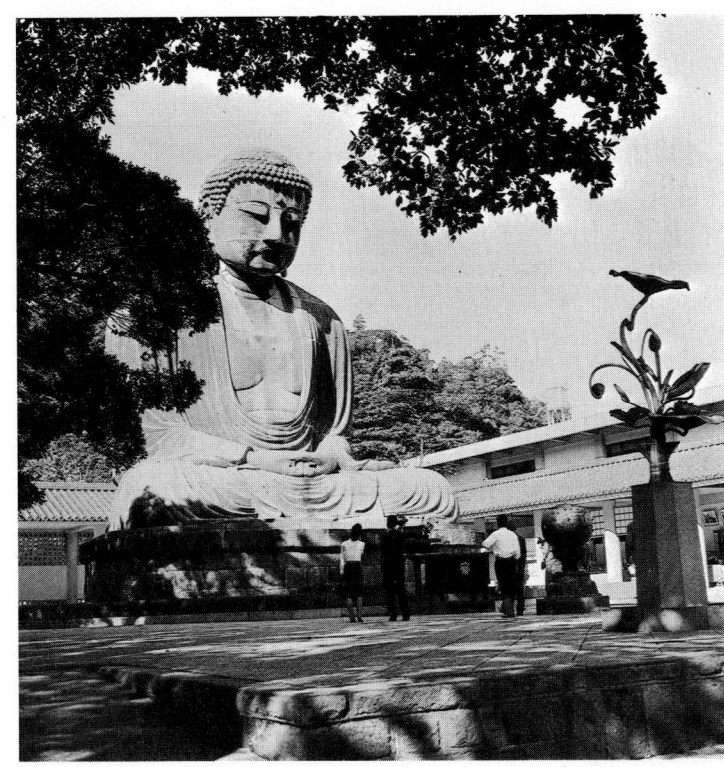

36 Engraving:
SOUS UN JÉSUS EN CROIX
OUBLIÉ LÀ
by Georges Rouault
from **Miserere,** c.1927
(City Museum and Art Gallery,
Birmingham)

37 Sculpture:
THE BUDDHA OF KAMAKURA
Japan, thirteenth century
(Japan National Tourist
Organisation)

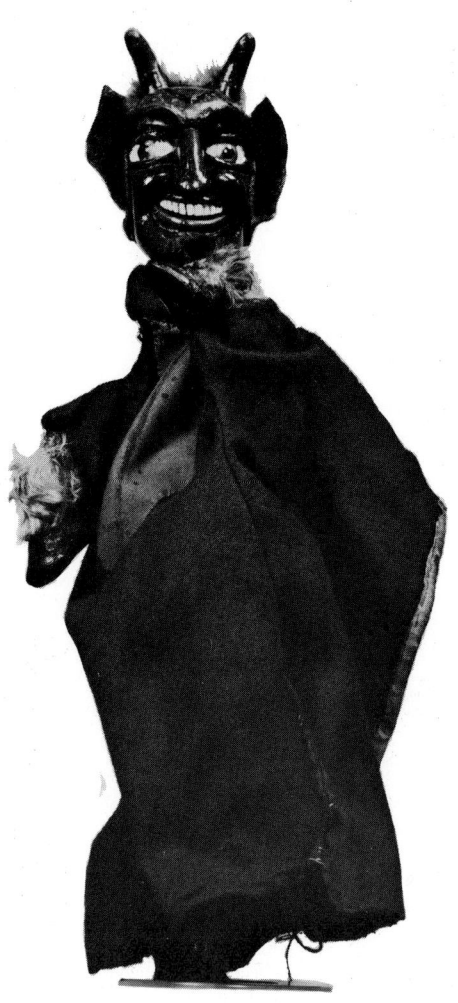

39 Sculpture:
HEAD OF THE GODDESS
MINERVA
Roman Britain
(Roman Museum, Bath)

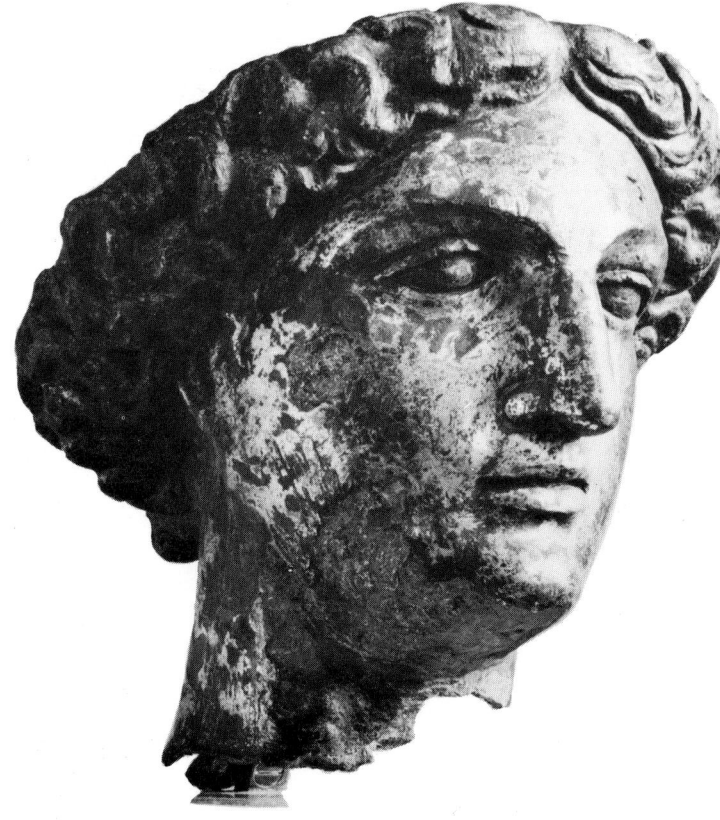

Pictures of gods or demons can be
intended to uplift the soul, terrify or
even entertain. In any such case the
meaning of the representation must
be visual in form, but the context and
the understanding of the viewer are
also important.

38 Puppet:
THE DEVIL
from a set of glove puppets for
a **Punch and Judy show**
(Museum of Childhood,
Edinburgh)

40 Sculpture:
MAHĀKOLA YAKSHA AND
HIS EIGHTEEN DEMONS OF
DISEASE
Ceylon, purchased 1899
(Pitt Rivers Museum, University
of Oxford)

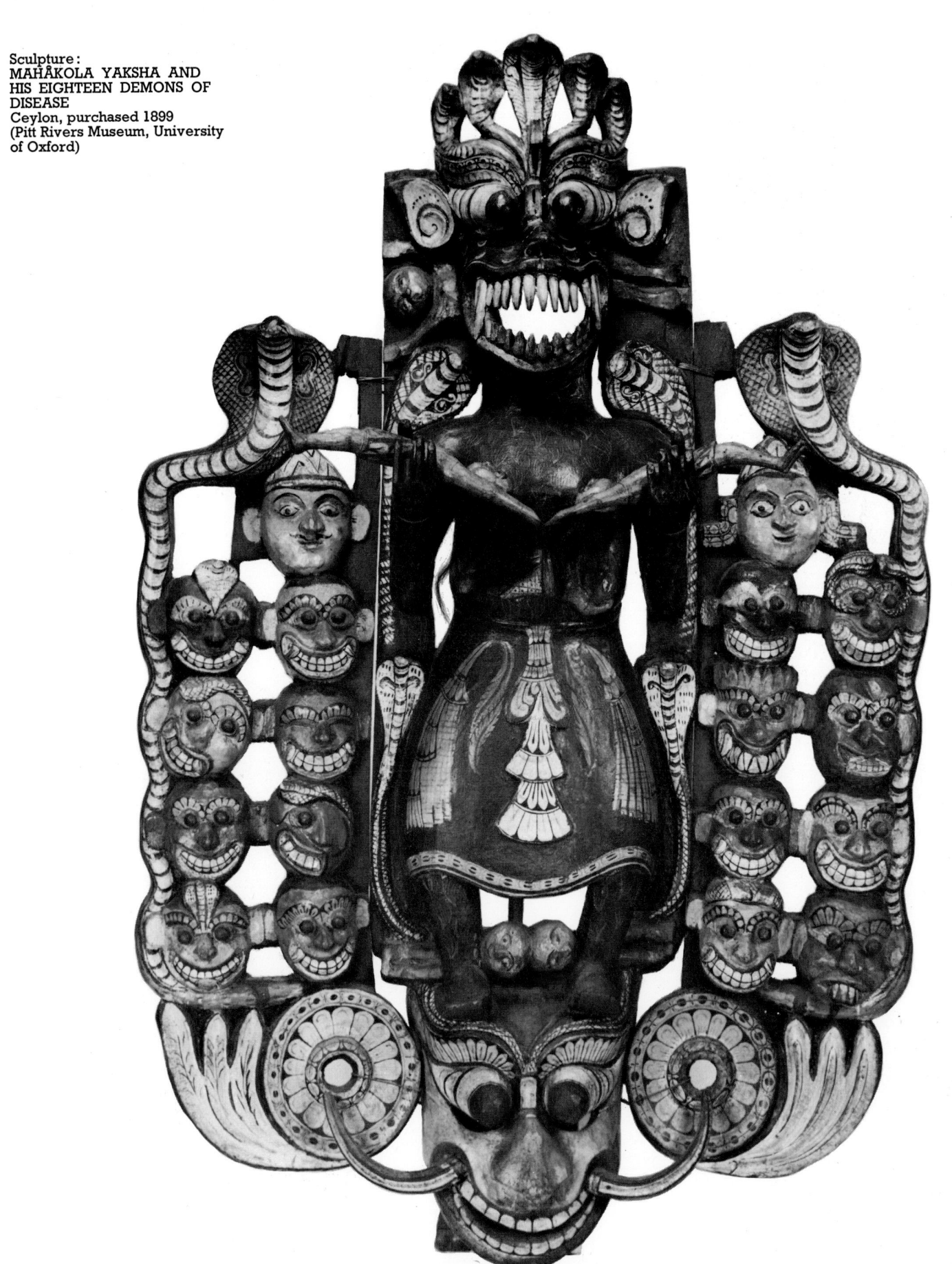

In most periods stories about gods have permeated every aspect of life, serving as the subject matter of applied decoration, play, and home crafts like weaving or needlework. This has, on one hand, made holy images commonplace and widely available and, on the other, made it difficult to distinguish between the sacred and the profane in the visual arts. In terms of the theme of past, present and future such representations make constant reference to the religious philosophy of any particular culture, reiterating time and again the basis of the relationship between God and man. They bring the past constantly into the present.

41 Playing cards:
    illustrating the EXPLOITS OF
    KRISHNA
    India
    (Horniman Museum, London)

43 Tapestry picture:
    THE FLIGHT INTO EGYPT
    Wales, early twentieth century
    (Ken and Kate Baynes)

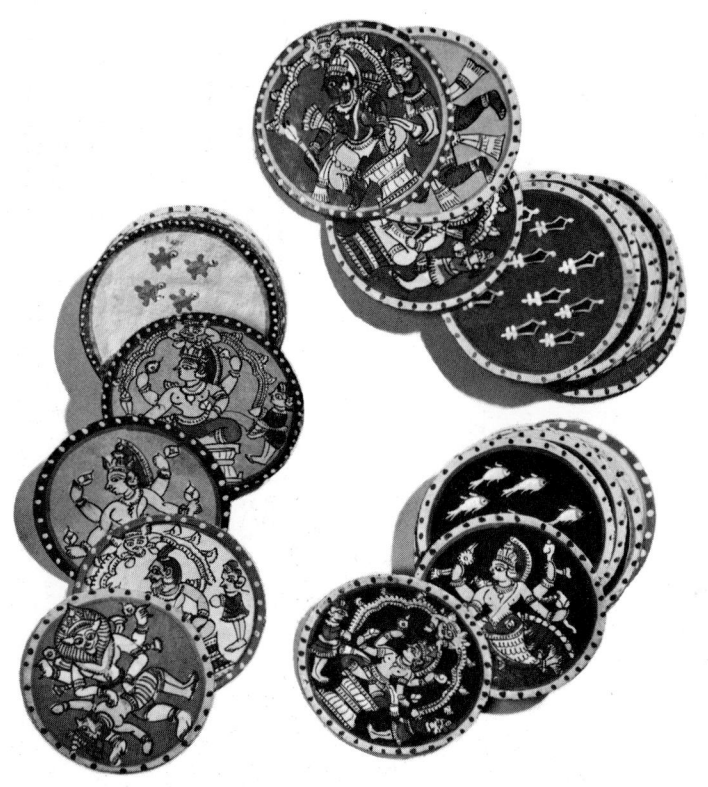

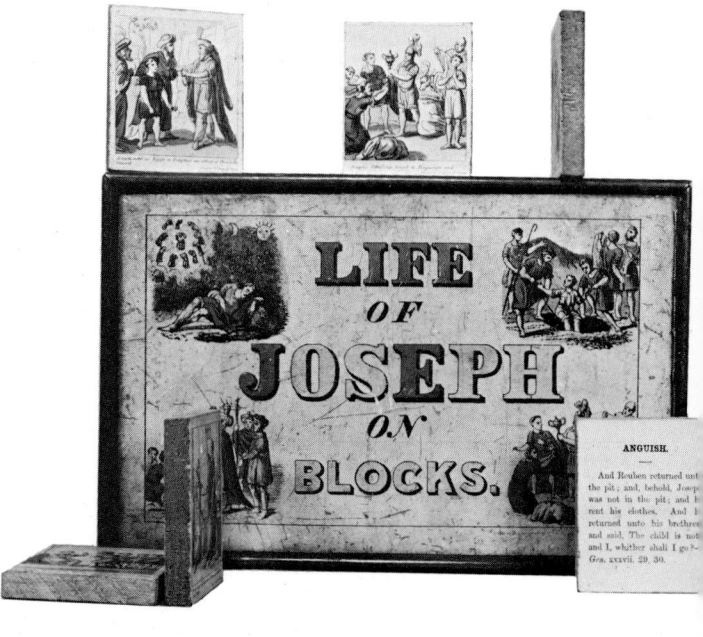

42 Building blocks:
    illustrating the LIFE OF JOSEPH
    (Museum of Childhood,
    Edinburgh)

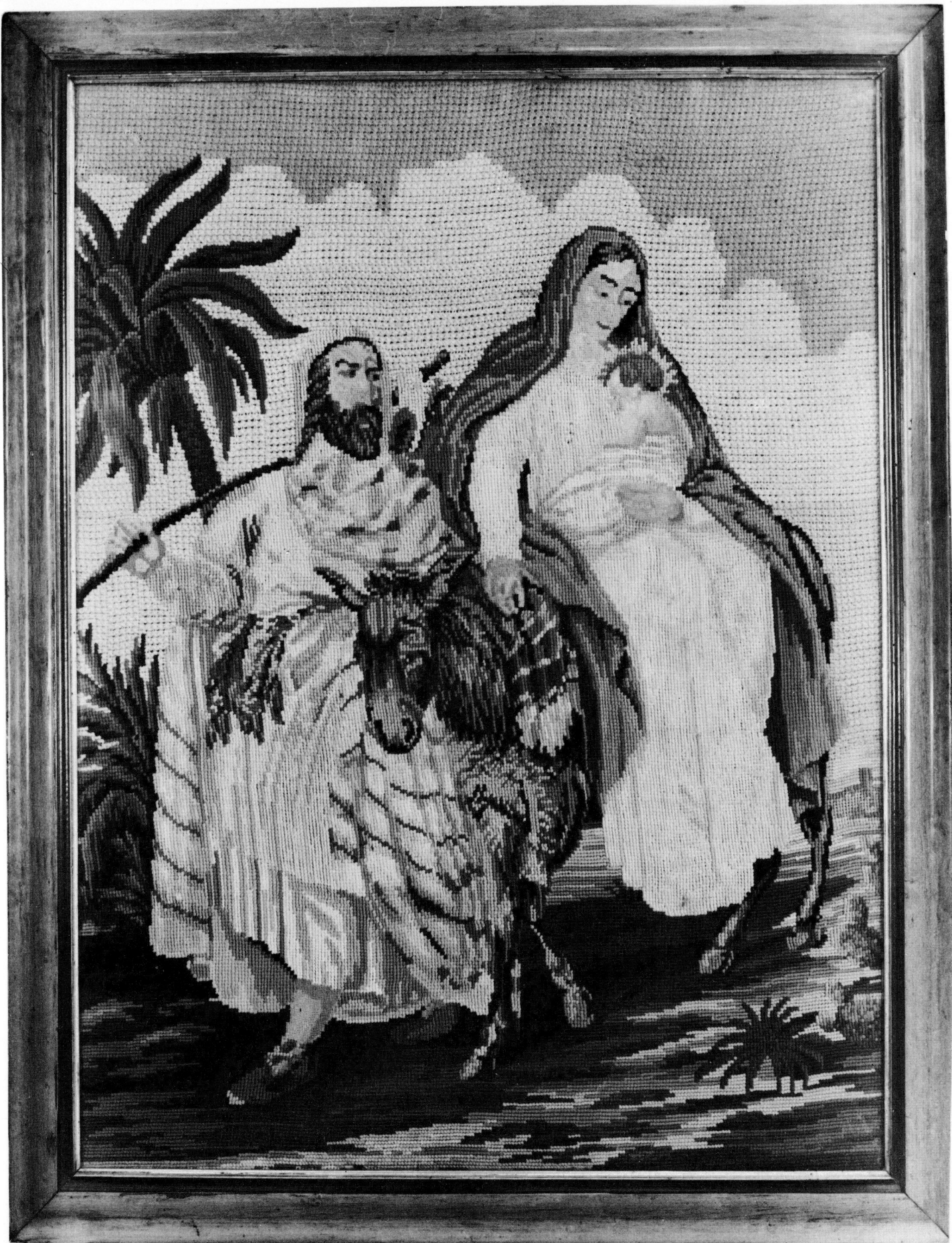

Words have a special place in the transmission of religious philosophy from past to present. They may actually be the 'word of God' and thus deserving of the most magnificent embellishment and the most splendid presentation. The illuminated manuscripts of medieval Europe are among the best known examples but every major religion has its superb holy books, and the Middle East has an architecture of sacred words where mosques are covered with decorations based on the texts of the Koran.

44 SCROLL OF ESTHER
German, seventeenth century
(The Jewish Museum, London:
photograph copyright the
Warburg Institute)

45 Sampler:
with BIBLE TEXTS
by Elizabeth Dun, 1723
(City Museum, City of St Albans)

46 Broadsheet:
JOSEPH EXPLIQUANT LES
SONGES DU ROI PHARAON
France
(Museum of Childhood,
Edinburgh)

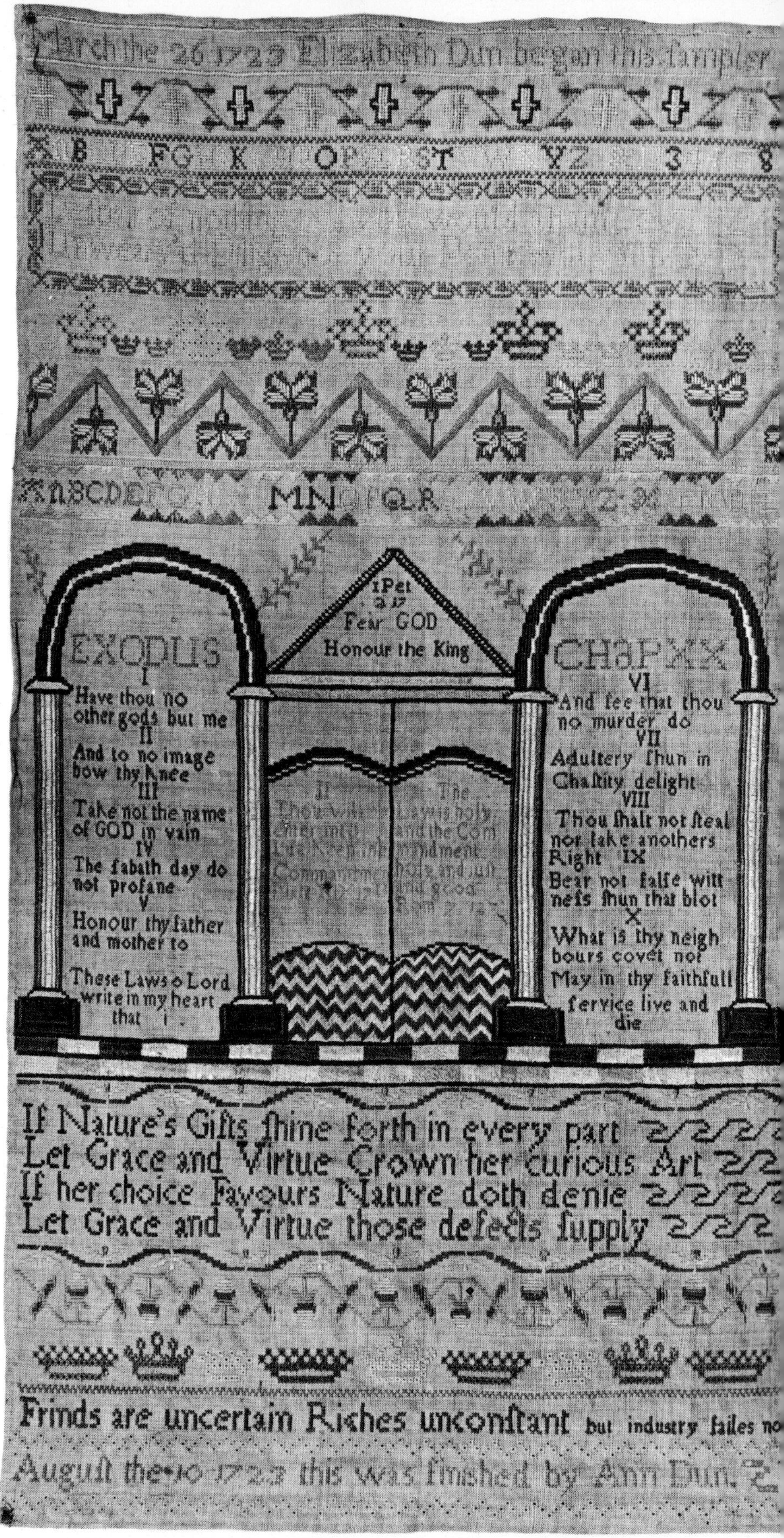

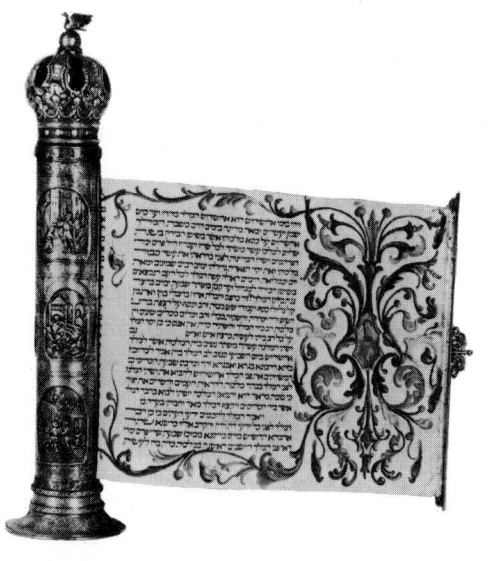

JOSEPH
EXPLIQUANT LES SONGES DU ROI PHARAON.

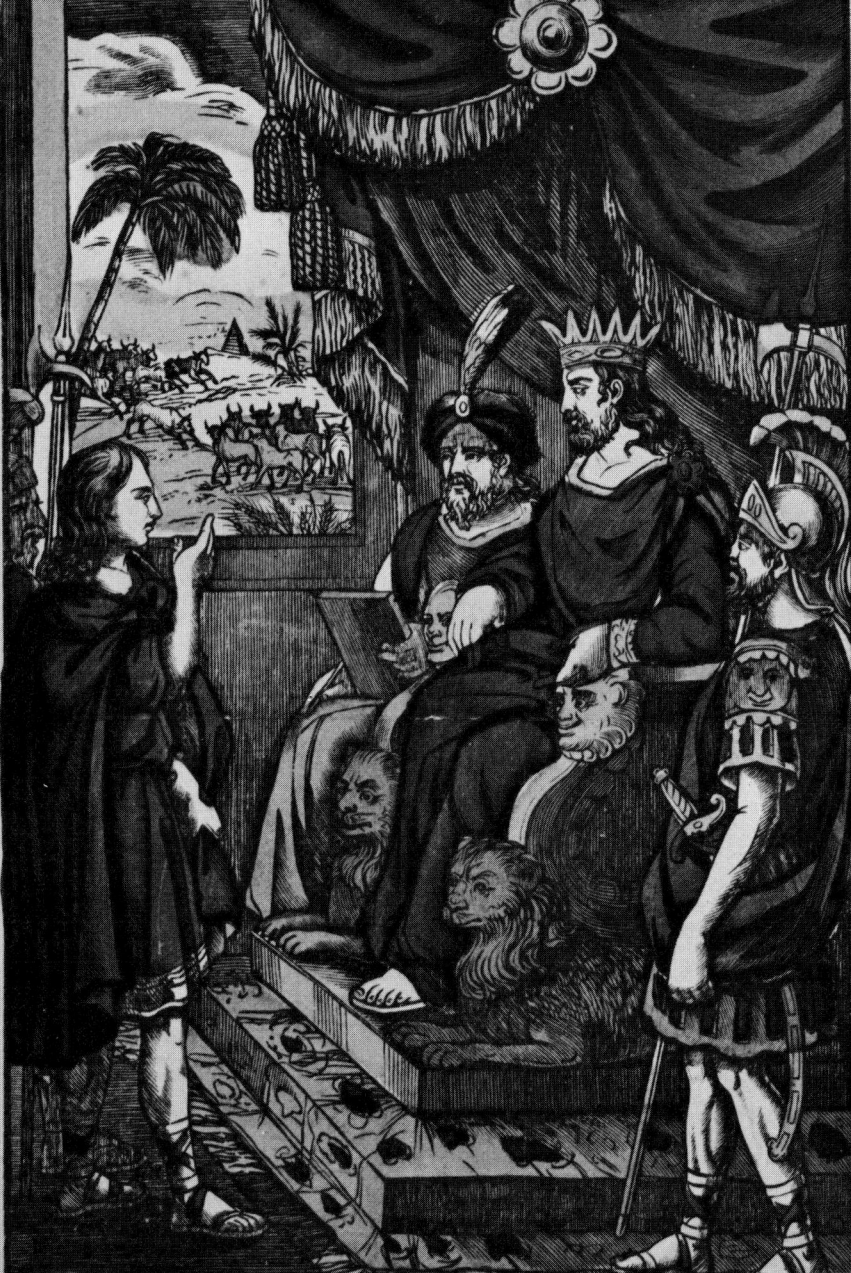

JOSEPH
ÉLEVÉ AUX HONNEURS
DE L'ÉGYPTE.

L'Échanson à Joseph.
Cans Joseph, bonne nouvelle, Par mon zèle Le roi te fait appeler, Quittes-là toutes les chaînes Que tu traînes, Viens à lui sans chanceler.

Joseph au Roi.
Quelle chose avez-vous, Sire, A me dire? Que désirez-vous de moi? Il n'est rien qu'avec la grâce Je ne fasse Pour obéir à mon roi.

Pharaon.
Il faut que tu pronostiques Et m'expliques Quelques songes que j'ai faits; On connaîtra ton mérite Dans l'Egypte Par mes signalés bienfaits.

Sept vaches grasses et alègres, Par sept maigres Mes yeux ont vu dévorer; Sept pleins épis par sept vides, Tous arides, Cela me fait soupirer.

Joseph.
Grand Prince, à sept ans fertiles, Sept stériles Aussitôt succéderont: Prévenez par l'abondance, L'indigence, Ou vos sujets périront.

Pharaon.
Joseph, je te fais le maître, Fais paraître Ta prudence à gouverner: Partage, pour récompense, Ma puissance, Je ne te veux point borner.

Joseph.
Que puis-je vous rendre, sire, Pour l'empire Que vous me donnez sur tous! Nonobstant cette fortune, Peu commune, Je veux être à vos genoux.

Pharaon.
Il suffit que tu me serves, Et conserves Tous les biens de mes états; Si j'apprends qu'on te traverse, Qu'on t'exerce, J'en punirai l'attentat.

Jacob à ses enfants.
Nous voici dans la famine, Sans farine, Et sans un grain de froment; Le bruit court qu'on en débite En Egypte, Allez-y promptement.

Les enfants.
Nous n'y connaissons personne, Qui nous donne Vers le prince un libre accès; Nous perdons déjà courage, Ce voyage N'aura pas un bon succès.

Le Père.
Faites comme il vous propose Toute chose, Dieu vous sera provident; Portez une bonne somme A cet homme Qu'on a fait surintendant.

Ses frères à Joseph.
Agréez, grand personnage, L'humble hommage Qu'en tremblant nous vous rendons; Nous venons vous reconnaître Pour vrai maître Des biens que nous possédons.

Joseph.
Ce ne sont que des souplesses, Des finesses, Pour épier le pays; Et si je ne vous accorde, Que la corde, Vous serez bien ébahis.

Ses Frères.
Que le ciel par sa justice Nous punisse, Si nous avons ce dessein; Nous ne sommes venus vite En Egypte Que pour acheter du grain.

Joseph.
Je veux qu'on vous emprisonne, Et j'ordonne La torture sans merci; Que chaque frère me dise Sans feintise, Si vous êtes tous ici.

Ses Frères.
Il reste encore notre père, Outre un frère Qui se nomme Benjamin; Pour Joseph le pénultième, Notre onzième, Il fit une triste fin.

Ruben à ses Frères.
Vous voulûtes satisfaire La colère, Vendant Joseph vingt deniers; Il est juste que Dieu venge Ce bel ange, Nous détenant prisonniers.

Ses Frères.
Souffrons tous la juste peine, De la haine Qui nous le fit vendre à tort, Et perdons toute espérance, Notre offense Mérite à bon droit la mort.

Joseph.
Juste ciel! leurs pleurs, leurs craintes, Leurs complaintes, Me contraignent à pleurer; Il faut donc que je me cache, Que je tâche De les faire renvoyer.

Trois fois saint Dieu de mon âme, Je me pâme Du plaisir que je reçois; La joie excite mes larmes, O quels charmes! J'ai mes frères avec moi.

Maître-d'hôtel, tout-à-l'heure, Sans mesure Allez remplir le sac de ces gens; Tâchez avec adresse Et vitesse D'y fourrer l'argent dedans.

Ses Frères.
Monseigneur, que le ciel vous rende La guirlande Qui répond à vos bienfaits; Vous méritez le couronne Que Dieu donne Aux hommes les plus parfaits.

Joseph.
Je te tiens dans l'esclavage, Pour ôtage, Simon sage et benin; Je prétends qu'il y demeure Jusqu'à l'heure Que je verrai Benjamin.

Réflexion.
Dieu permet que l'on t'abaisse, Qu'on t'oppresse, Garde-toi de perdre cœur; L'adversité de ce monde, Te seconde Pour demeurer le vainqueur.

Si l'orage et la bonace, Par la grâce, Sont dans ton cœur bien d'accord; Tu ne feras pas naufrage, Car l'orage Te conduira dans le port.

FIN.

ROMANCE DE JOSEPH. — Air connu.

A peine au sortir de l'enfance,
Quatorze ans au plus je comptais:
Je suivis avec confiance
De méchans frères que j'aimais.
A Sichem, au gras pâturage,
Nous paissions de nombreux troupeaux;
J'étais simple comme au jeune âge,
Timide comme mes agneaux.

Près de trois palmiers solitaires
J'adressais mes vœux au Seigneur,
Quand saisi par ces méchans frères
(J'en frémis encore de frayeur).
Dans un froid et humide abyme
Ils me plongent dans leurs fureurs,
Quand je n'opposais à leur crime
Que mon innocence et mes pleurs.

Hélas! près de quitter la vie,
Au jour enfin je fus rendu;
A des marchands de l'Arabie
Comme un esclave ils m'ont vendu.
Tandis que du prix de leur frère
Ils comptaient l'or qu'ils partageaient,
Hélas! moi je pleurais mon père
Et les ingrats qui me vendaient.

Fabrique de PELLERIN, Imprimeur-Libraire, à ÉPINAL.

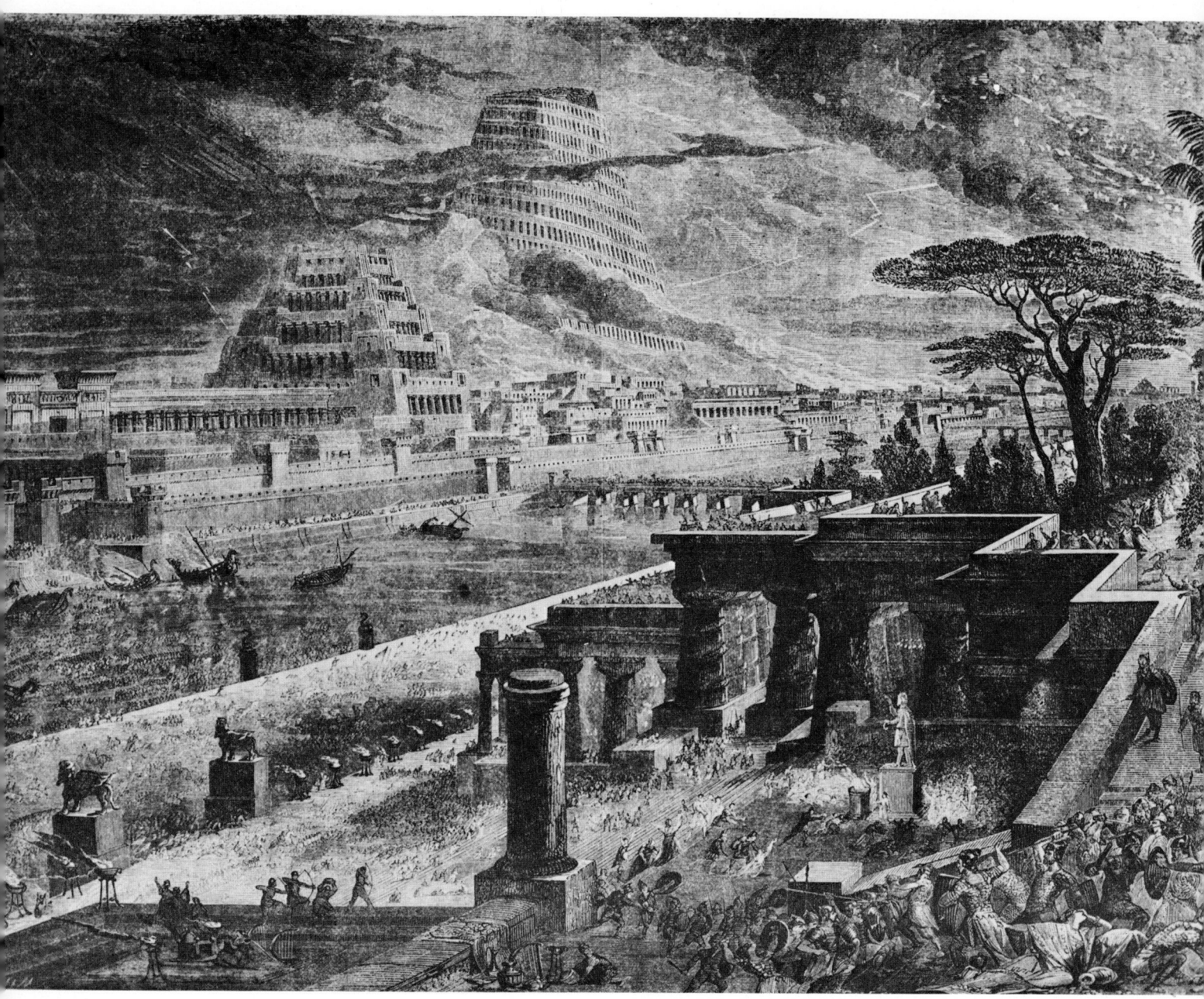

In the nineteenth and twentieth
centuries the pace of transmission of
images and stories of every kind has
been vastly increased. In the process
the meaning of many religious
themes has changed from religious
entertainment to entertainment pure
and simple. At the same time the
pressure of scepticism has pushed
religion into a more attacking,
propagandist stance.

47   ILLUSTRATION FROM A
     FAMILY BIBLE
     1863, see also figs 31 and 66
     (Mrs Joy Goodfellow)

48   Film still:
     from INTOLERANCE
     Directed by D W Griffiths, 1916
     (National Film Archive)

49   Film still:
     from LA PASSION DE JEANNE
     D'ARC
     Directed by Carl Dreyer, 1927
     (National Film Archive, Societé
     Generale de Films)

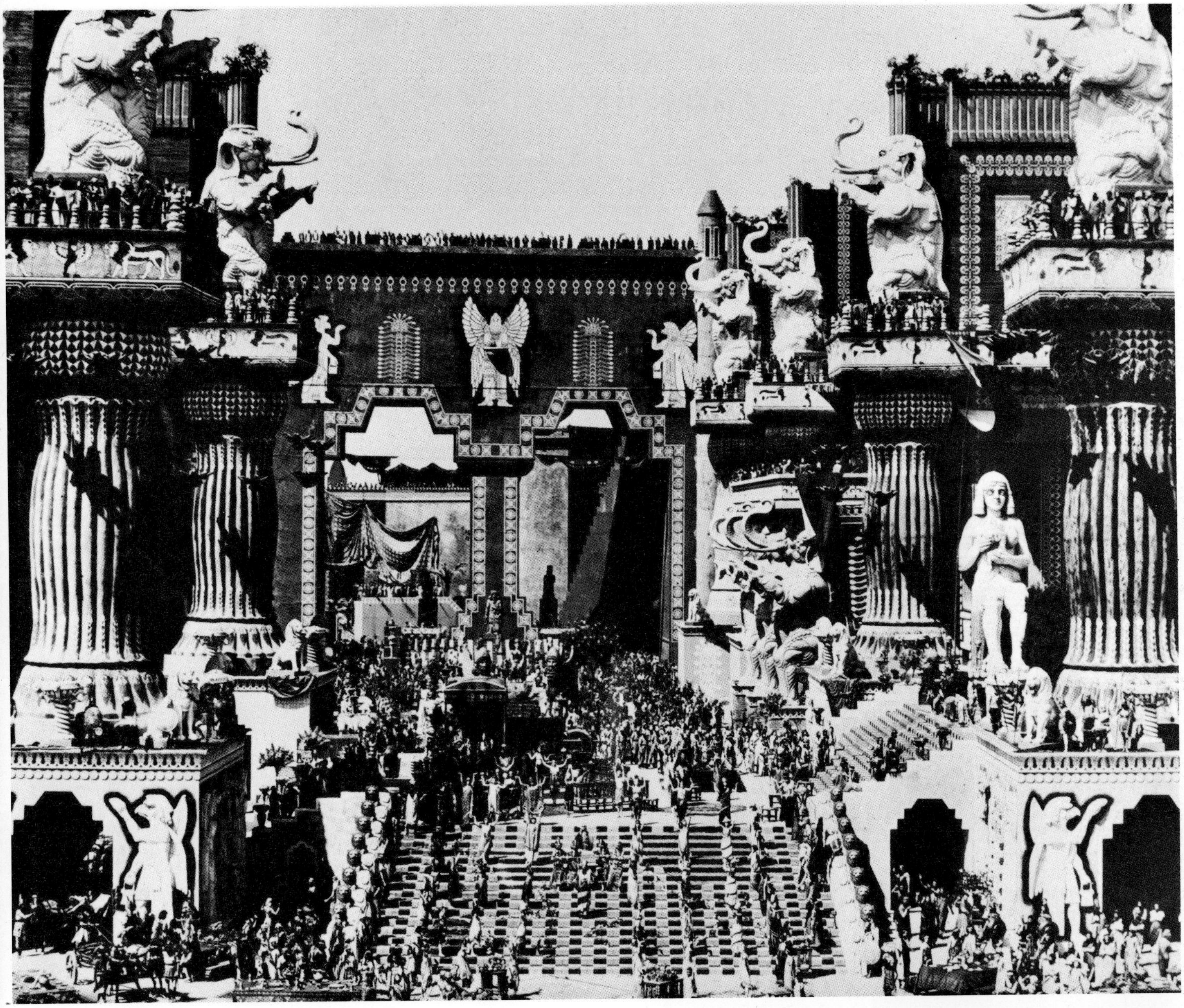

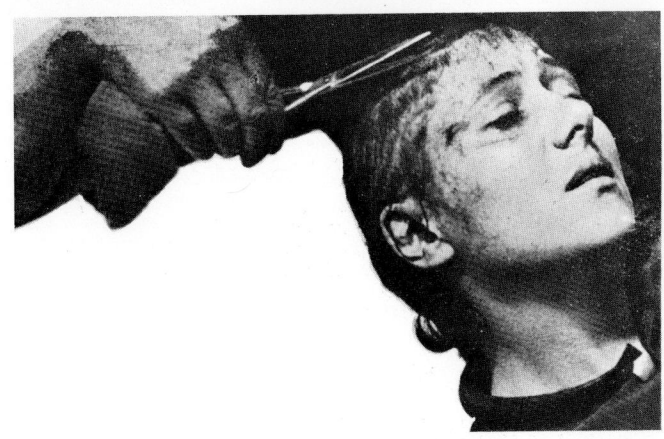

After arranging to stay with the priests at the foot of the mountain, I climbed to the temple situated near the summit. The whole mountain was made of massive rocks thrown together, and covered with age-old pines and oaks. The stormy ground itself bore the colour of eternity, paved with velvety moss. The doors of the shrines built on the rocks were firmly barred and there was not a sound to be heard. As I moved on all fours from rock to rock, bowing reverently at each shrine, I felt the purifying power of this holy environment pervading my whole being.

In the utter silence
Of a temple,
A cicada's voice alone
Penetrates the rocks.

from The Narrow Road to the Deep North by the Japanese poet Bashō (1644-94). Translated by Nobuyuki Yuasa and published as a Penguin Classic, 1966.

Come, Dionysus!
Come, and appear to us!
Come like a bull or a
Hundred-headed serpent,
Come like a lion snorting
Flame from your nostrils!
Swoop down, Bacchus, on the
Hunter of the Bacchae;
Smile at him and snare him;
Then let the stampeding
Herd of the Maenads
Throw him and throttle him
Catch, trip, trample him to death!

from the Bacchae by Euripides, translated by Philip Vellacott and published as a Penguin Classic in 1954.

Now what shall we say of these rich citizens of London? What shall I say of them? Shall I call them proud men of London, malicious men of London, merciless men of London? No, no I may not say so; they will be offended with me then.

Yet must I speak. For is there not reigning in London as much pride, as much covetousness, as much cruelty, as much oppression, and as much superstition, as was in Nebo? Yes, I think, and much more too. Therefore I say, repent, O London; repent, repent. Thou hearest thy faults told thee, amend them, amend them.

Hugh Latimer, from the Sermon on the Plough, preached at the Shrouds, St Paul's 18 January 1548 and quoted by Paul A Welsby in Sermons and Society, a Pelican original, 1970.

Present

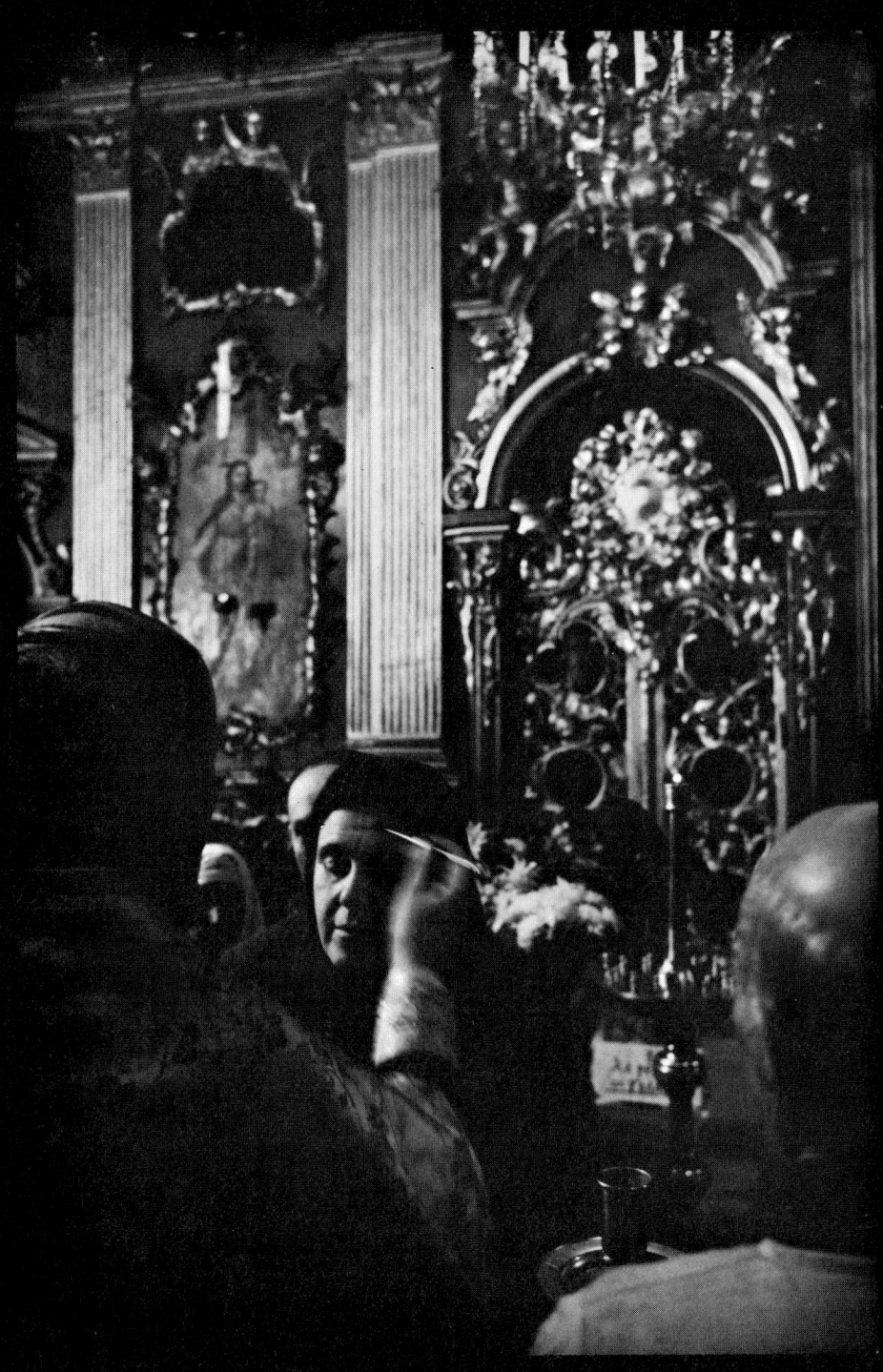

50 Photograph:
SCENE IN A CHURCH IN
KIEV
by Cornell Capa
(The John Hillelson Agency Ltd)

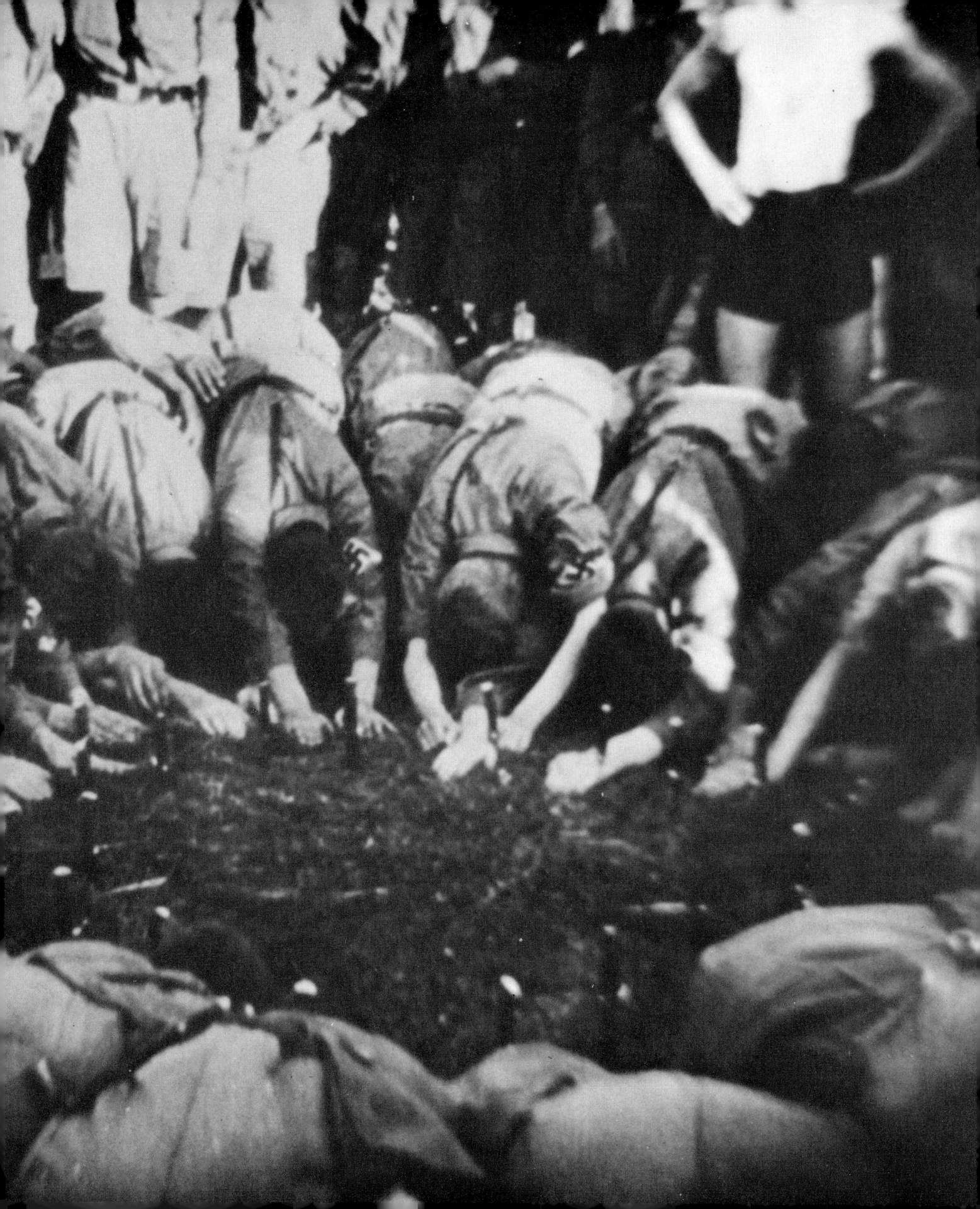

At the centre of the idea of worship is ceremony. In a series of formalized activities – like dance or drama or mime – the reality of religious philosophy is brought to earth. From the necessities of such ceremonies have been born theatre and music and, perhaps also, the use of clothing as a symbol for unity, power or status. In detail the functions of the ceremonies vary, and so, therefore, do the forms of movement and gesture, the words and the artefacts. The aim may be the union of a single worshipper with God: or it may be the reassertion in mass feeling of old or new truths. The outcome may be reassuring and purifying, or it may be dangerously hysterical. In any event, the resulting combination of forms is one of the most powerful uses of art so far devised by humanity.

52 Photograph:
    JAPAN'S WARRIORS OF THE
    MIND
    by Takamasa Inamura
    (Camera Press Ltd, London)
A student monk says a prayer before his meal in a monastery.

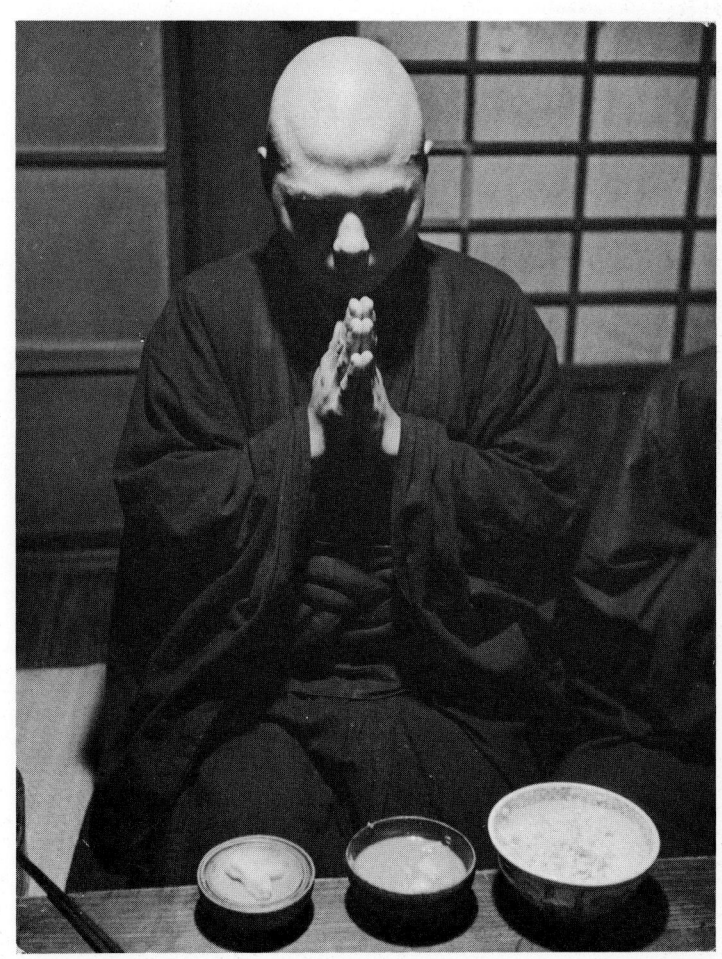

51 Film still:
    from TRIUMPH OF THE WILL
    Directed by Leni Riefensthal,
    1935
    (National Film Archive)
A group of Nazis worship their daggers.

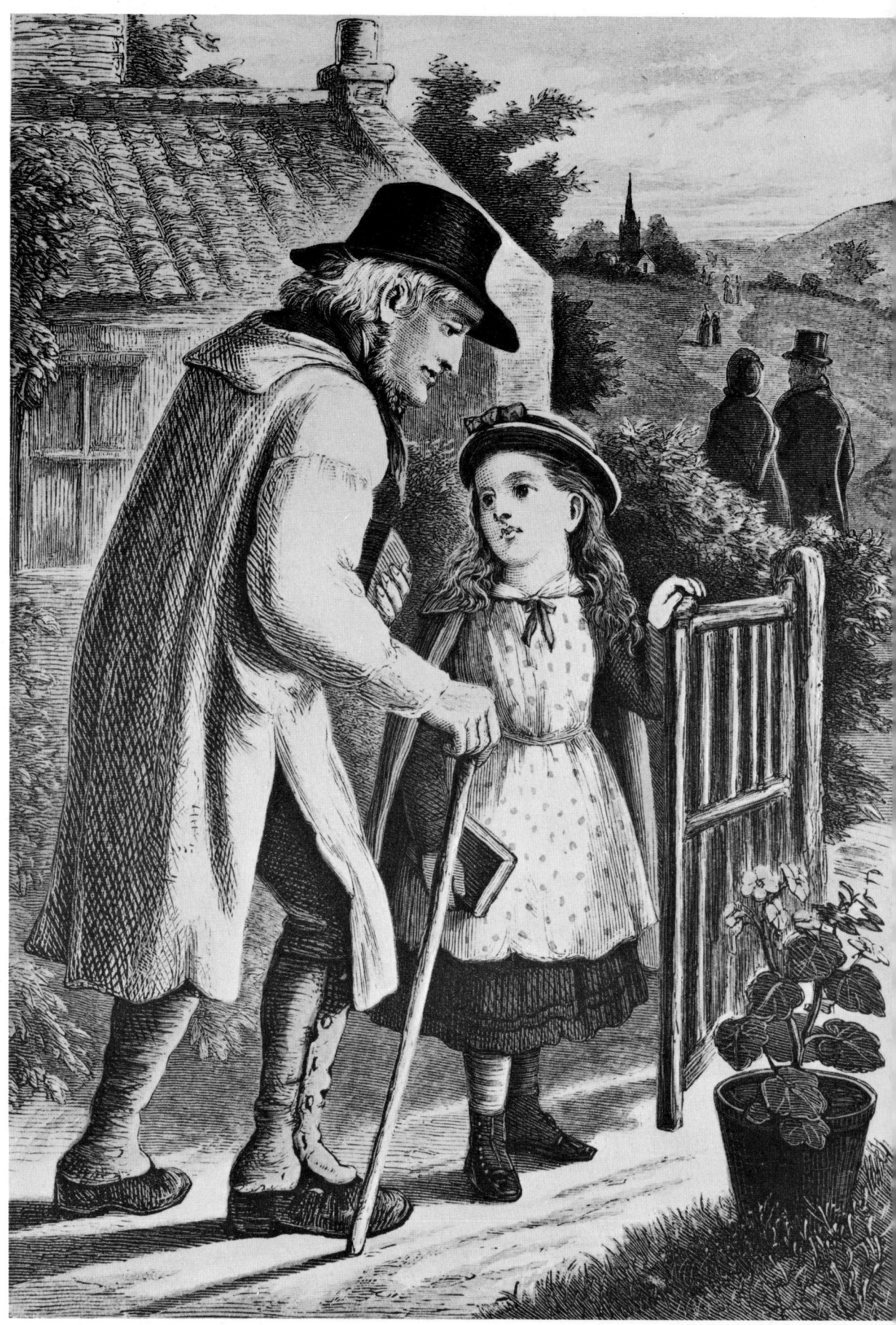

53 Lithograph:
SUNDAY MORNING
late nineteenth century
(Mansell Collection)
The act of worshipping at the centre
of the family life of the community.

55 Sculpture:
THE NATIVITY
from Chartres Cathedral,
eleventh–thirteenth century
(French Government Tourist
Office: photograph by Hélène
Adant)
The Virgin and the animals worship
the infant Christ.

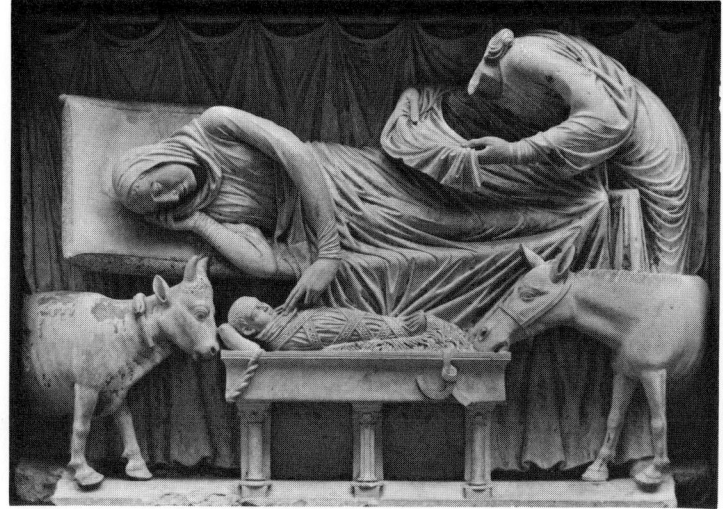

54 Photograph:
AUDIENCE AT A
PERFORMANCE BY THE
BEATLES
by David Hurn
(David Hurn)
The worship of a human ideal.

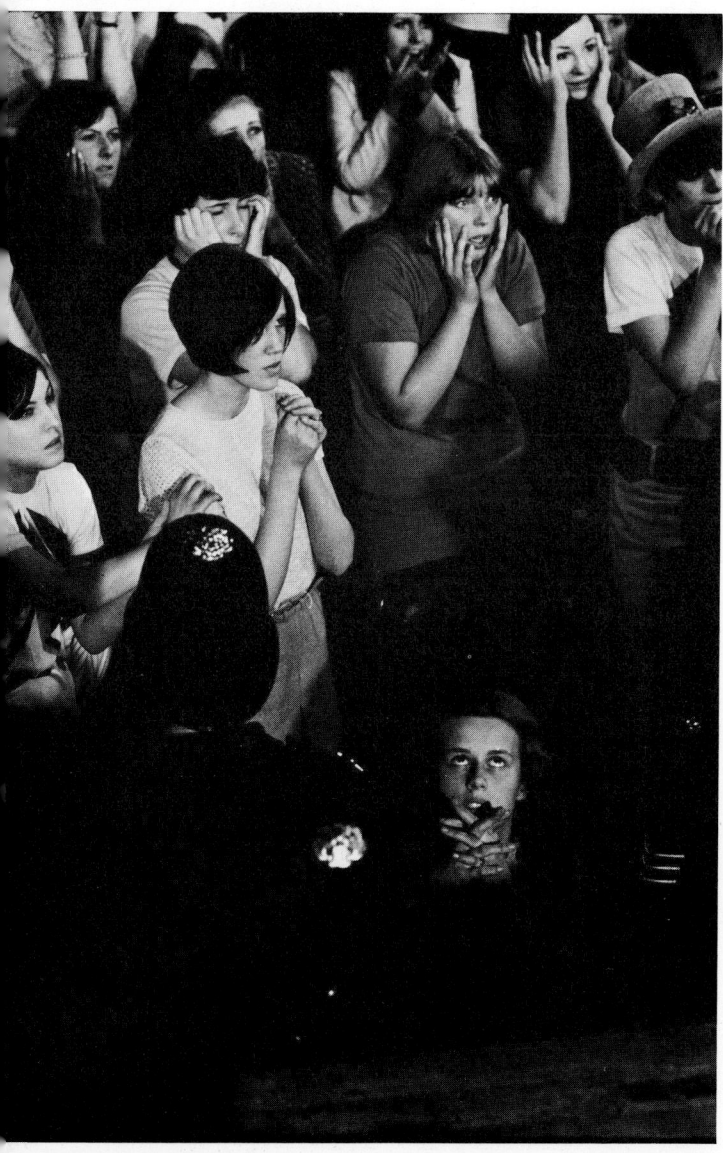

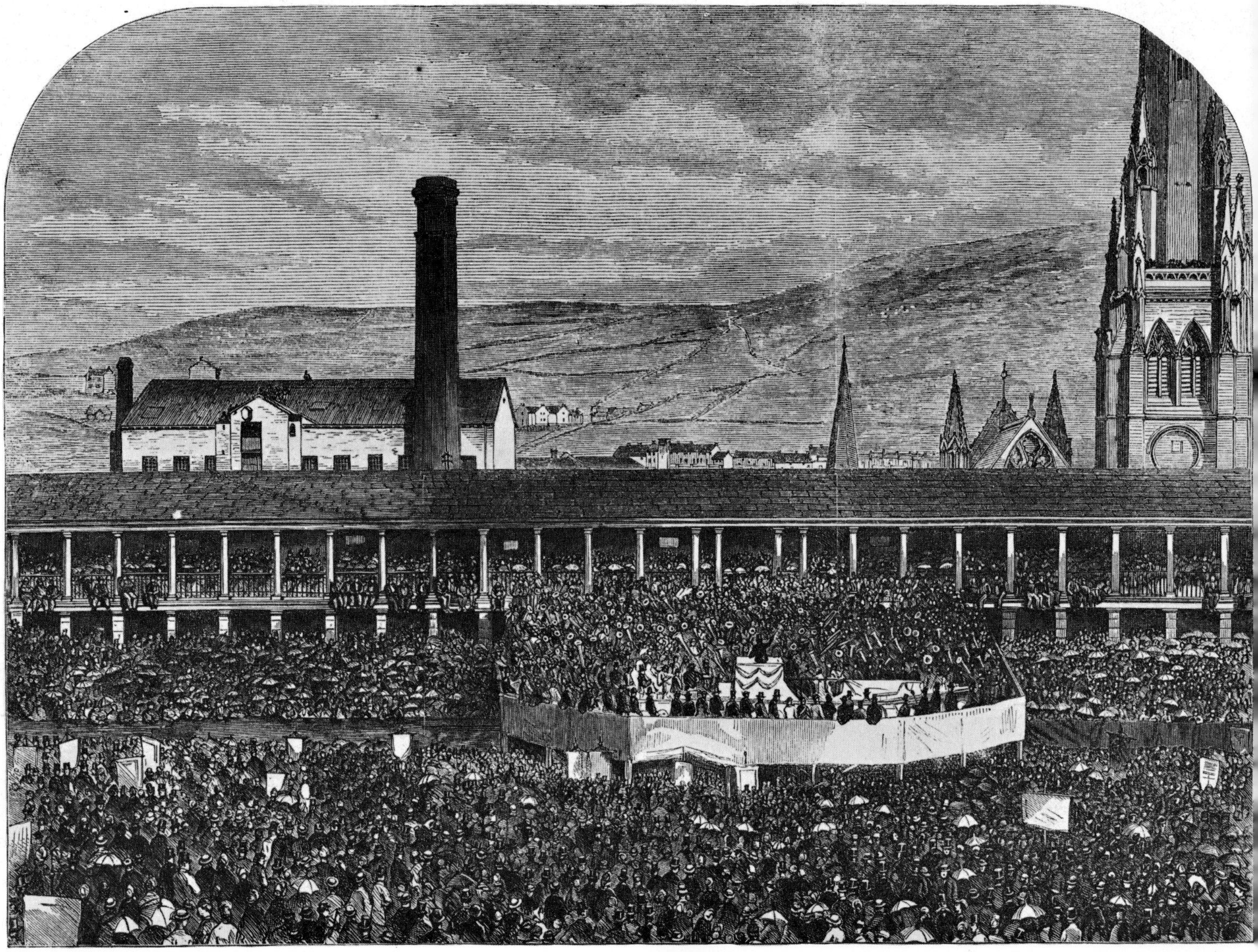

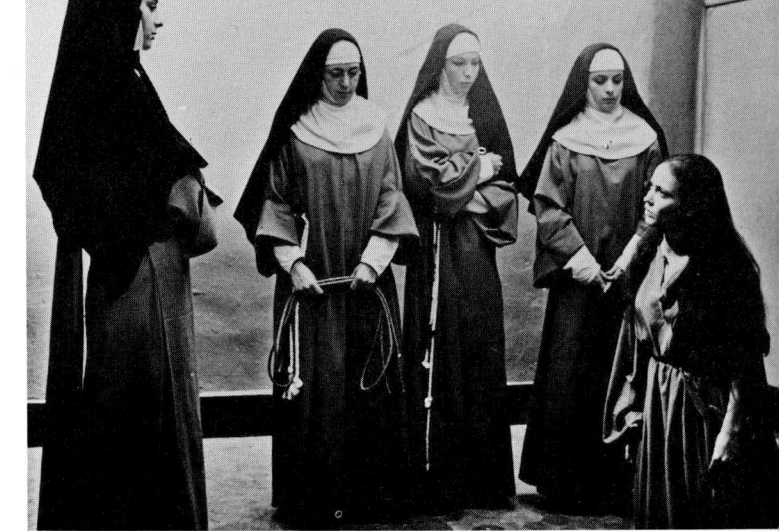

It is partly through the involvement of young people in the ceremonies and disciplines of worship that the religious link between past, present and future has been made real.

56 Illustration:
SUNDAY-SCHOOL JUBILEE
COMMEMORATION IN THE
PIECE HALL, HALIFAX
from the **Illustrated London News,** 1866
(Mansell Collection)

57 Film still:
from LA RELIGIEUSE
Directed by Jacques Rivette, 1965
(National Film Archive, Gala Film
Distributors Ltd)

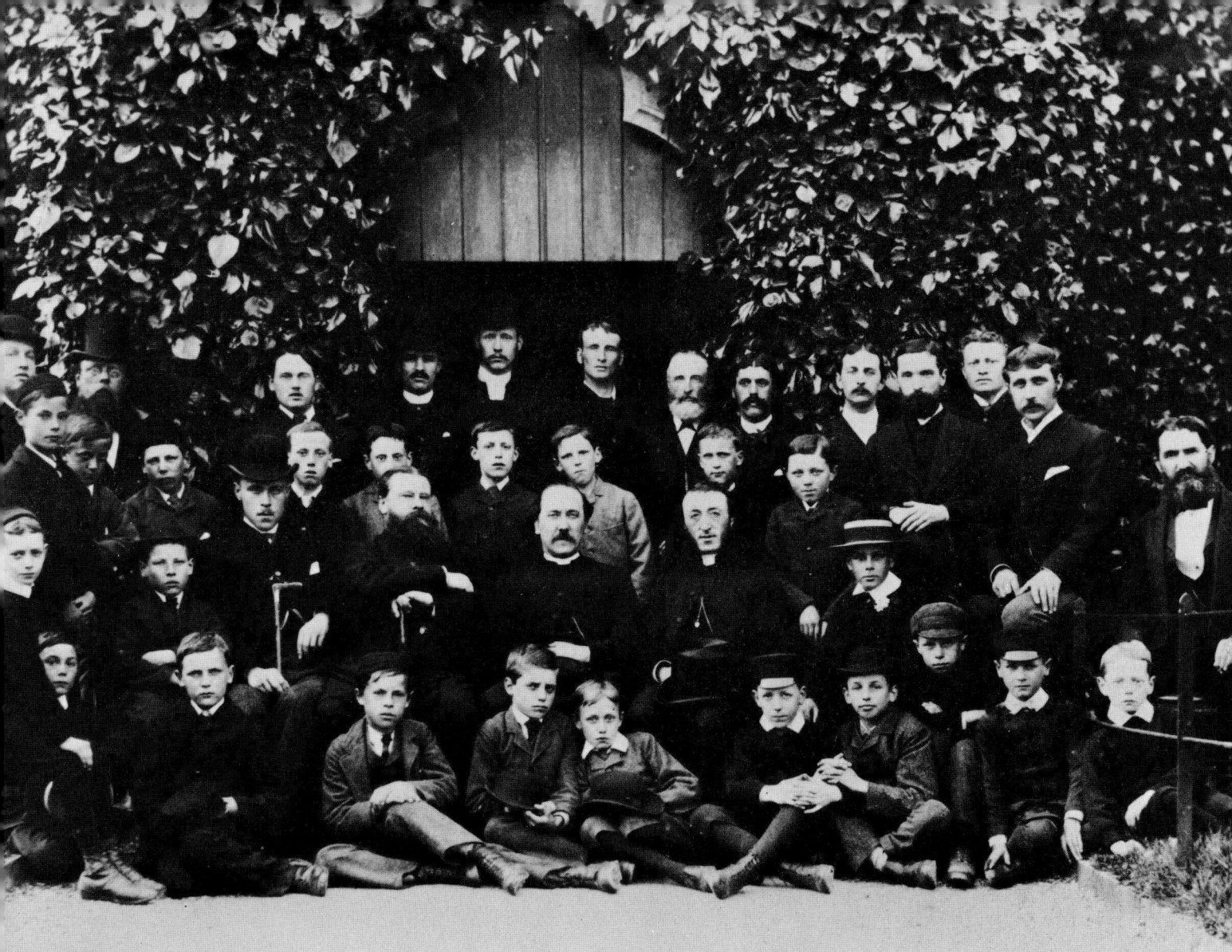

58 Photograph:
JOINT CHOIRS OF ST JOHN'S
BURGESS HILL AND THE
CHAPEL ROYAL
1884
(Mansell Collection)

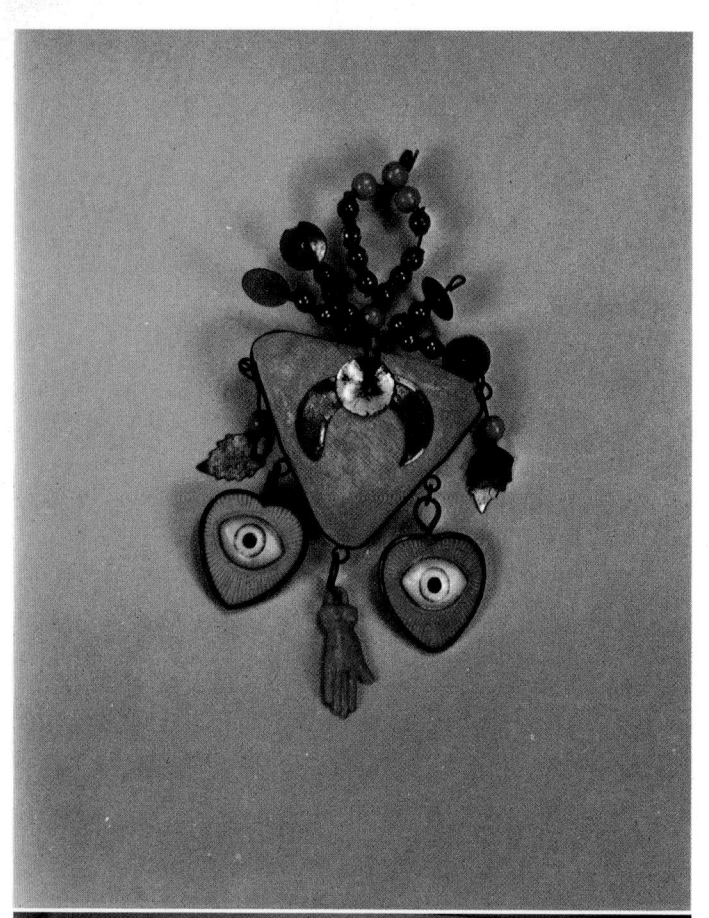

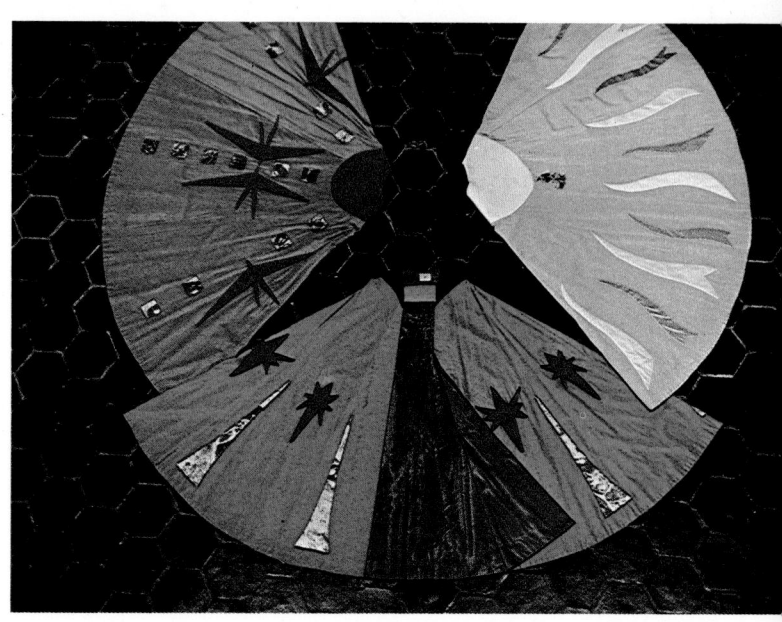

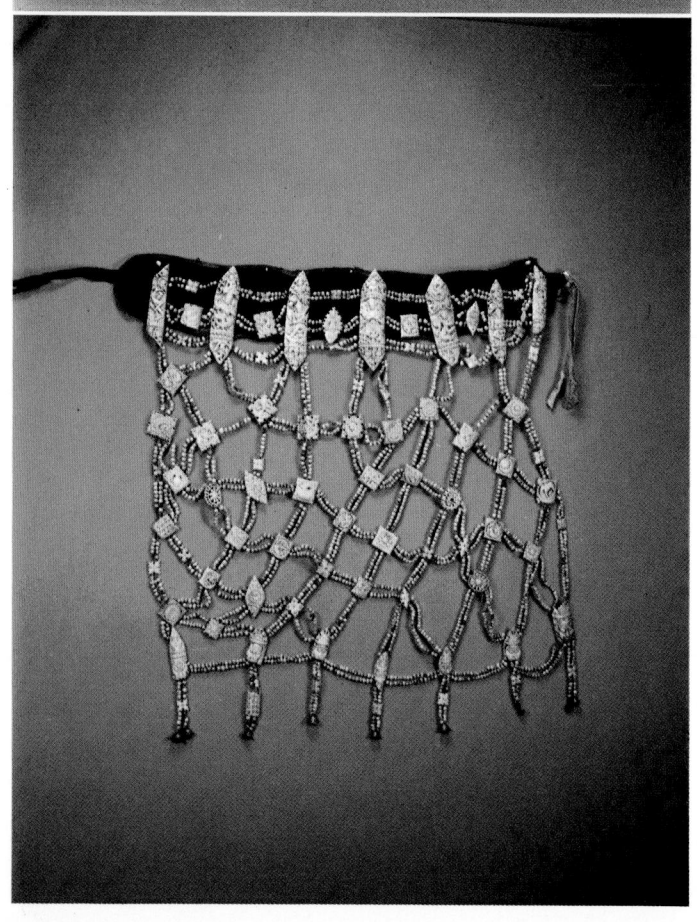

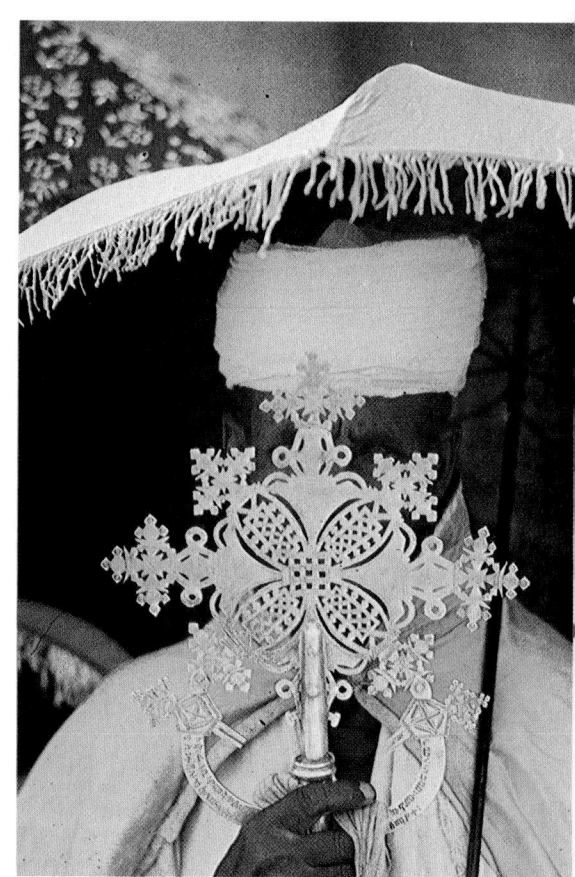

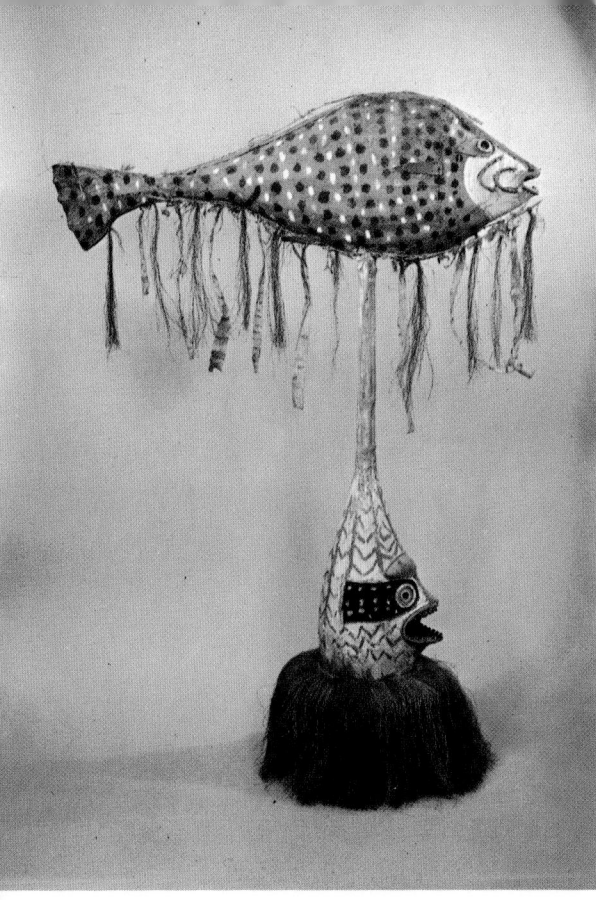

Ceremony is a work of art. But within that embracing form an astonishing variety of other works are included, each with a particular use, each acting as a particular focus of activity, sentiment or thought.

59 CHARM
    hung in motor-cars in the Aleppo area of Syria, contemporary
    (Pitt Rivers Museum, University of Oxford, Coll. P Copeland)
Travellers seem always to have needed the reassurance of talismans : sometimes these have acted as portable shrines making possible small, unavowed acts of worship in everyday life.

60 Costume :
    LAMA'S APRON
    Tibet
    (Pitt Rivers Museum, University of Oxford)
This apron was worn by exorcists.

61 COPES
    by John Piper, made by Louis Grosse for Coventry Cathedral
    (Provost and Chapter of Coventry Cathedral)

62 Photograph :
    ETHIOPIAN CHRISTIAN CARRYING A CROSS
    by John Bulmer
    (Camera Press Ltd, London)

63 Mask :
    EHARO
    New Guinea
    (Pitt Rivers Museum, University of Oxford)
This mask carries a fish totem and was used in ceremonies which re-enacted mythical events. The long stalk is a functional part of the mask's role in the dance, for the wearer sometimes bent forward thrusting the totem to the ground.

64 Painting :
    EX VOTO, MARIA BEINBERG
    Bavaria, 1850
    Photographed by Claus Hansmann
    (Claus Hansmann)
This painting was a votive offering.

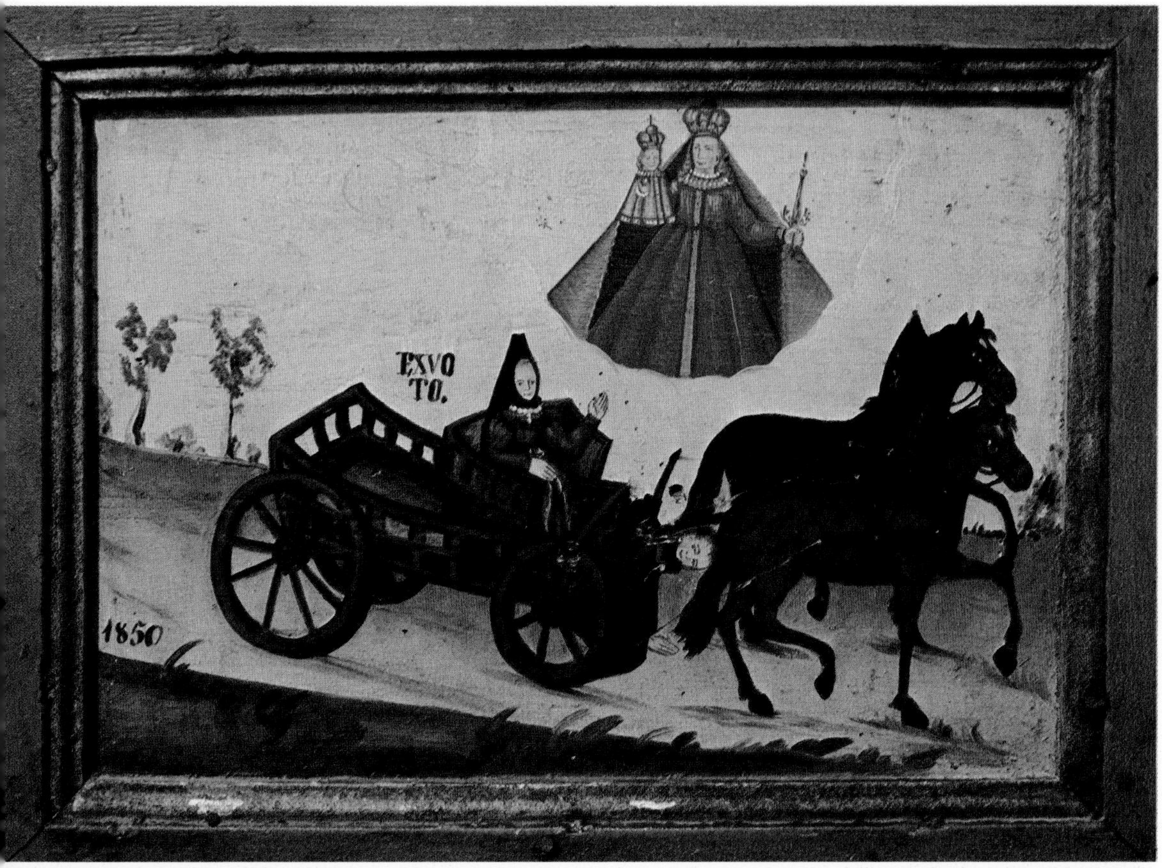

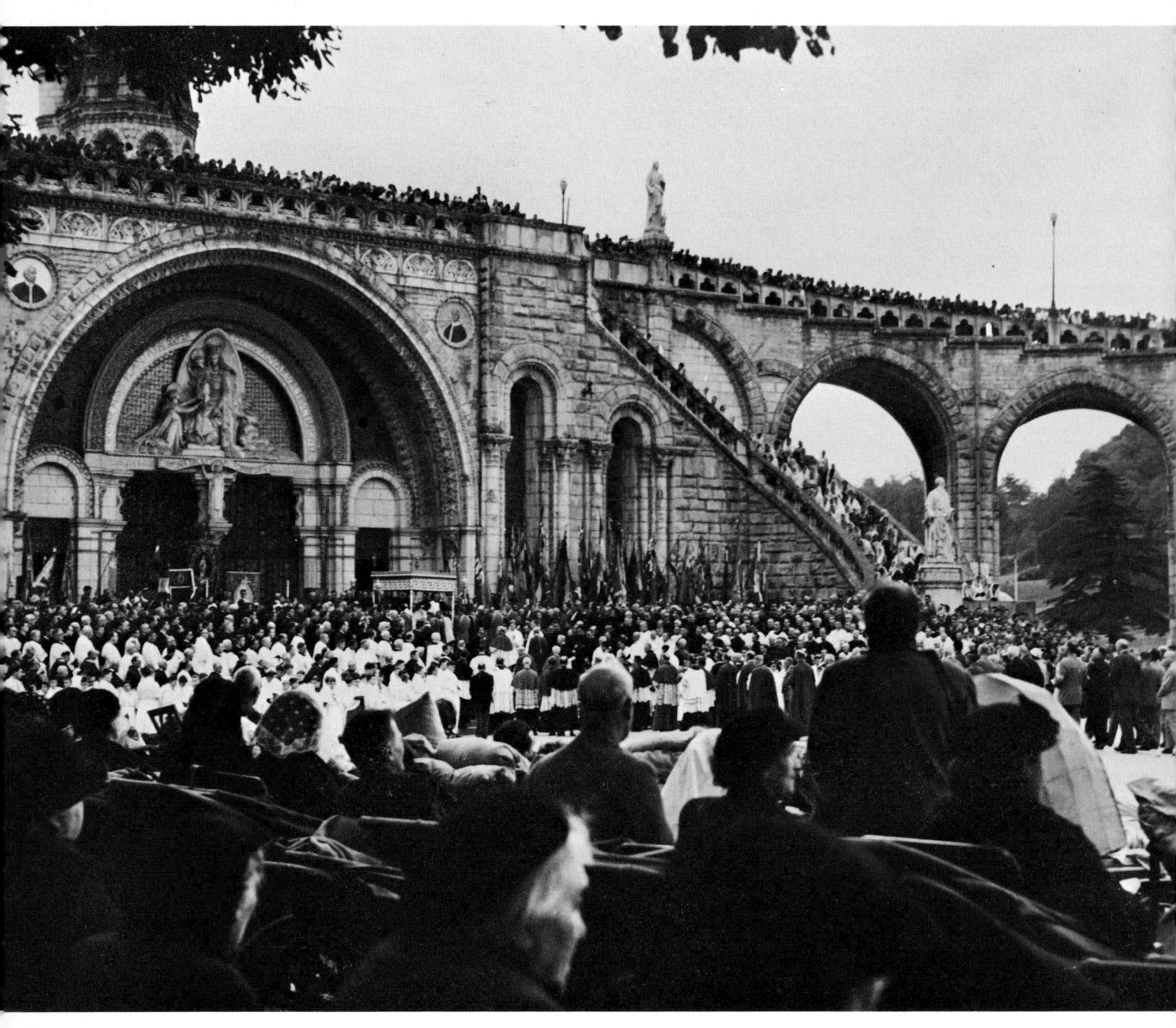

65 Photograph:
PROCESSION OF THE BLESSED
SACRAMENT, LOURDES
by Peter Tynan-O'Mahony
(Camera Press Ltd, London)

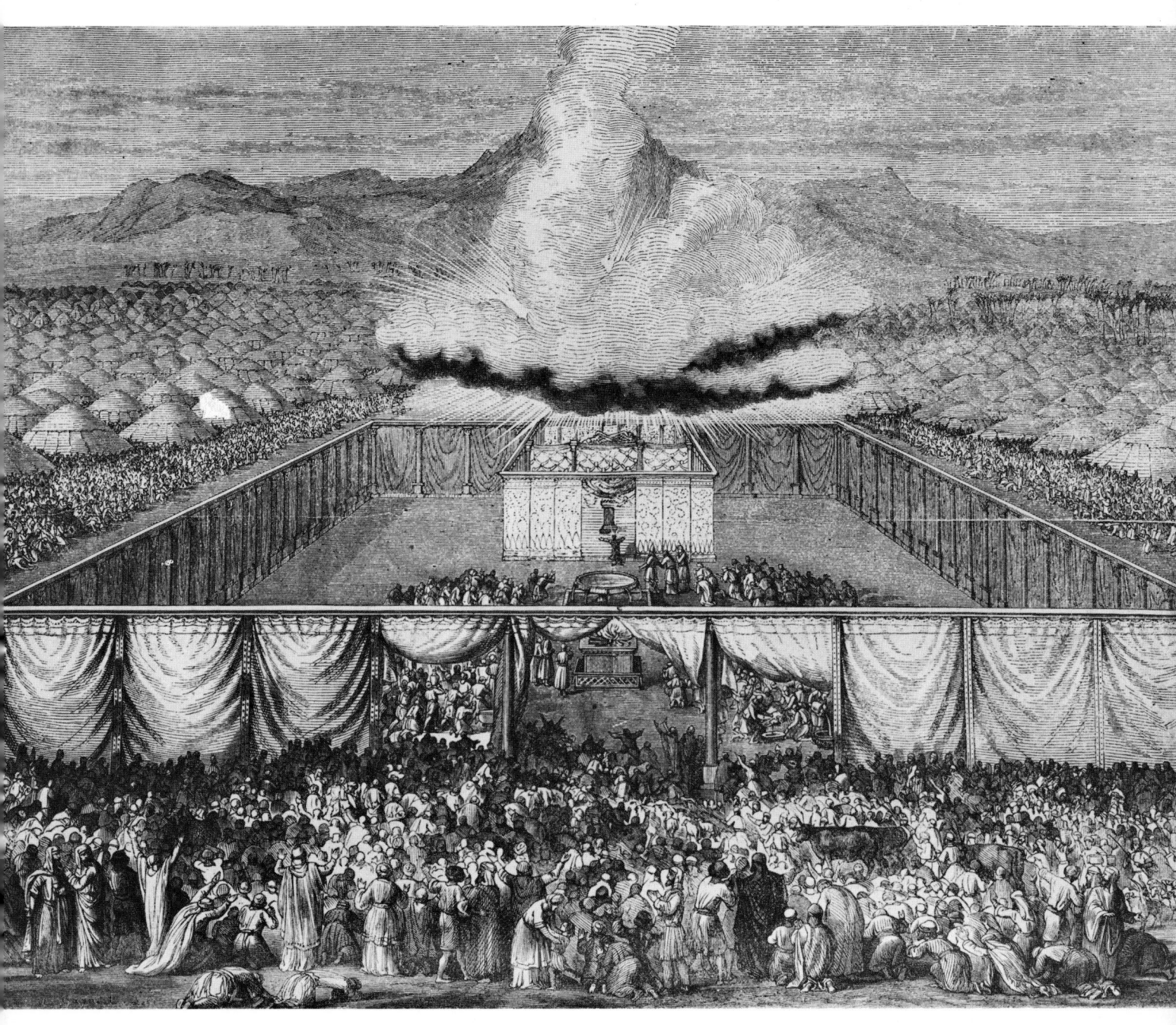

66 ILLUSTRATION FROM A
FAMILY BIBLE
1863, see also figs 31 and 47
(Mrs Joy Goodfellow)

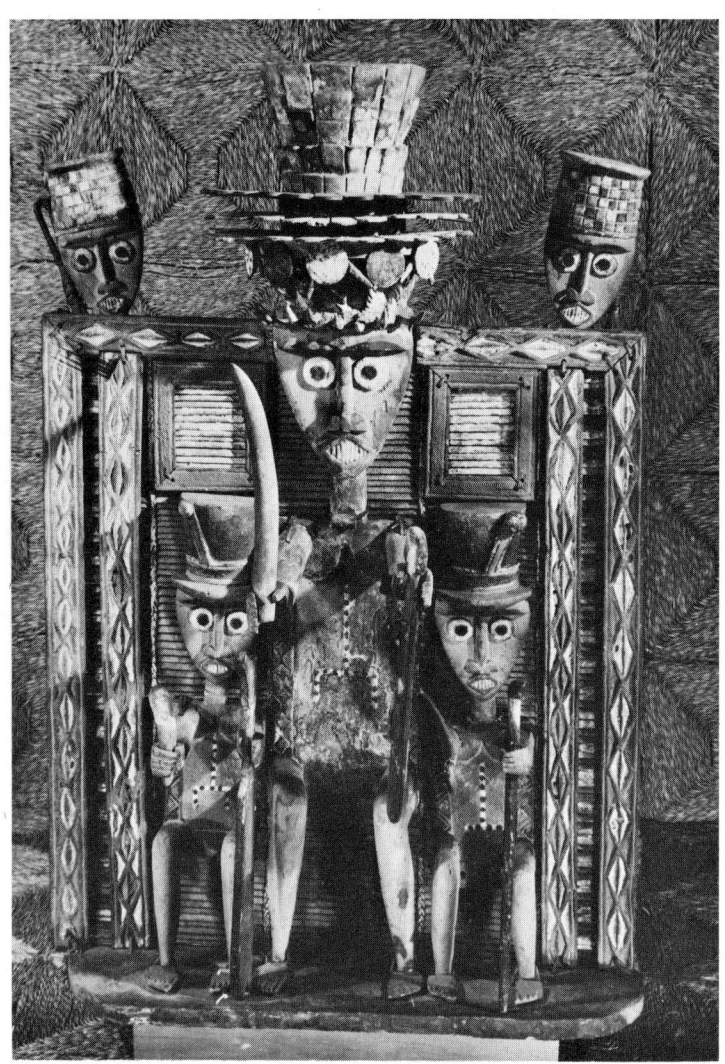

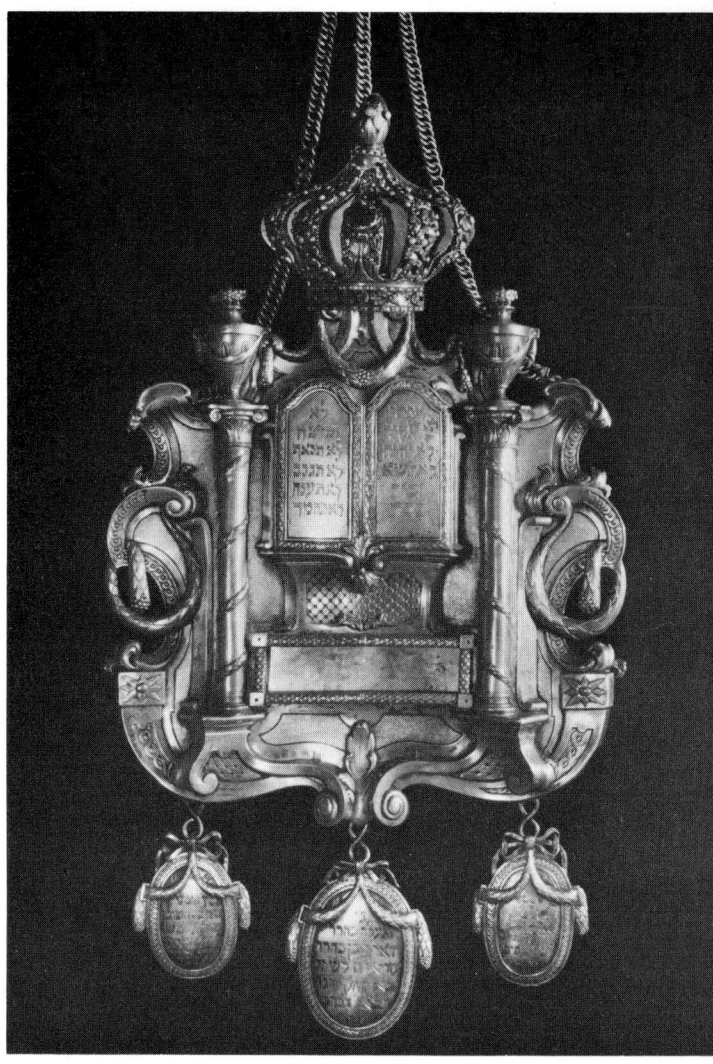

Ceremonial objects, particularly
shrines and altars, have inevitably
been the subject of a specially high
standard of craftsmanship, love and
care. However, the function of such
objects is primarily symbolic and
only takes on its true meaning when
it is vivified by the presence of
worshippers.

67 Sculpture:
    DUEN FOBARA
    Kalabari Ijo Tribe, Nigeria
    (Pitt Rivers Museum, University
    of Oxford)
This is an ancestral shrine
commemorating a chief of the Ekine
or Sekiapn Society.

68 TORAH SHIELD WITH
    EMERALDS, RUBIES AND
    PEARLS
    by R Fleischmann
    Prague, Czechoslovakia, 1784
    (State Jewish Museum, Prague:
    photograph by Vladimír Soukup)

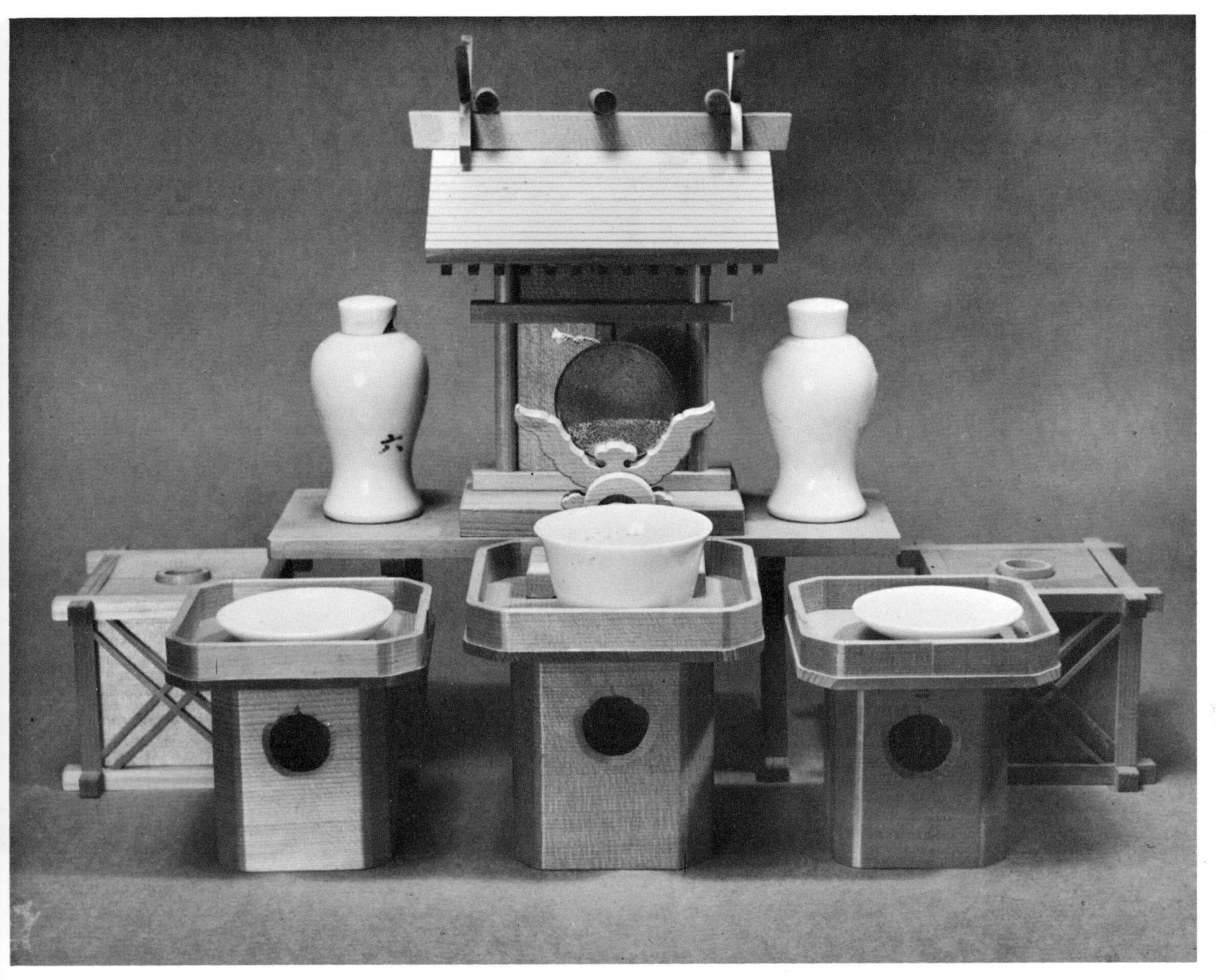

69 SHINTO SHRINE
Japan
(Pitt Rivers Museum, University
of Oxford)
The miniature shrine has vessels for
offerings to the deceased, and was
used in periods of mourning.

70 DANCE MASK
Japan
(Pitt Rivers Museum, University
of Oxford)

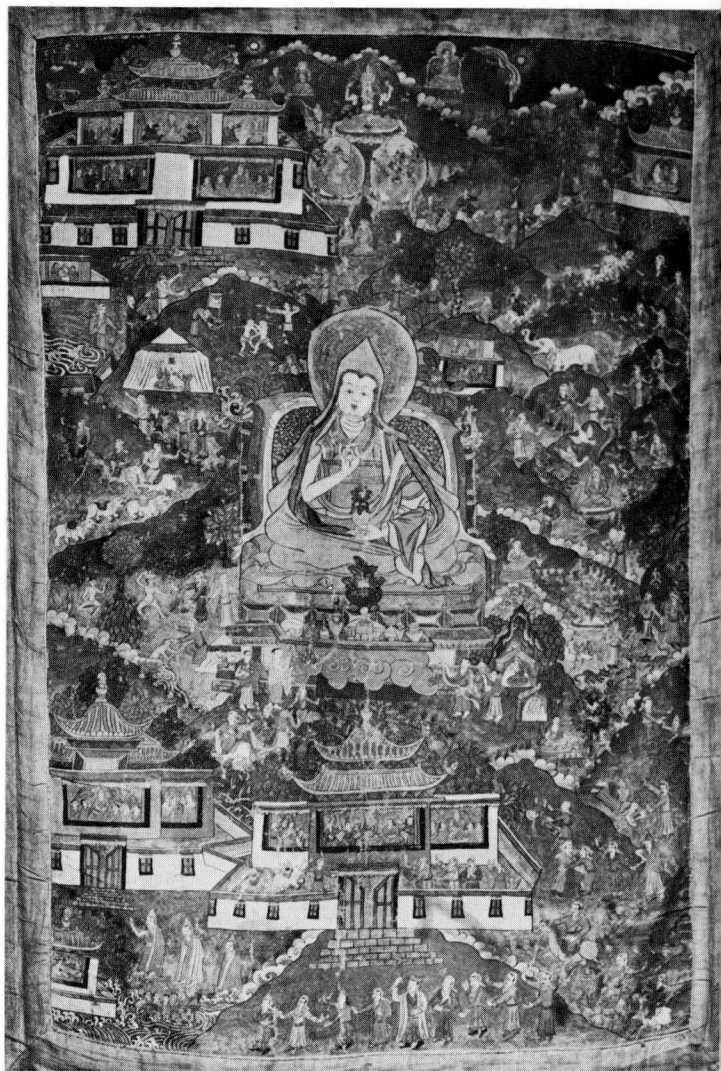

**71 TEMPLE BANNER OF A HIGH
LAMA, PROBABLY
TSONG-KA-PA**
Tibet
(Horniman Museum, London)

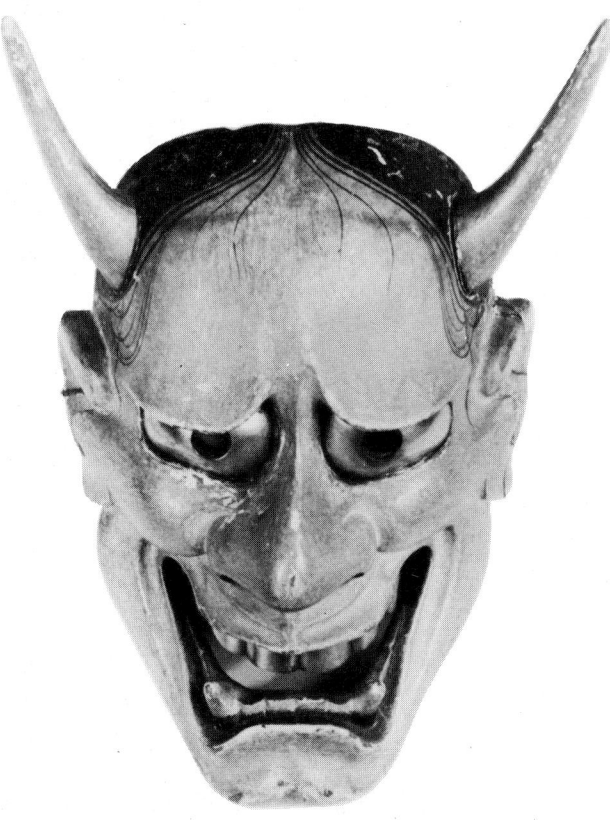

72 DEVIL MASK (with painted
electric light bulbs for eyes)
Oruro, Bolivia
(Horniman Museum, London)

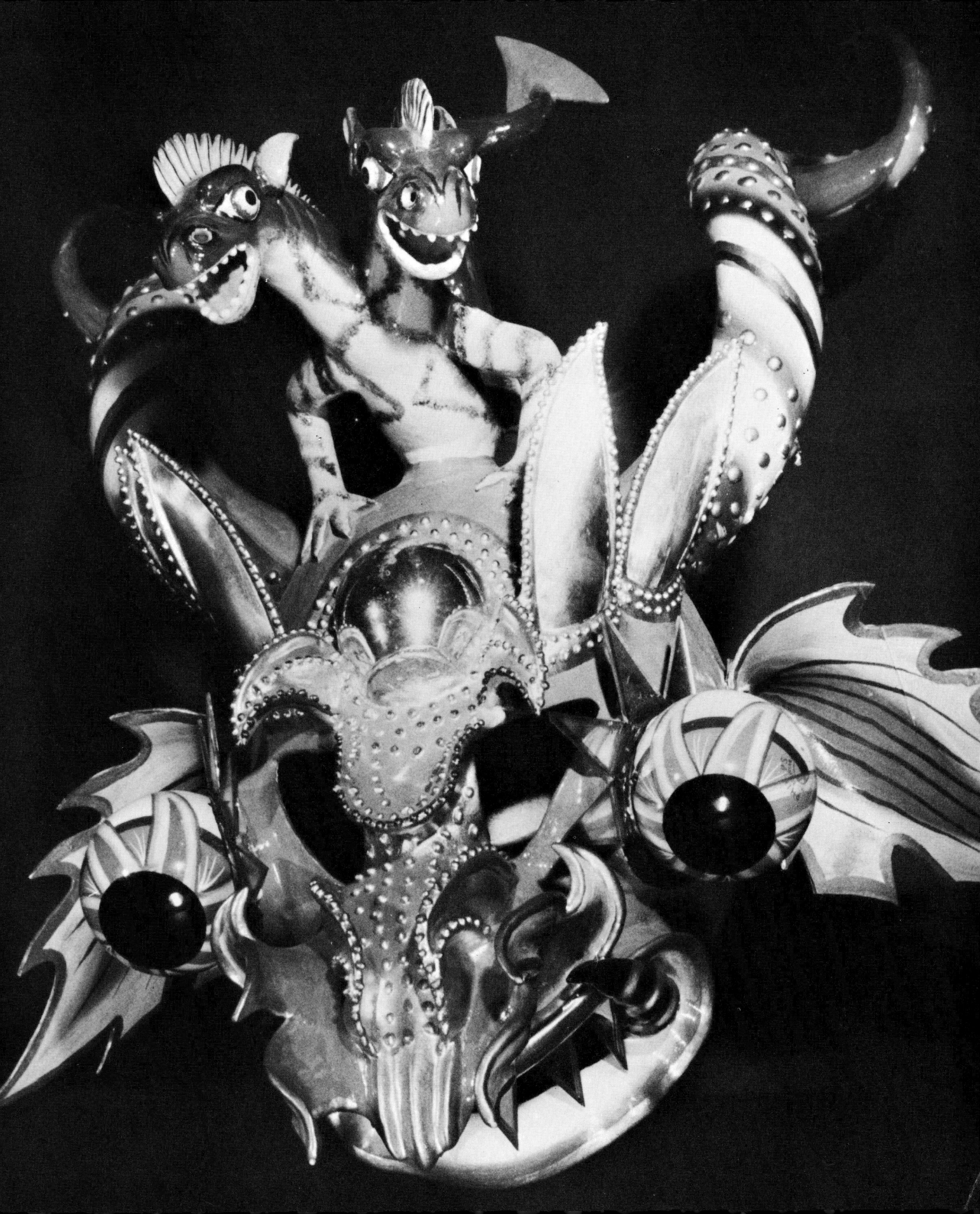

Priests, witch doctors, and wise men.

73 Lithograph:
THE REVEREND WILLIAM WILLIAMS
OF PANT-Y-CELYN
(National Library of Wales)

74 Sculpture:
A PRIESTESS SACRIFICING
Roman Britain, second or third
century
(Museum of Antiquities, University of Newcastle
and Society of Antiquaries, Newcastle upon Tyne)

75 TV still:
THE QUESTION WHY
with Malcolm Muggeridge
(BBC-TV)

76 Sculpture:
A SHAMAN OF THE HAIDA
TRIBE
British Columbia
(Wellcome Institute of the History
of Medicine, London)

77 Film still:
DON CAMILLO'S LAST
ROUND
with Fernandel as Don Camillo
1955
(National Film Archive, Films de
France)

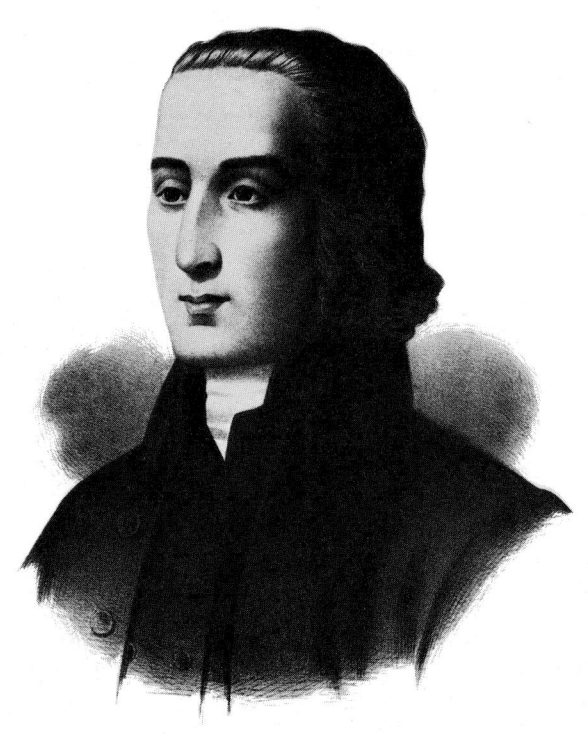

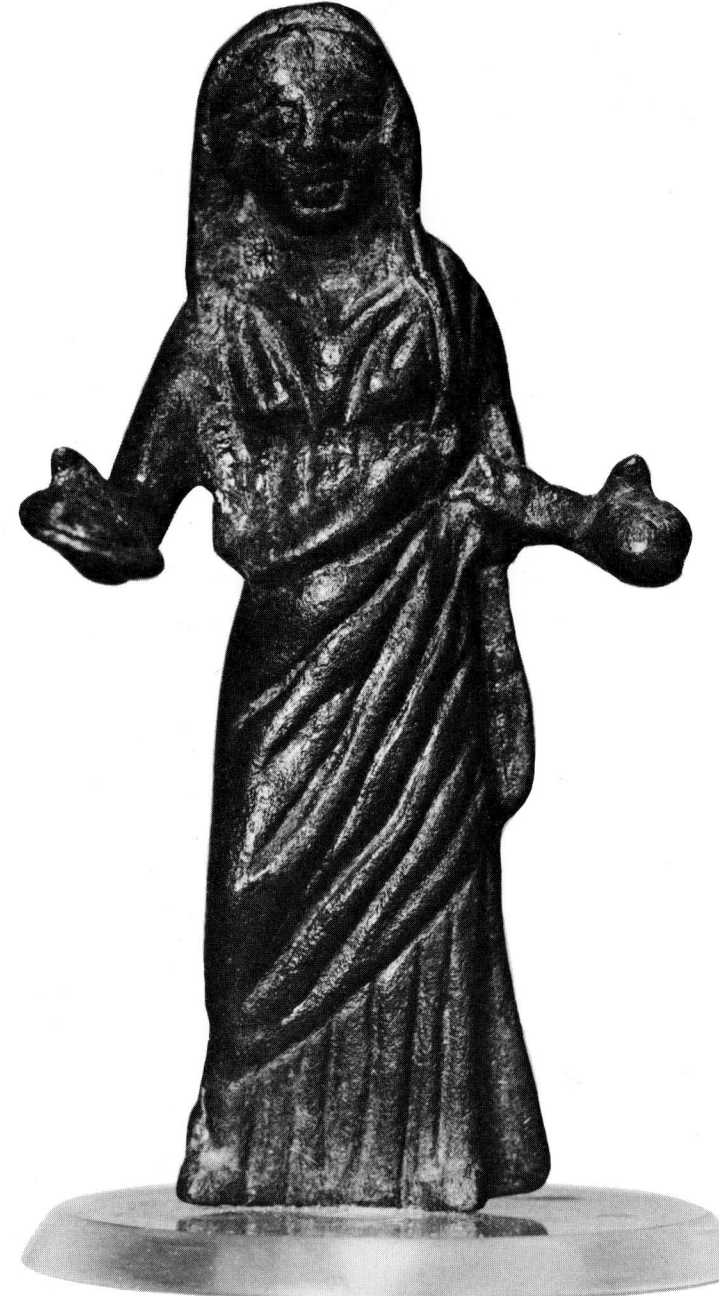

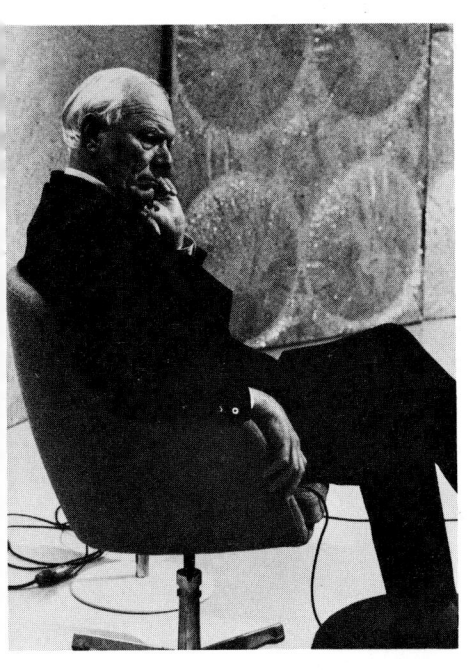

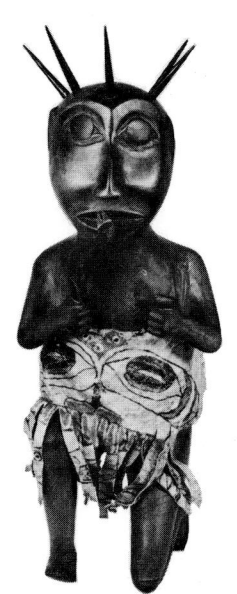

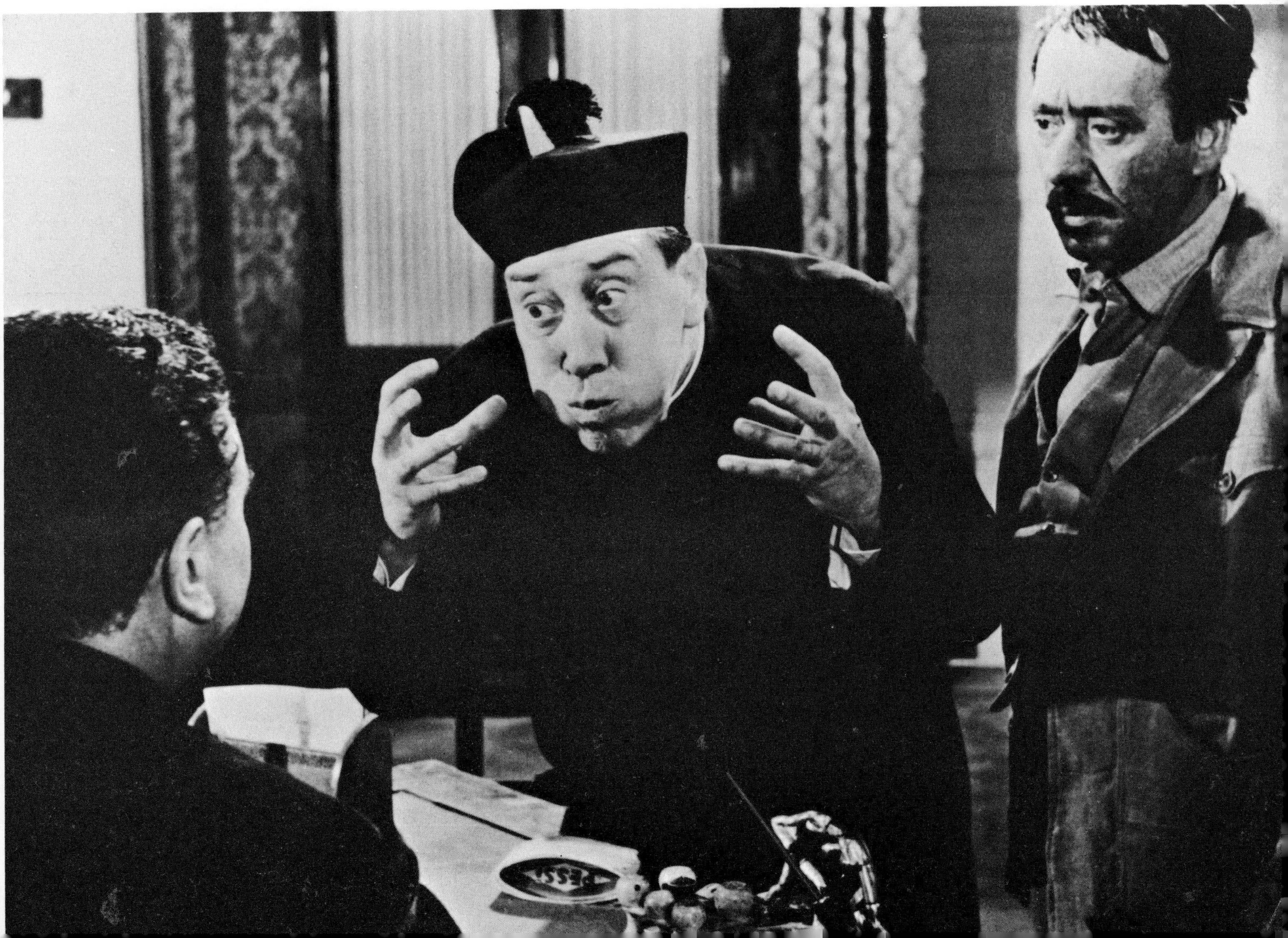

78 A PRAYER
Tibet
(Anthropological Museum,
University of Aberdeen)

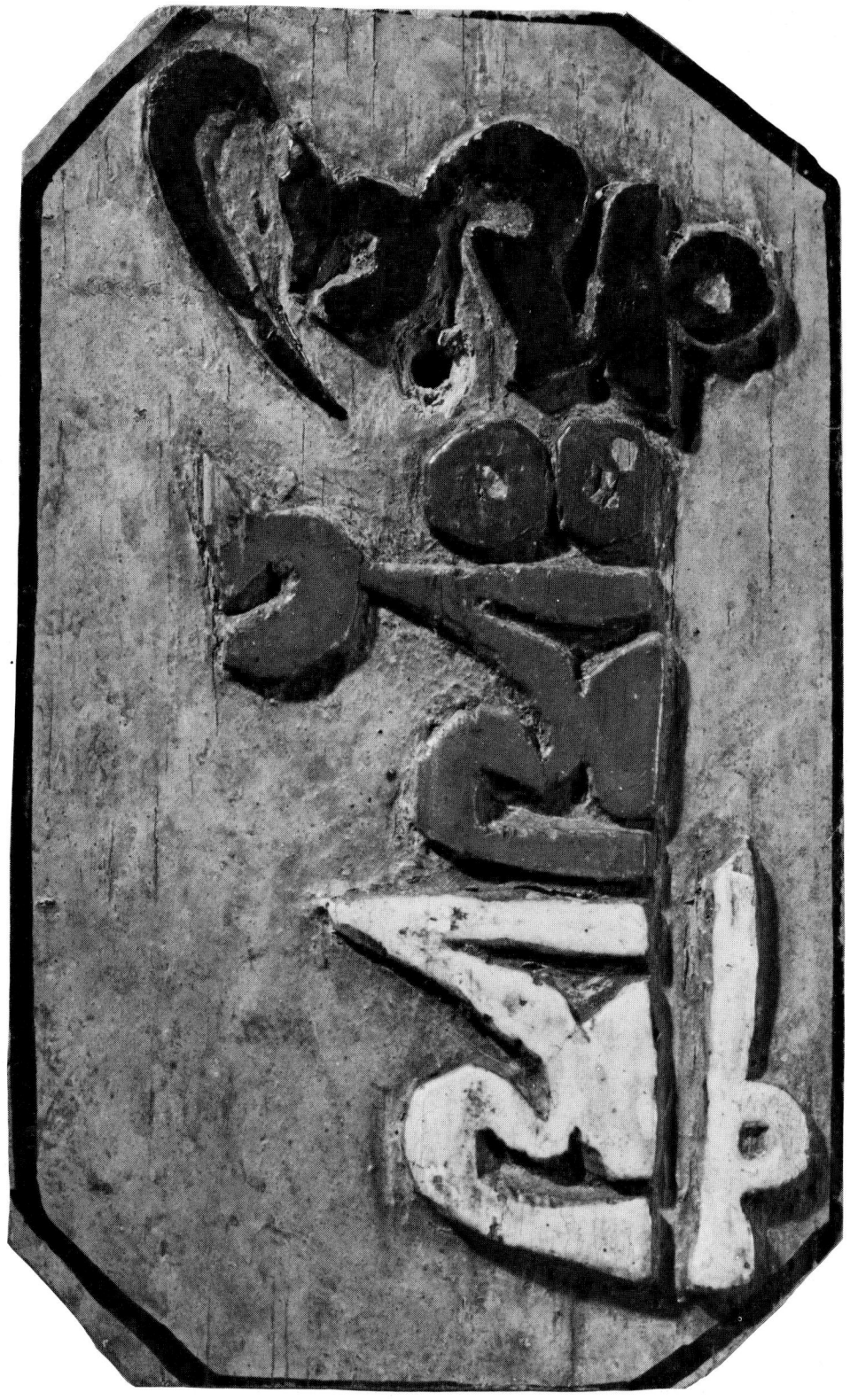

79 WOMAN'S PRAYER STICK
Norway, 1655
(Pitt Rivers Museum, University
of Oxford)

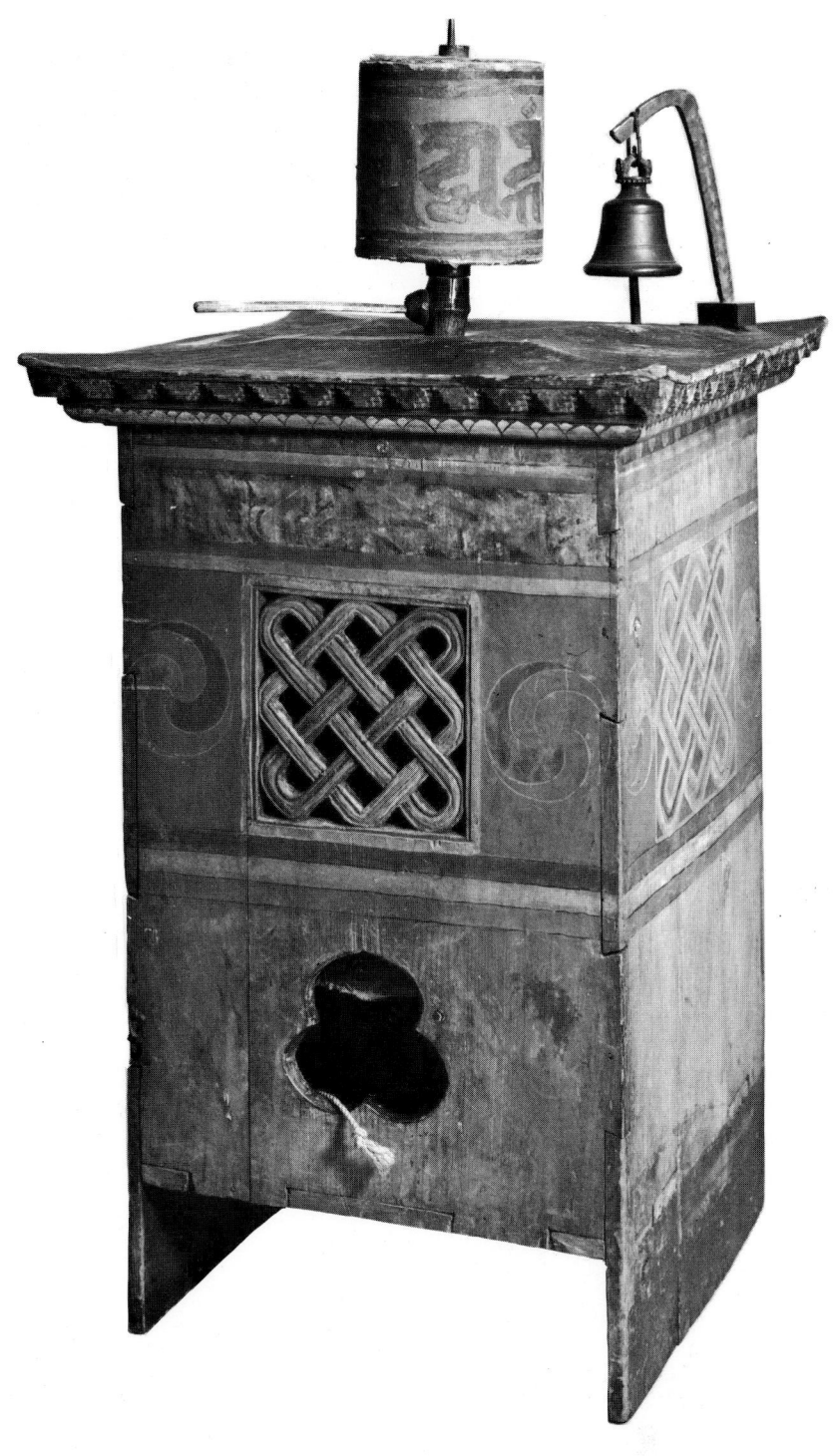

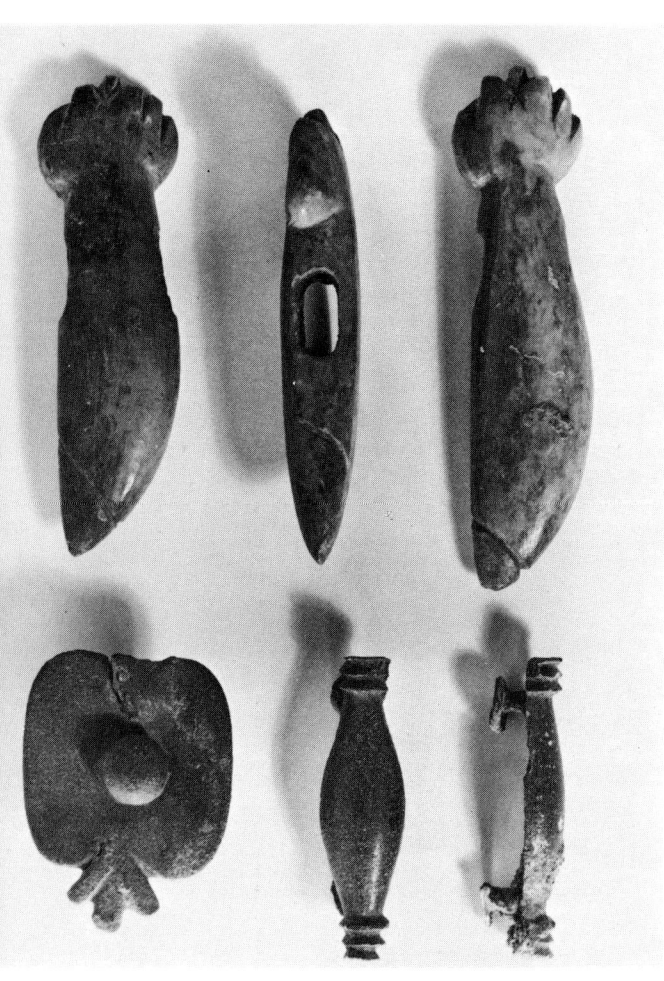

81 Sculpture:
CHARMS TO AVERT THE
EVIL EYE
Roman Britain, first century
(Verulamium Museum, City of
St Albans)

82 Sculpture:
SCARAB
Egypt, XXII Dynasty
(Anthropological Museum,
University of Aberdeen)

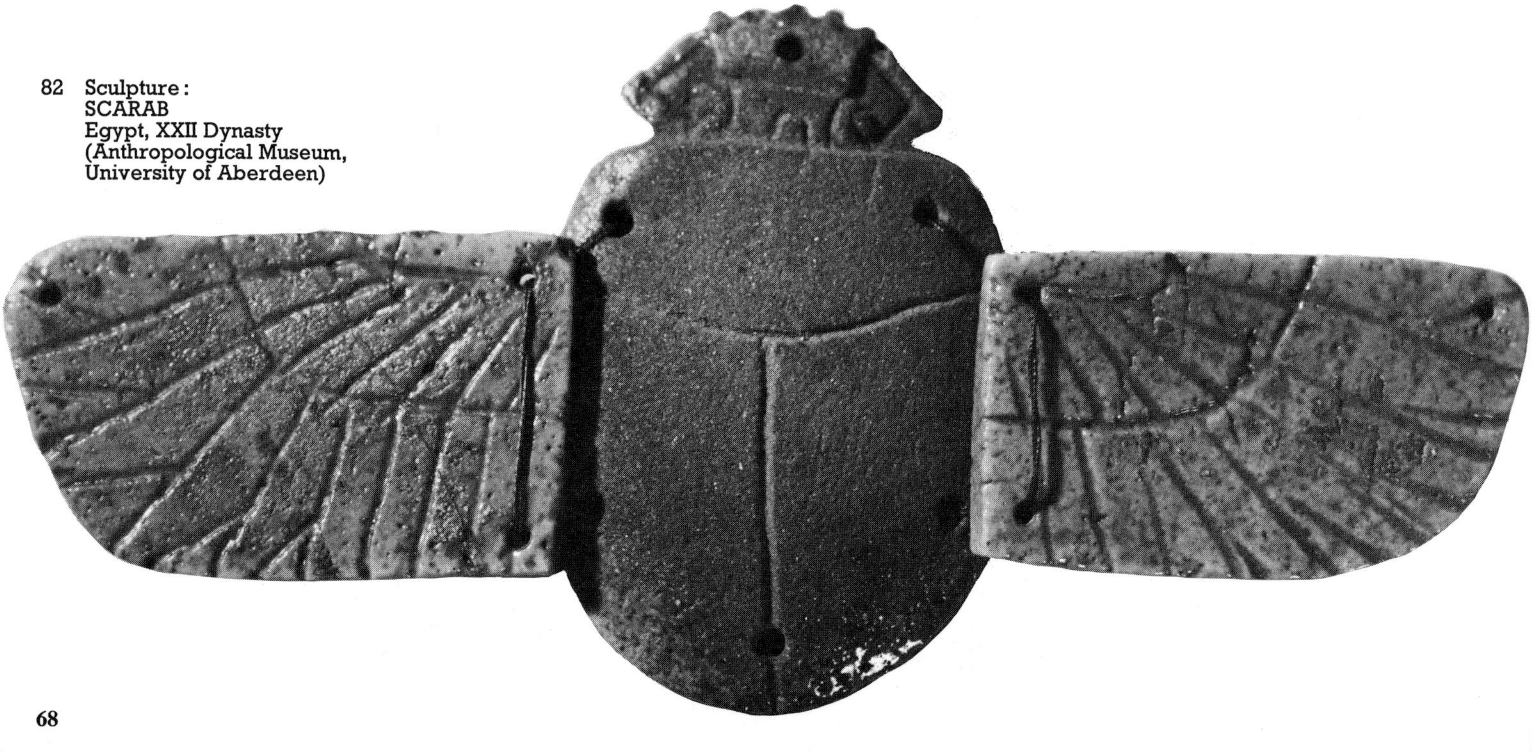

68

83 Pictures on various substances:
VOTIVE OFFERINGS
German, nineteenth century
(Horniman Museum, London)

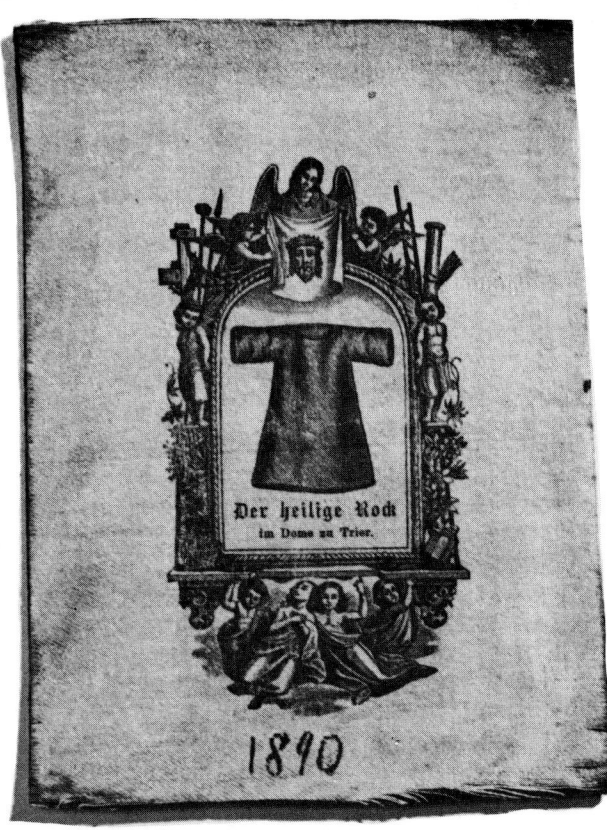

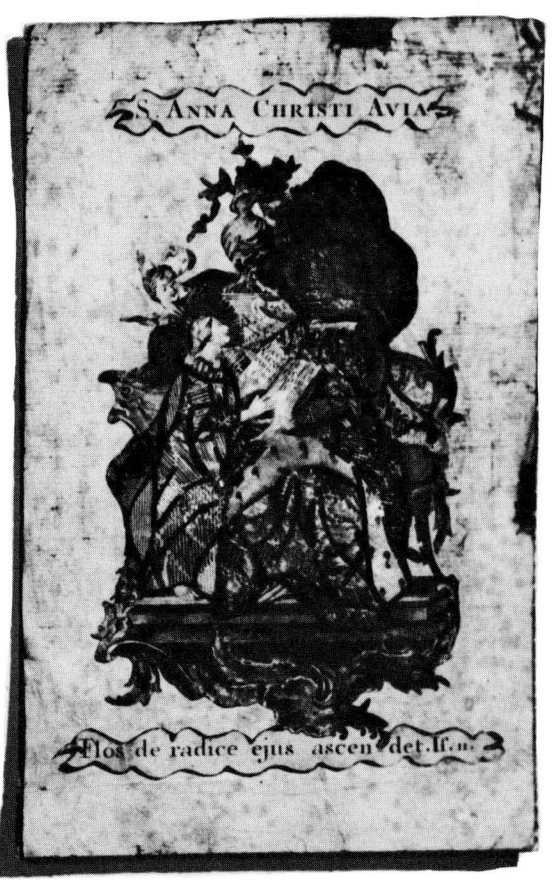

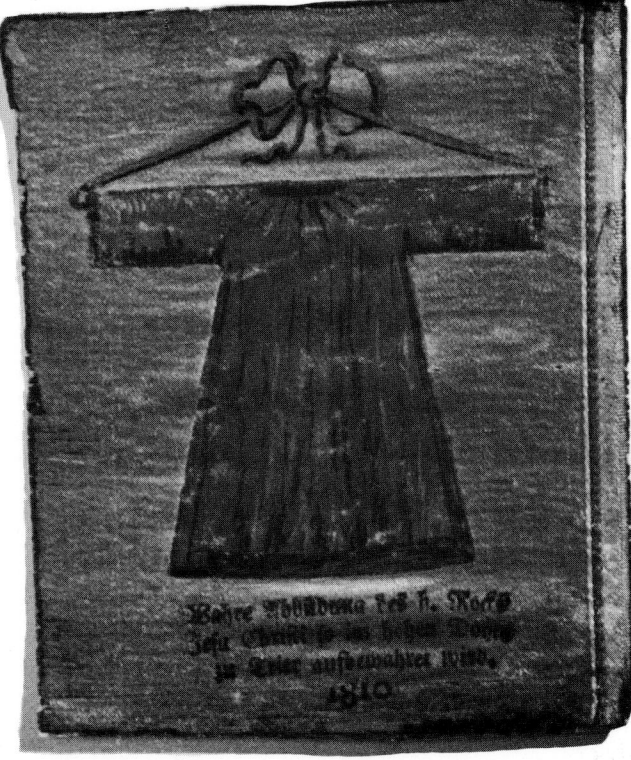

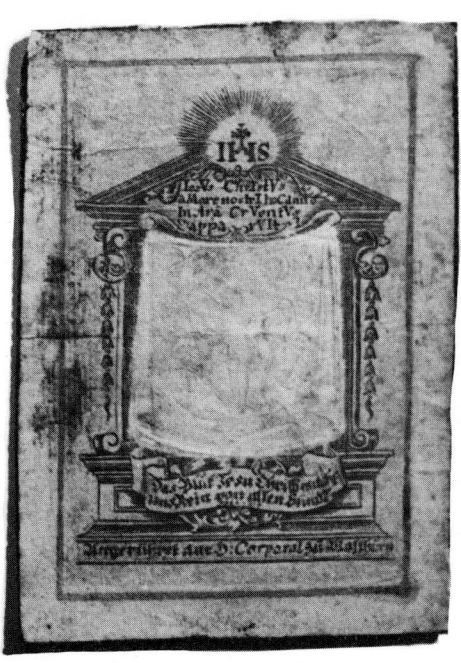

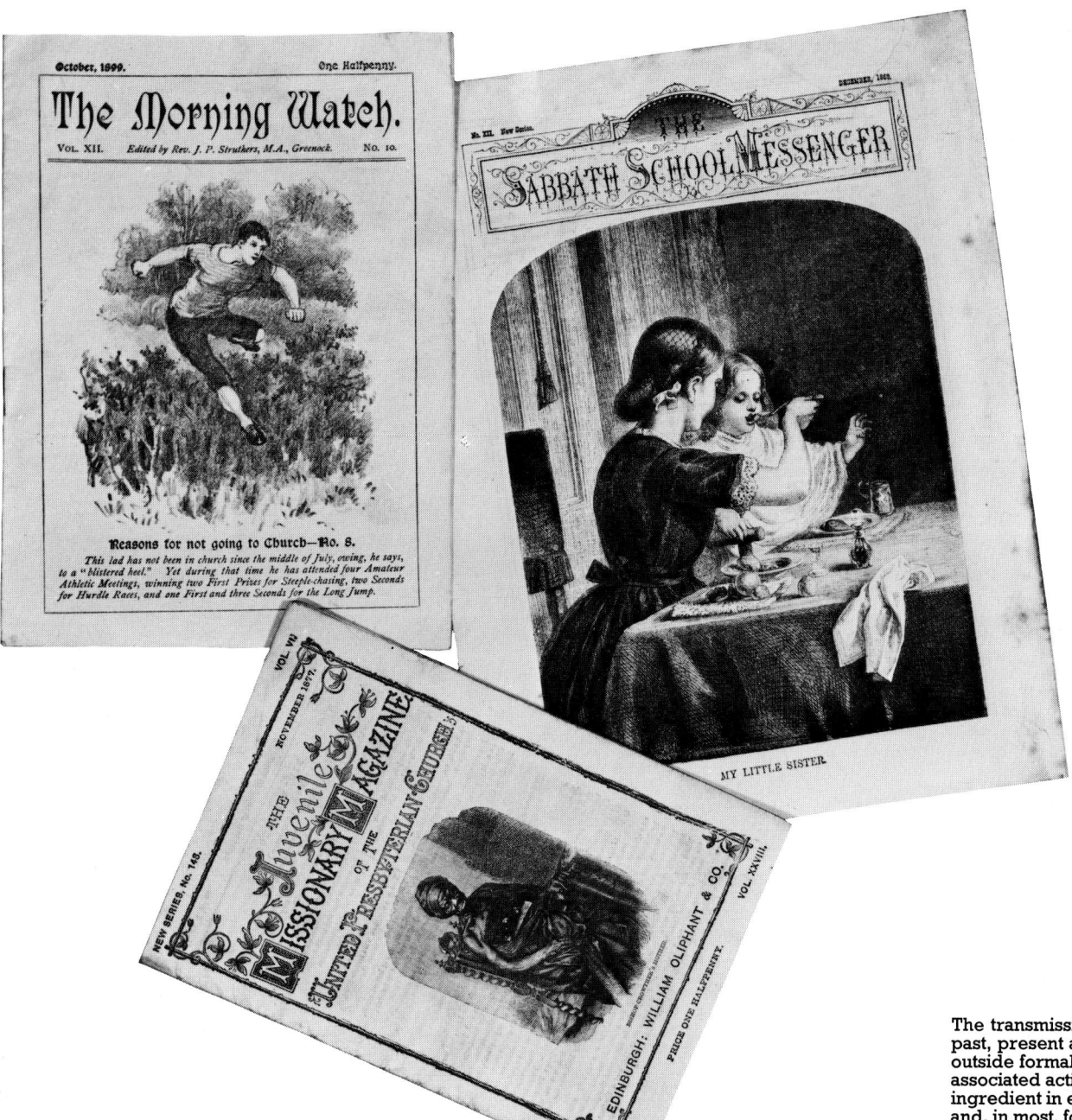

MY LITTLE SISTER.

The transmission of the concept of past, present and future extends far outside formal worship and its associated activities. It is an important ingredient in education in all societies and, in most, forms a part of domestic and play activity.

84 Magazines for children:
THE MORNING WATCH,
October 1899
THE SABBATH SCHOOL
MESSENGER, December 1869
THE JUVENILE MISSIONARY
MAGAZINE OF THE UNITED
PRESBYTERIAN CHURCH,
November 1877
(Museum of Childhood,
Edinburgh)

85 Sampler:
REMEMBER NOW THY
CREATOR IN THE DAYS OF
THY YOUTH
by Mary Ann Blandford, aged 13
1841
(Museum of Childhood,
Edinburgh)

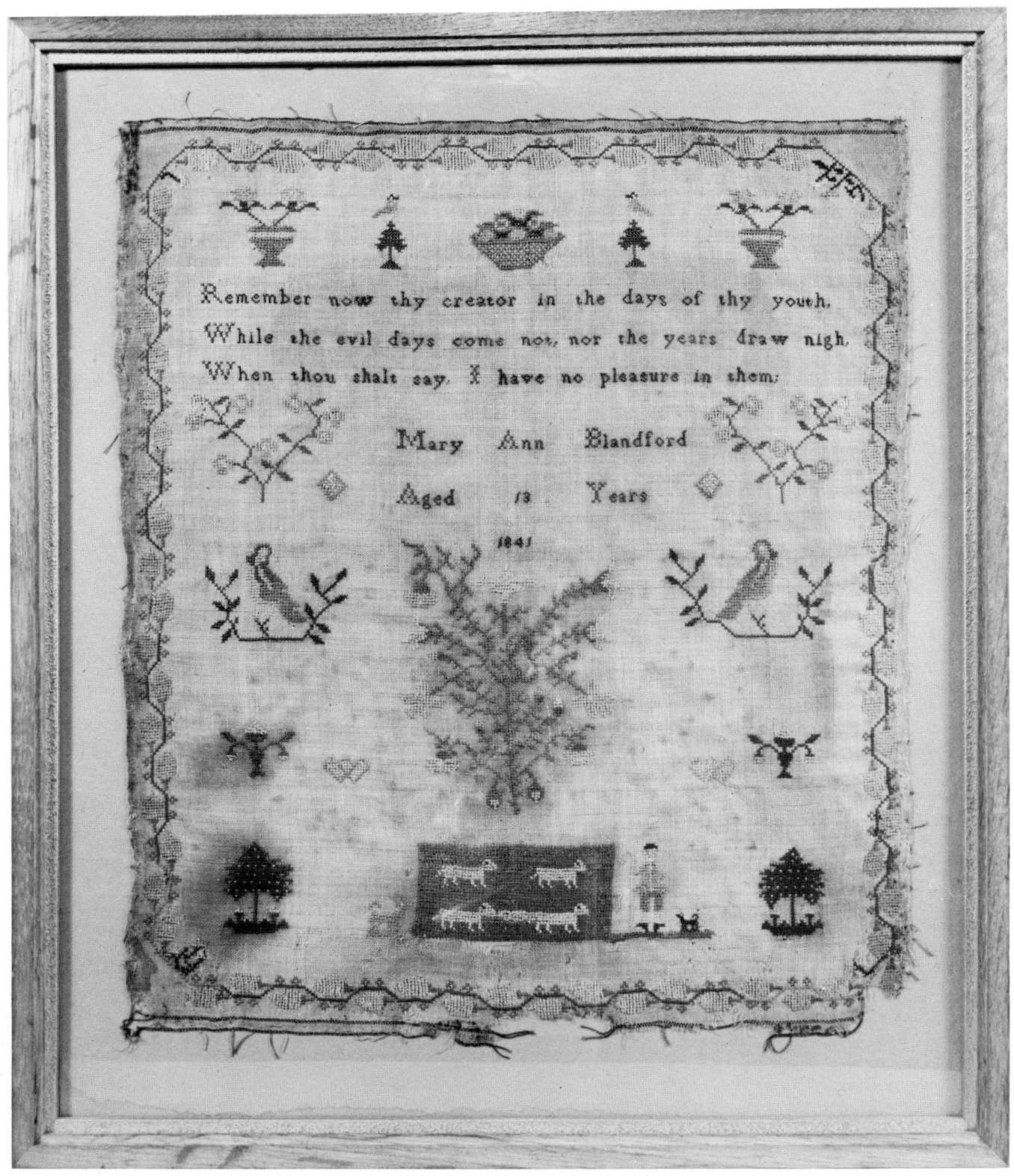

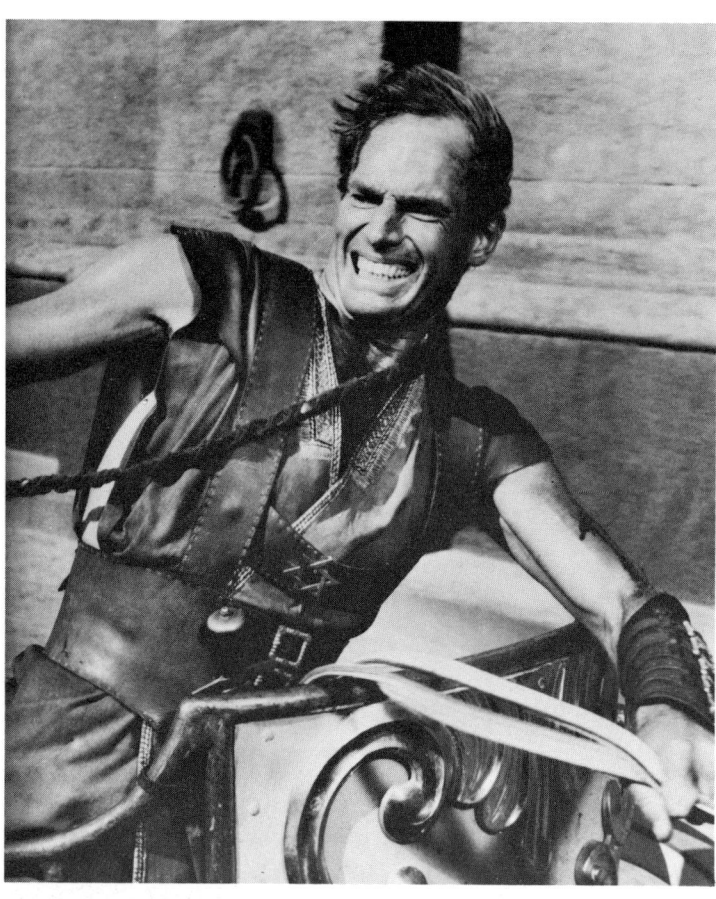

As used in this book the category 'present' is seen in relation to the impact of religion on everyday life, and the experience of individuals in the secular world. Here there is a basic tendency to drama, sentiment, humour or romance which has been taken to its most extreme since the industrial revolution.

86   Film still:
      from BEN HUR
      with Charlton Heston, 1959
      (National Film Archive, MGM)

87   Film still:
      from INTOLERANCE
      Directed by D W Griffiths, 1916
      (National Film Archive)

88   Painting:
      I AM AFLOAT
      by G F Watts
      (Walker Art Gallery, Liverpool:
      photograph by John Mills)

89   Painting:
      THE SCAPEGOAT
      by Holman Hunt
      (City Art Gallery, Manchester)

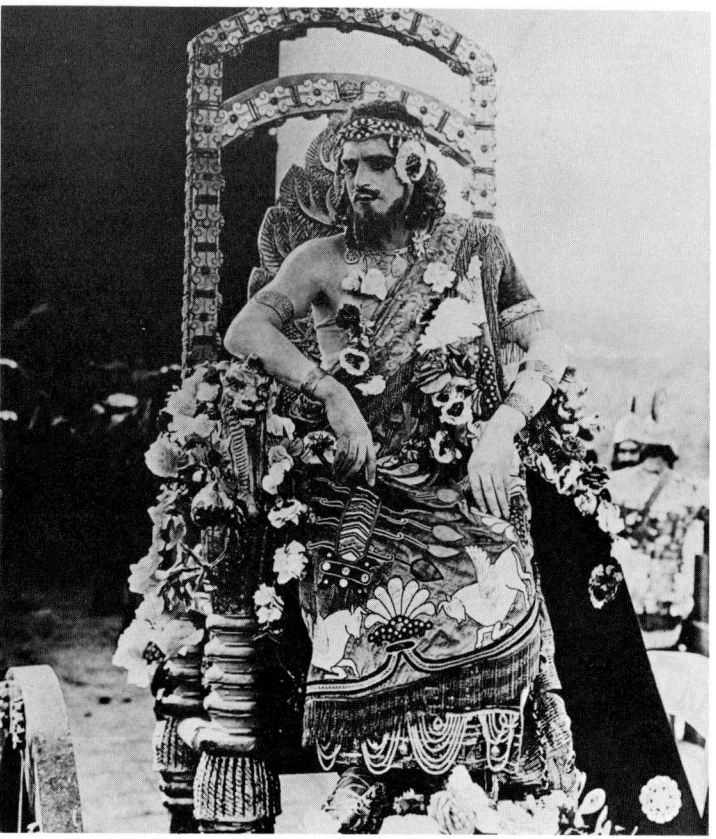

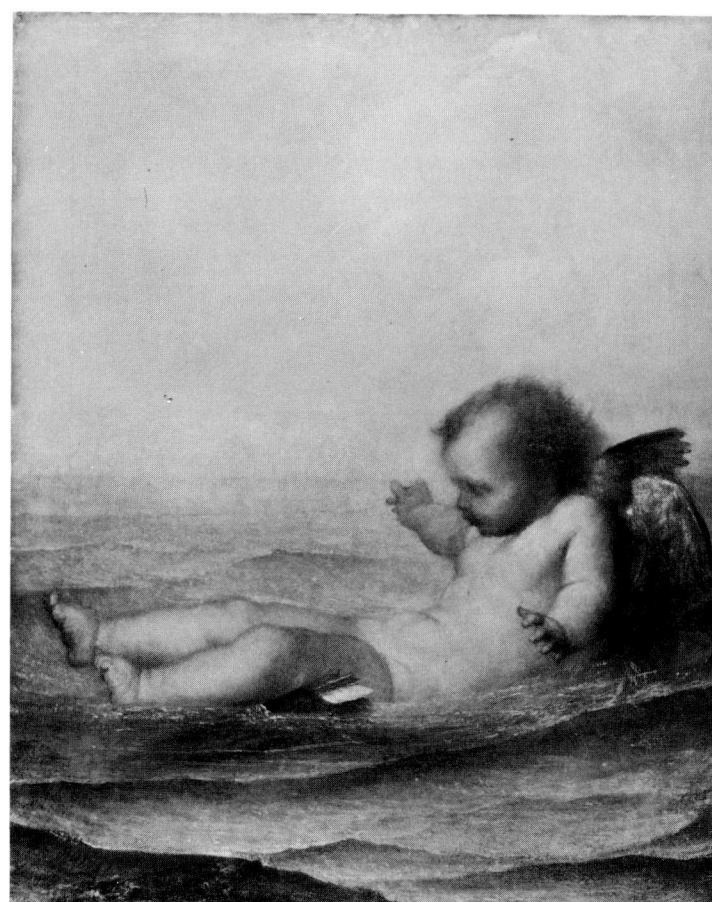

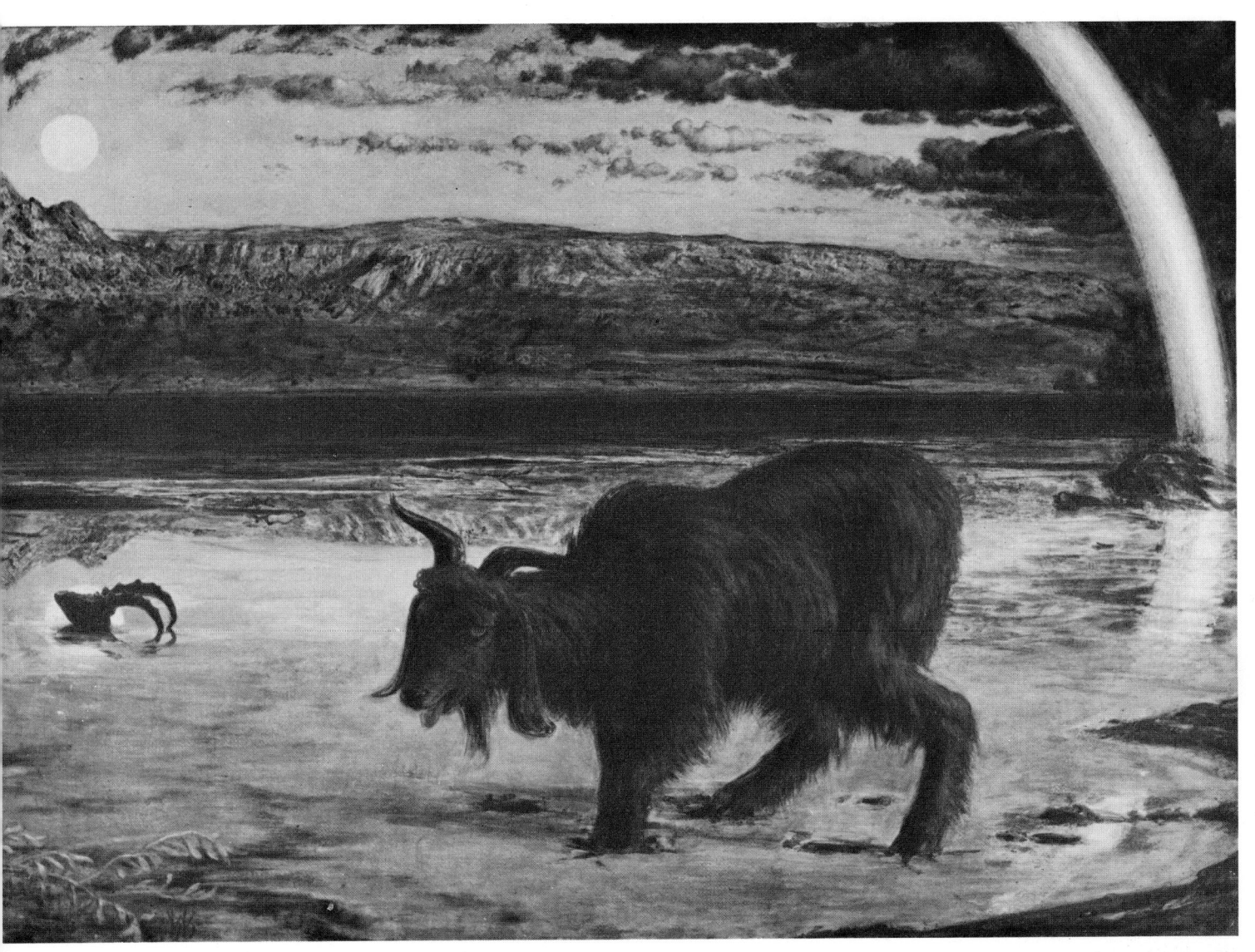

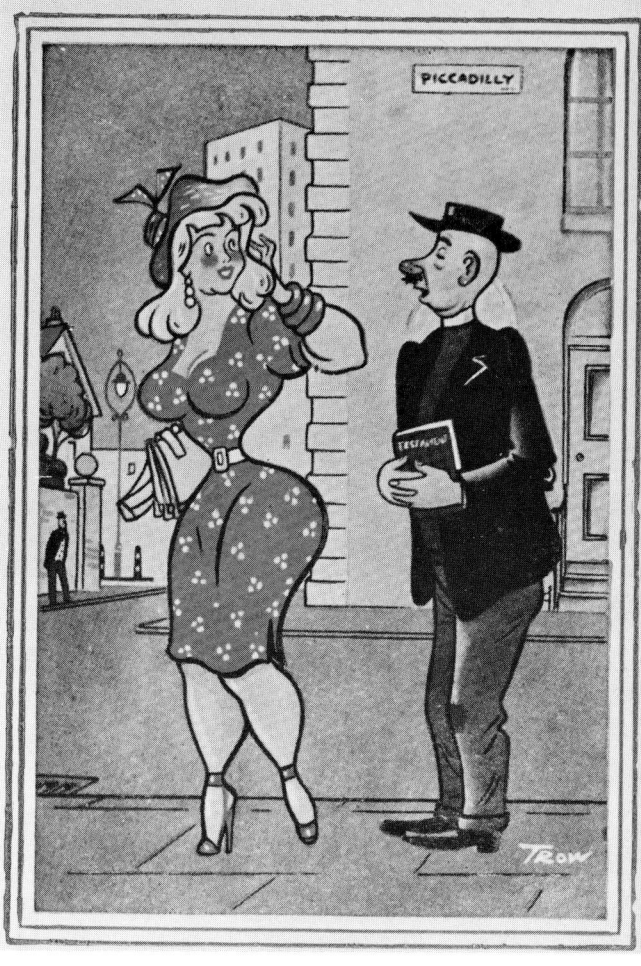

"I prayed for you last night, Sister! Why didn't you phone, Brother?"

90 Film still:
from DAVID AND BATHSHEBA
with Susan Hayward, 1951
(National Film Archive, 20th
Century Fox)

91 Postcard:
'I PRAYED FOR YOU LAST
NIGHT, SISTER!'
'WHY DIDN'T YOU PHONE,
BROTHER?'
by Trow
(Peter Jones)

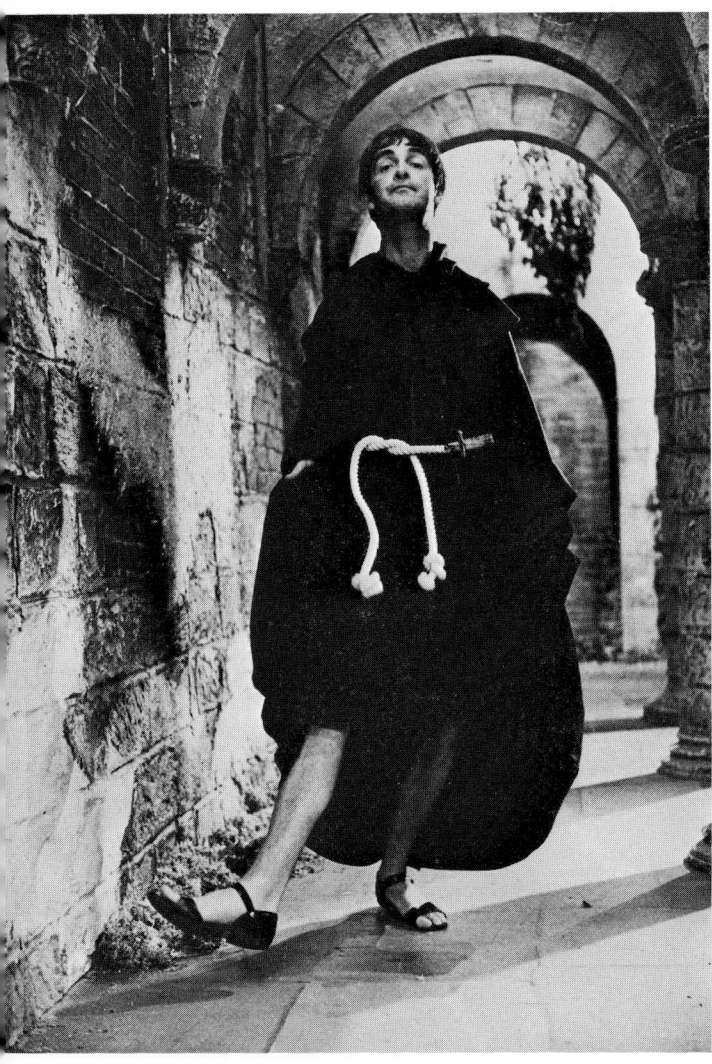

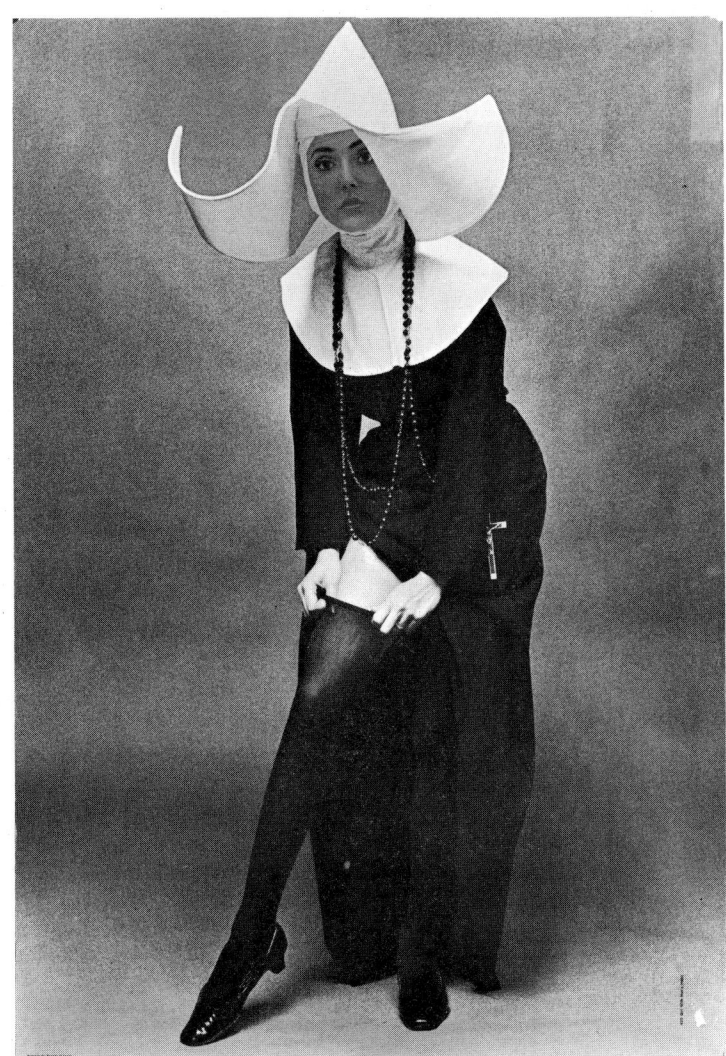

92　Television still:
from OH, BROTHER
with Derek Nimmo as Brother
Dominic
(BBC-TV)

93　Poster:
GIRL WITH NUN'S HABIT
(Personality Posters UK.Ltd)

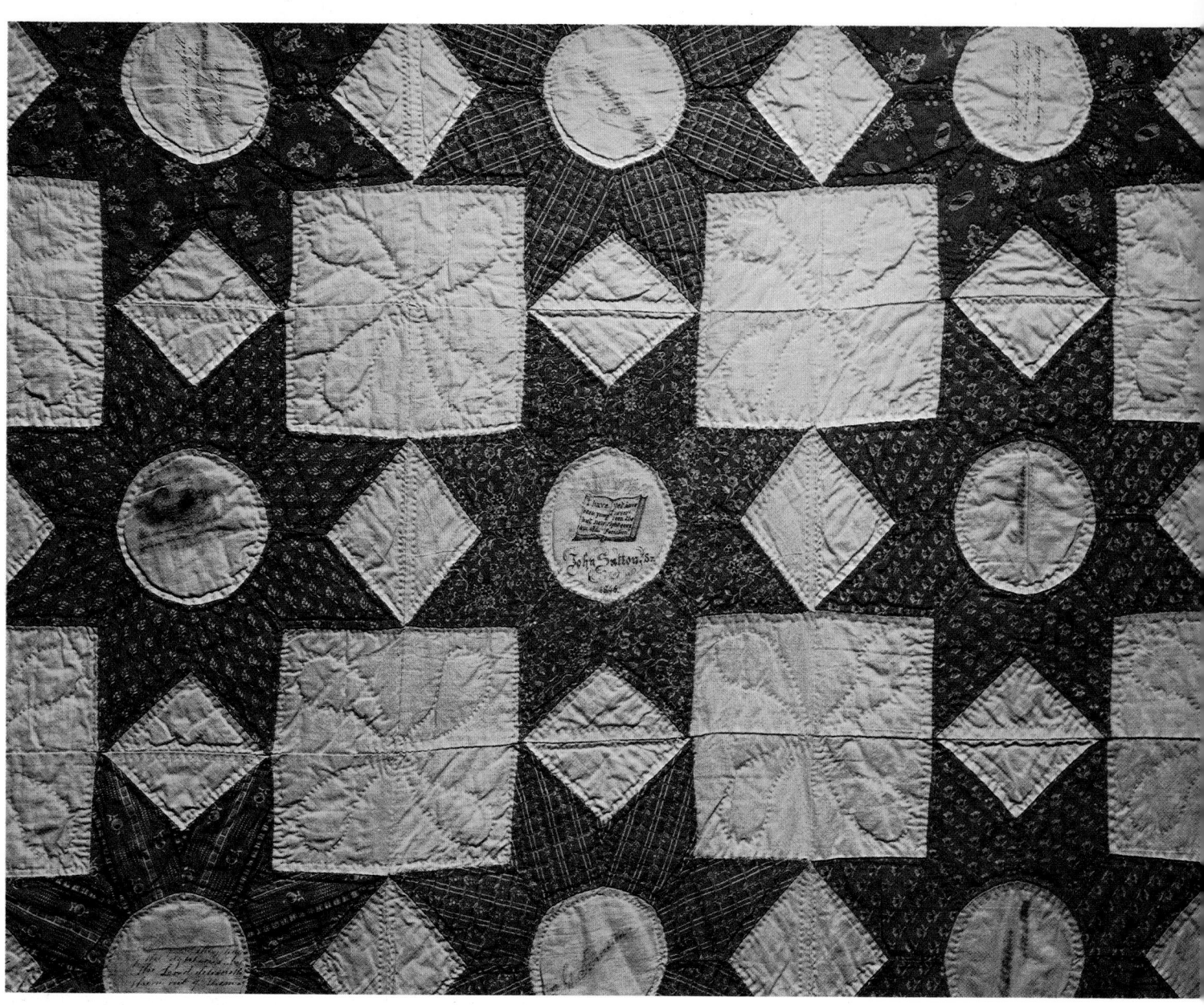

While handcraft methods lasted, religious imagery provided the major source for decoration on every kind of domestic utensil.

94 BIBLE QUILT
United States, 1846–7
(The American Museum in Britain, Bath)
In America, in the mid-nineteenth century, the making of quilts was a social occasion in which neighbours would join. It was an opportunity for friendly gossip. This quilt has biblical quotations written on it, and also (as was common) the names of those who came together to make it.

95 BREAD STAMP
Greece, purchased in 1922
(Anthropological Museum, University of Aberdeen)
This stamp was carved by monks on Mount Athos, but apparently similar objects were to be found in every Greek household. Two compartments of the stamp symbolize Jesus Christ, one the nine archangels, and one the Virgin Mary.

96 Cake-form:
CHRIST IN A CARRIAGE DRAWN BY A LAMB
Hungary, seventeenth or eighteenth century
(Museum of Arts and Crafts, Budapest)

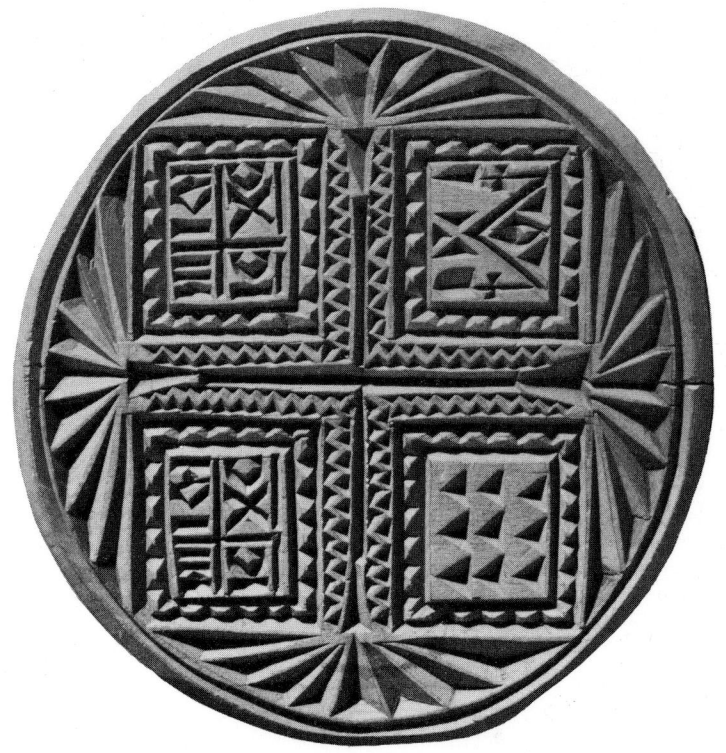

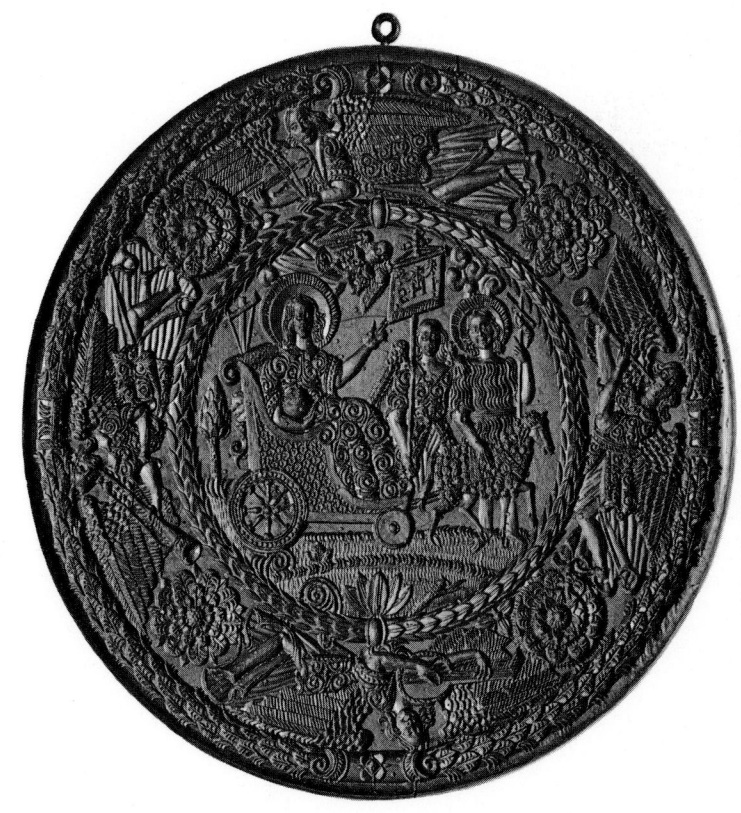

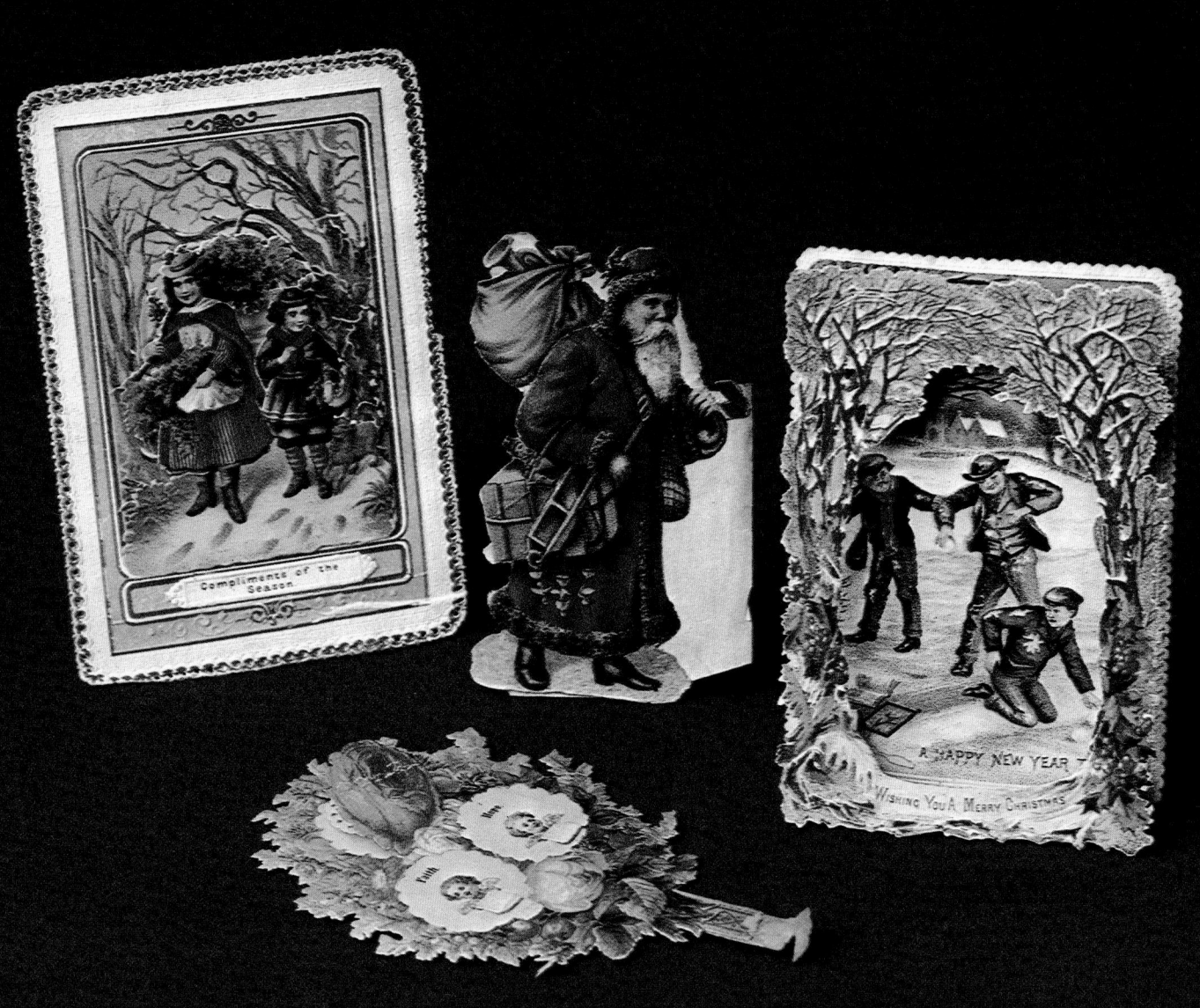

Christmas, and the elaboration of its exquisite story into a combined religious and secular festival in church and home, is one of the most extraordinary of human creations, involving art at every point. In terms of past, present and future it is particularly powerful, enshrining, as it does, a climactic birth which is celebrated in a primarily family occasion.

7 CHRISTMAS CARDS
   nineteenth century
   (Mansell Collection)

8 BREAD DOLLS
   Equador, contemporary
   (from **Cookies and Breads: The Baker's Art,** Museum of Contemporary Crafts, New York: photograph by Ferdinand Boesch)

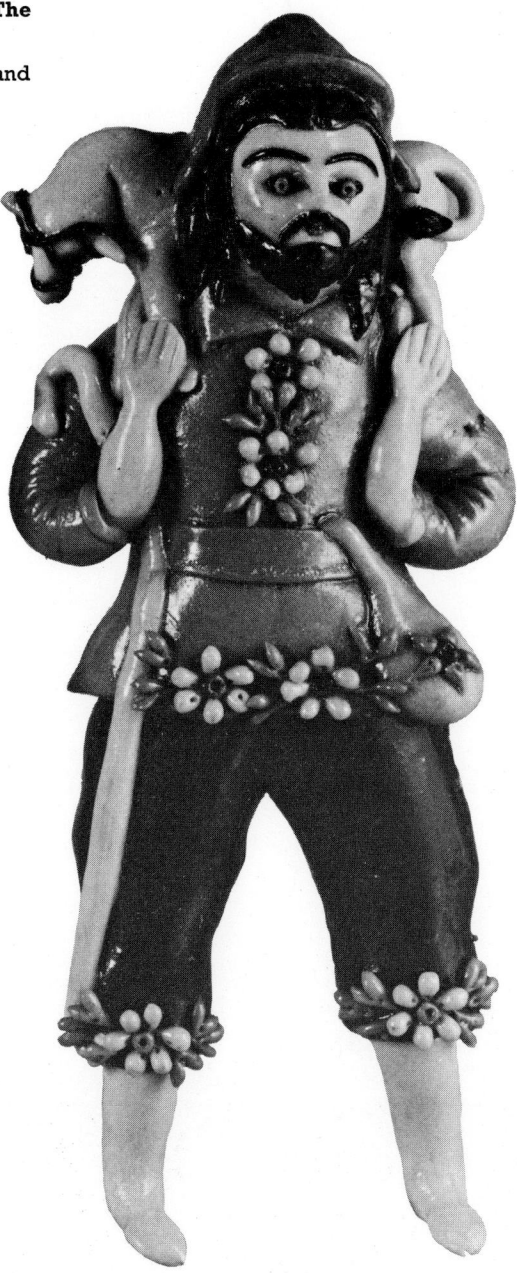
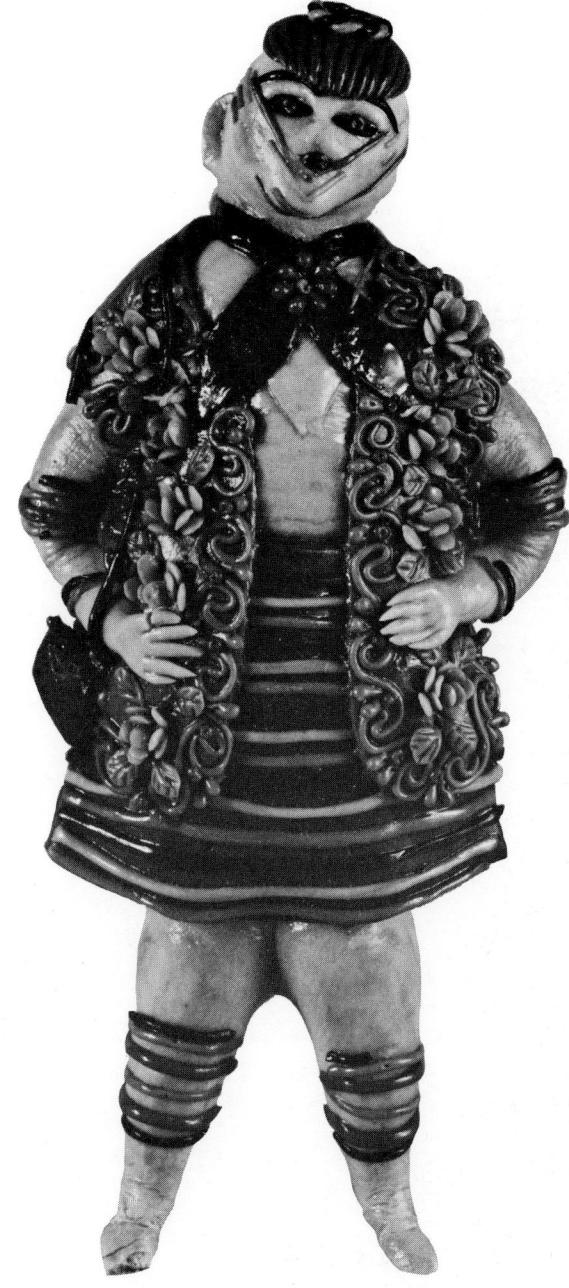

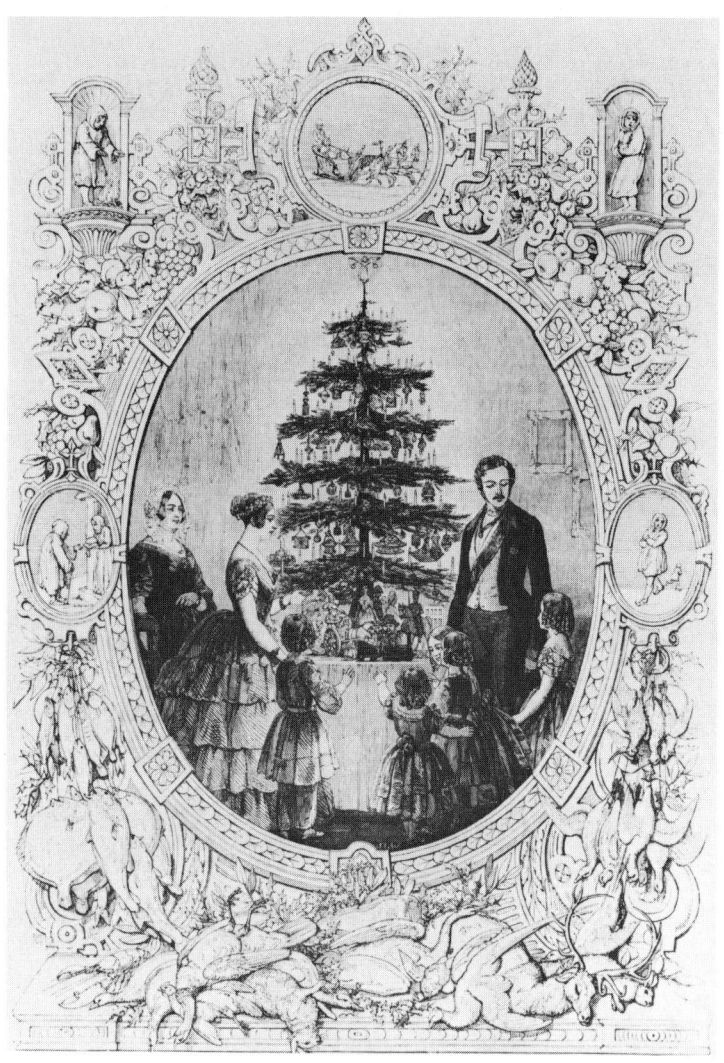

99 Illustration:
CHRISTMAS TREE AT
WINDSOR CASTLE
by J L Williams
1848
(Mansell Collection)

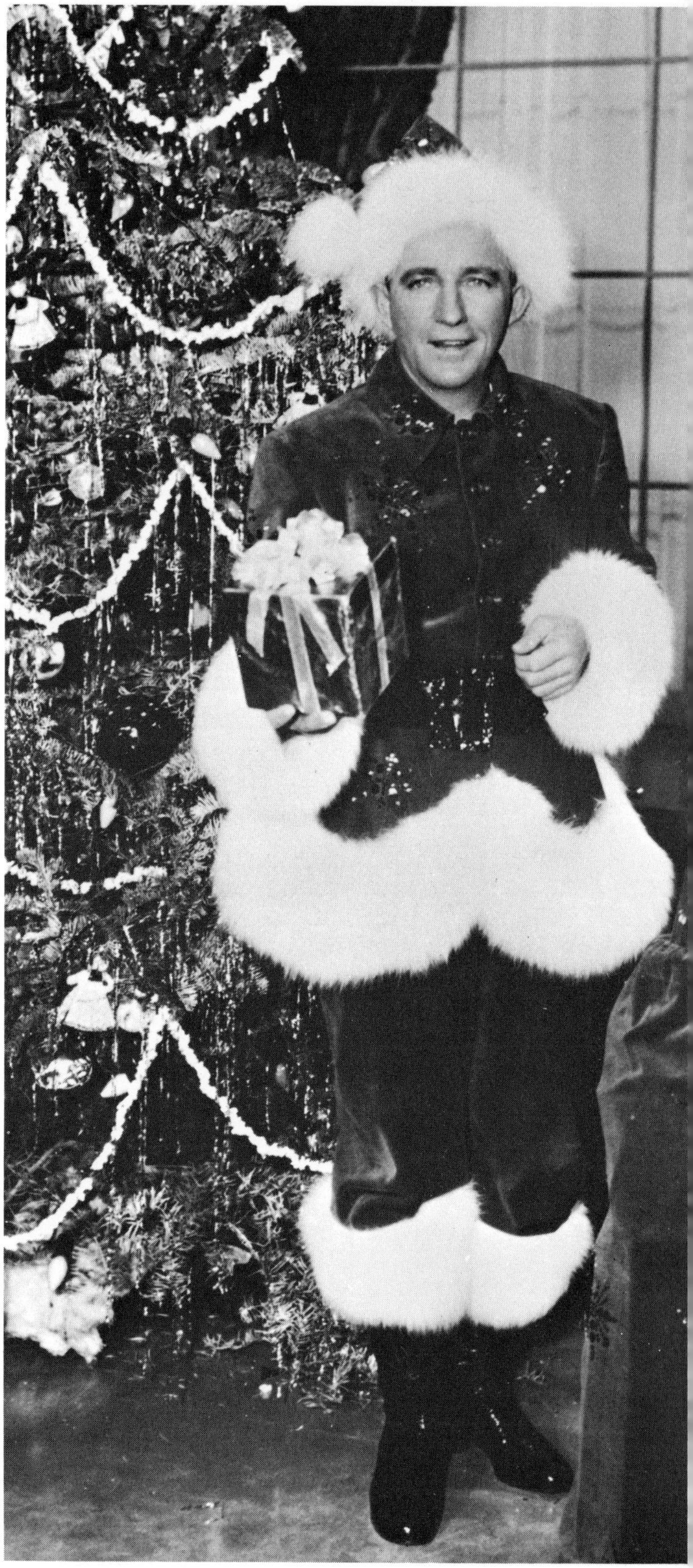

100 Film still:
from WHITE CHRISTMAS
with Bing Crosby, 1954
(National Film Archive, BBC)

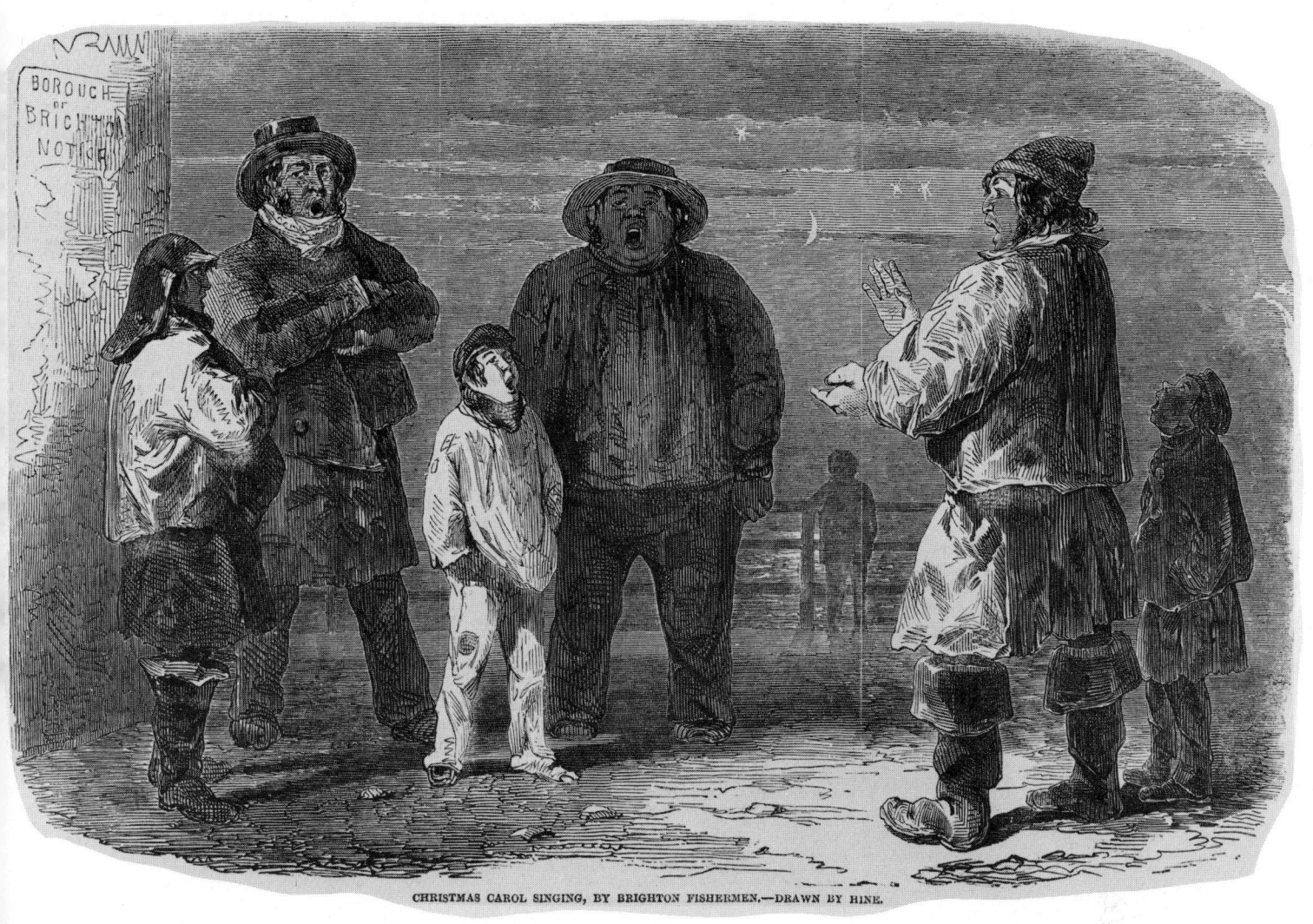

CHRISTMAS CAROL SINGING, BY BRIGHTON FISHERMEN.—DRAWN BY HINE.

101 Illustration:
CHRISTMAS CAROL SINGING,
BY BRIGHTON FISHERMEN
by Hine
nineteenth century
(Mansell Collection)

As religion can only be made evident to men in the secular world, it inevitably becomes involved in that world, with its grand issues and with its trivia. On the one hand religious imagery may be applied to the most surprising objects: on the other it may be identified with the whole concept of nationality and become a part of the fabric of social policy.

102   Glass paperweight:
      JERUSALEM
      CONGREGATIONAL CHURCH,
      GRANVILLE N.Y.
      (Gwilym Rees Hughes)

103   Poster:
      OURS . . . TO FIGHT FOR
      by Norman Rockwell, Second
      World War, issued by the
      American Office of War
      Information
      (Imperial War Museum)

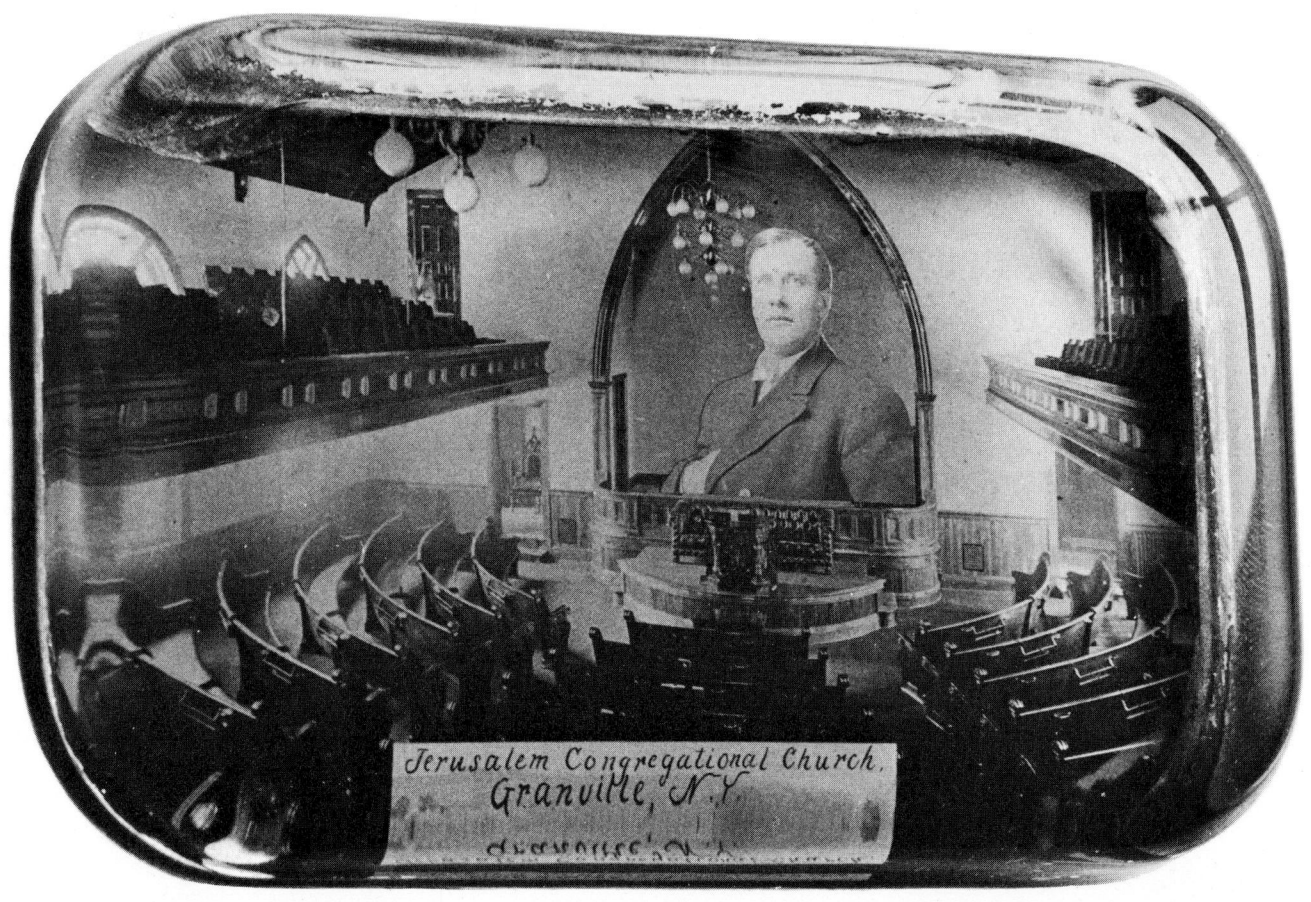

OURS...to fight for

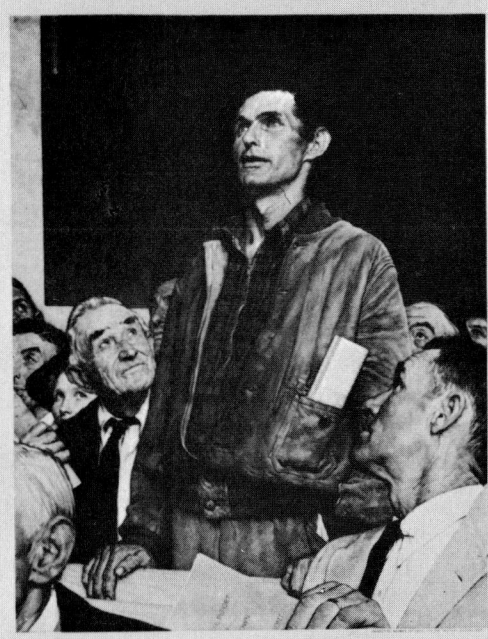

Freedom of Speech

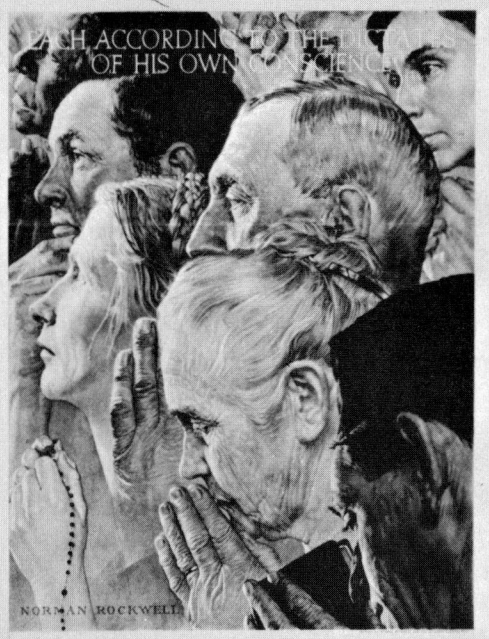

Freedom of Worship

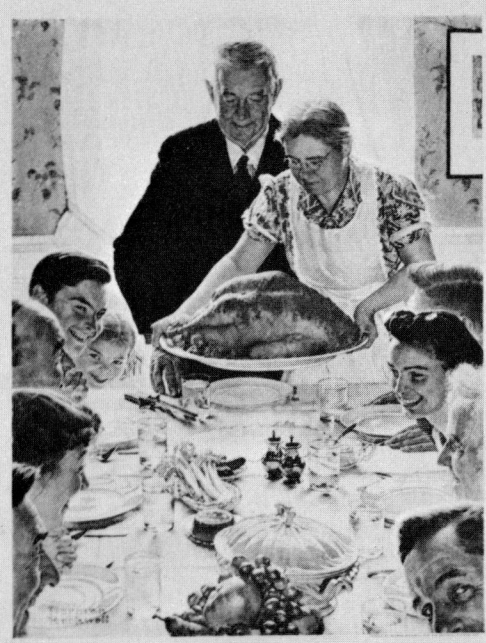

Freedom from Want

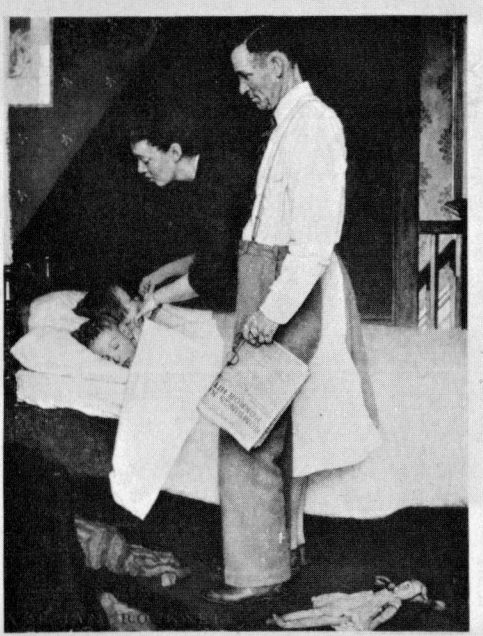

Freedom from Fear

I have tried to suggest the circumstances of the resurrection through a harmony between the quick and the dead, between the visitors to a cemetery and the dead rising from it.

Stanley Spencer describing his picture Resurrection: Reunion painted in 1945.

The sky is overcast, the stars are beclouded . . . the [very] bones of the earth-god tremble . . . when they see [this dead man] appear animated as a god who lives on his fathers and feeds on his mothers . . . [He] is the one who eats men and lives on gods . . . [He] is the one who eats their magic and devours their glory. The biggest of them are for his breakfast; their middle-sized are for his dinner; and the smallest of them are for his supper.

from the ancient Egyptian Cannibal Hymn. Quoted by John A Wilson in Before Philosophy 1949.

Goddess unseen, and Lord of the Sons of Darkness,
Aidoneous! Aidoneous!
If such a petition may be heard:
Grant to our friend a passing with no pain,
No grief, to the dark Stygian home
Of those who dwell in the far invisible land.
Out of the night of his long hopeless torment
Surely a just God's hand
Will raise him up again.

from Oedipus at Colonus by Sophocles, translated by E F Watling and published as a Penguin Classic, 1947.

Future

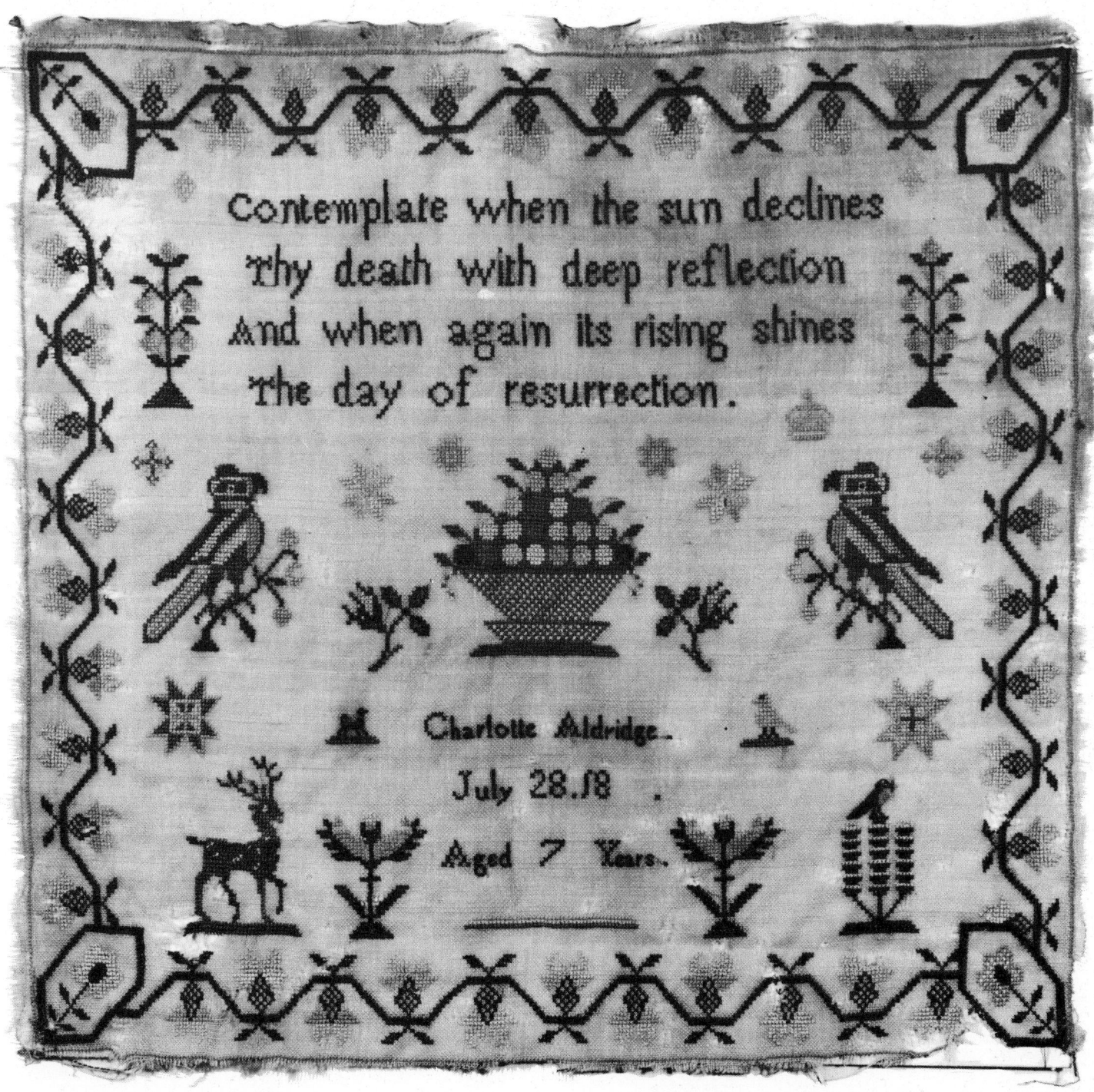

Contemplate when the sun declines
Thy death with deep reflection
And when again its rising shines
The day of resurrection.

Charlotte Aldridge
July 28.18
Aged 7 Years.

104 Sampler:
CONTEMPLATE WHEN THE
SUN DECLINES . . .
by Charlotte Aldridge, aged 7
1818
(City Museum, City of St Albans)

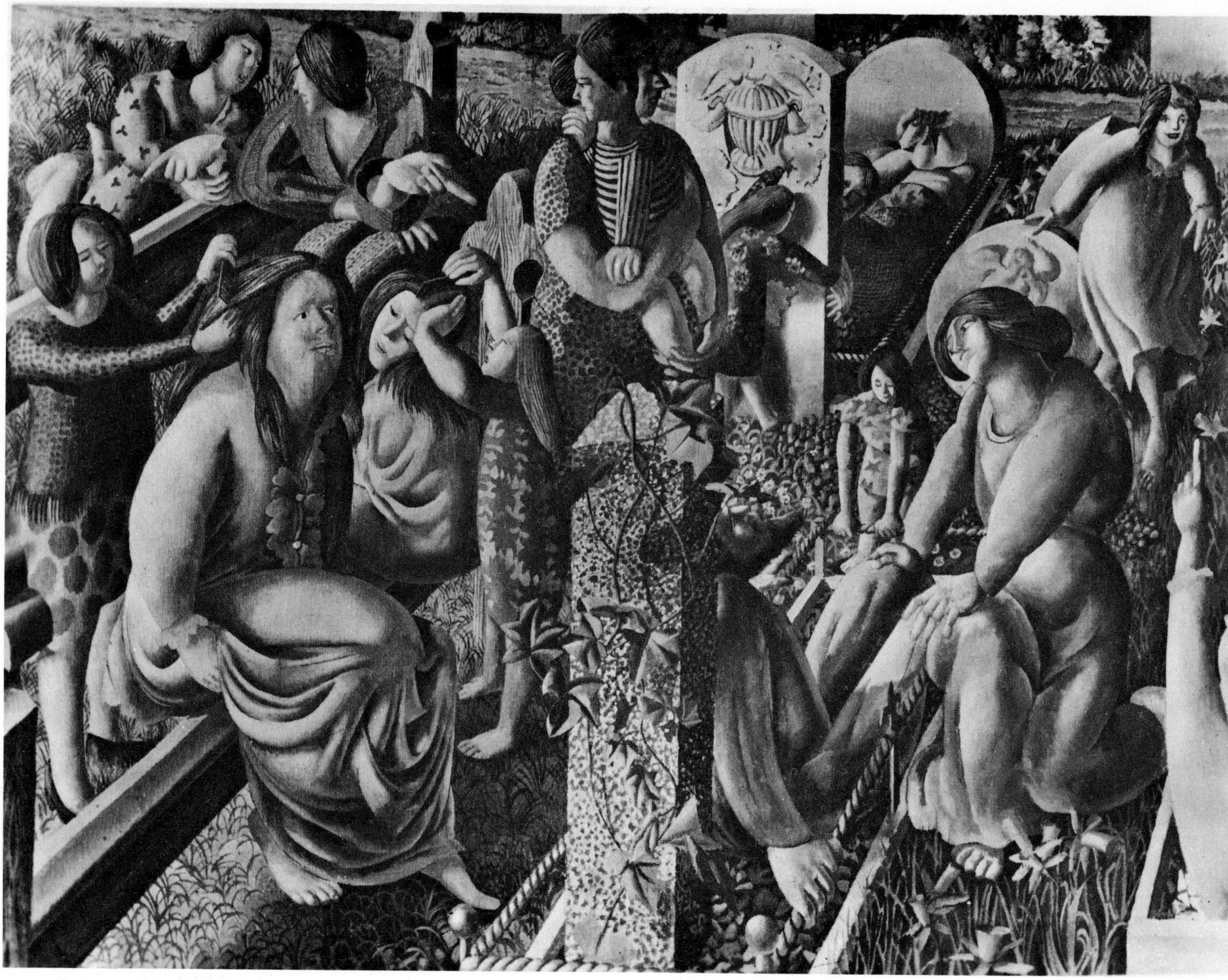

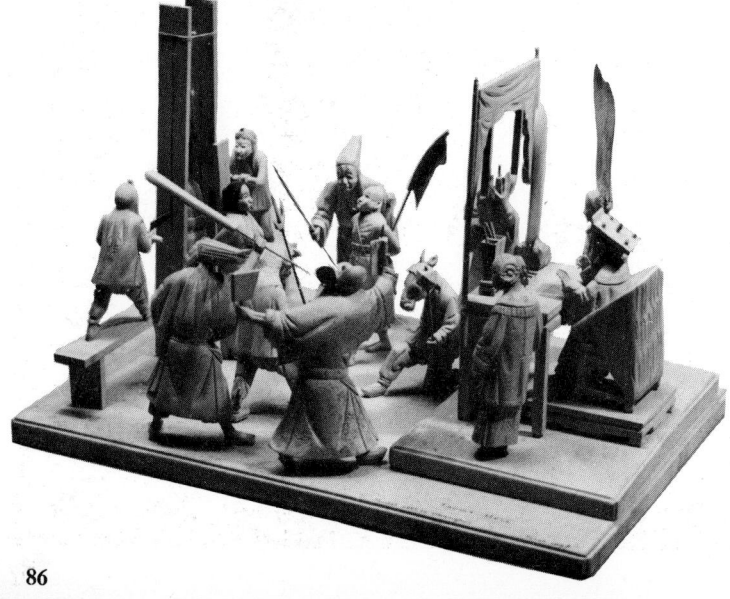

One of art's religious functions is to picture the future which lies in wait for the individual soul after death. This vision may be reassuring or frightening, but the idea of continuity beyond the grave is a fundamental one that art has consistently helped to make real.

105 Painting:
RESURRECTION: TIDYING
by Stanley Spencer, 1945
(City Art Gallery, Birmingham)

106 Sculpture:
TAOIST HELL
purchased in Shanghai
(Pitt Rivers Museum, University of Oxford)

107 Cut-out:
CHRIST RISEN FROM THE TOMB
Greece, contemporary
(Museum of Childhood, Edinburgh)

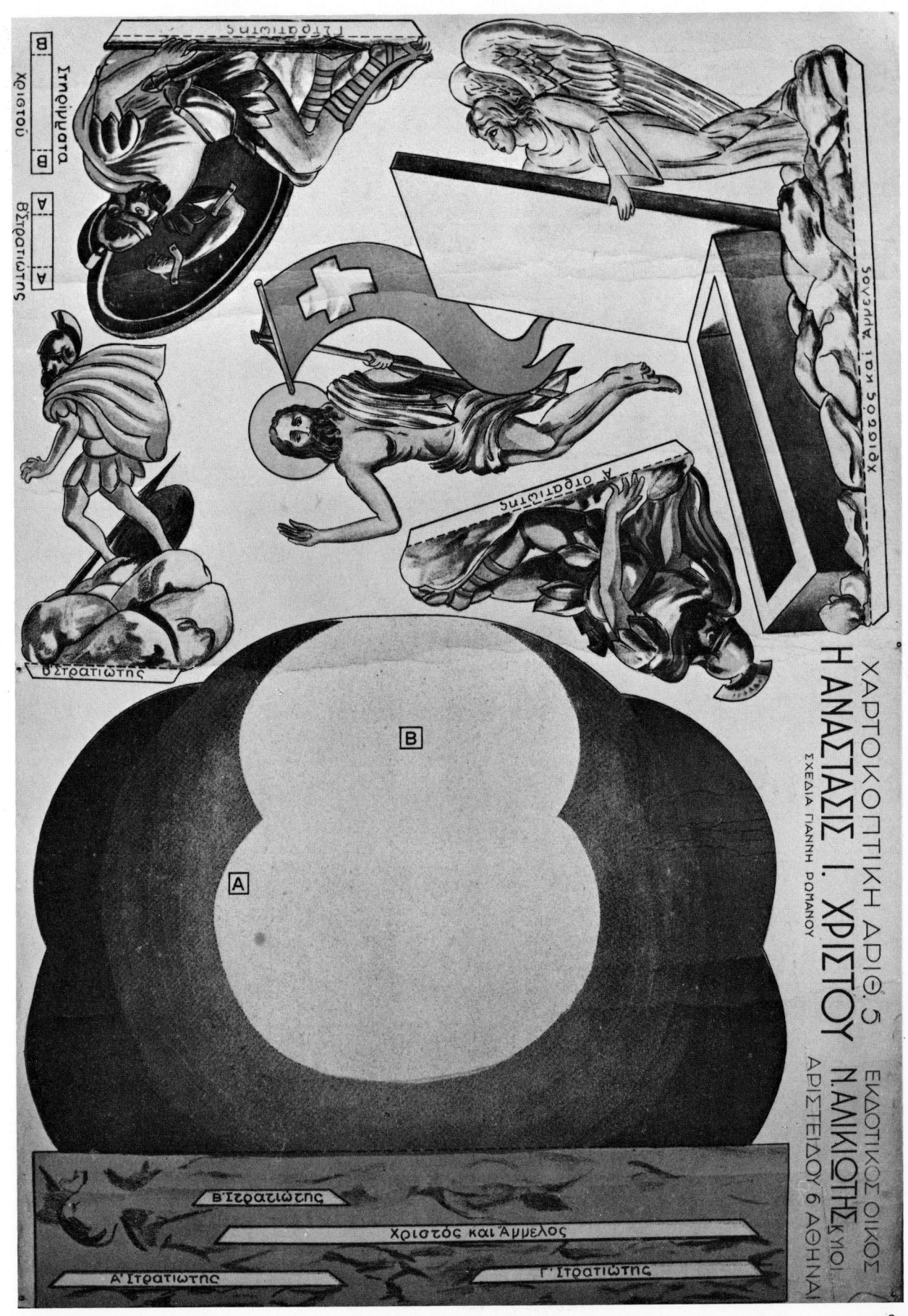

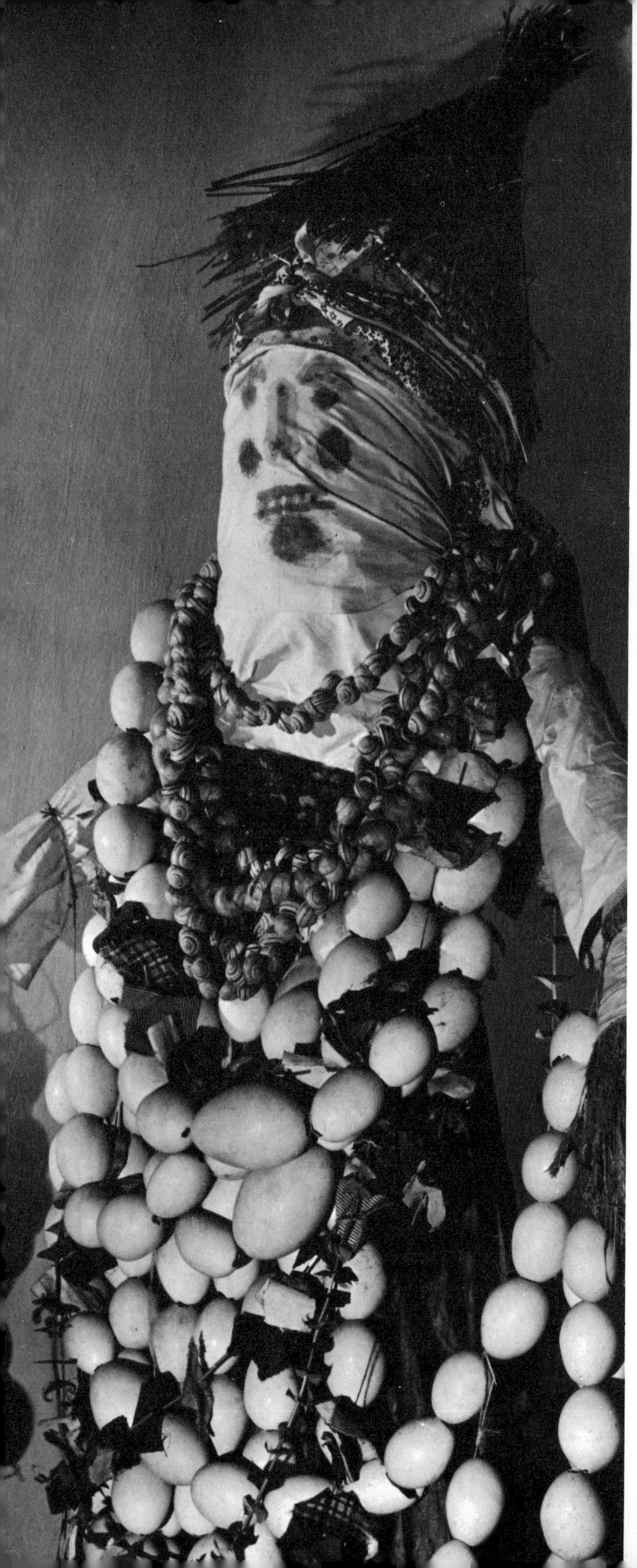

108 Sculpture:
SPRING FESTIVAL FIGURE
Czechoslovakia
(National Museum, Prague)

109 Sculpture:
HARVEST FESTIVAL FIGURE,
MADE FROM THE LAST
SHEAF OF CORN
Czechoslovakia
(National Museum, Prague)
These two superb figures, made of
the actual materials the continuity of
which they symbolize, stand for the
centuries old identification between
the immortality of man and the
seasonal immortality of nature. This
idea has been as powerful in
Christian eras as in pagan ones,
showing how inescapable is the
farmer's reverence for fertility.

110 Sculpture:
USHABTI FIGURES WITH BOX
Egypt, XXVI and XXVII–XXIX
Dynasties
(Anthropological Museum,
University of Aberdeen)
Ushabti figures were buried with a
deceased person to serve him in his
future life.

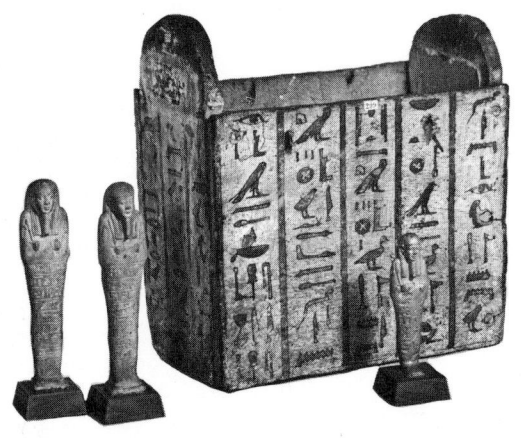
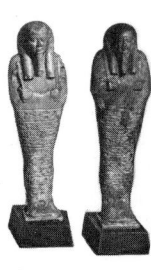

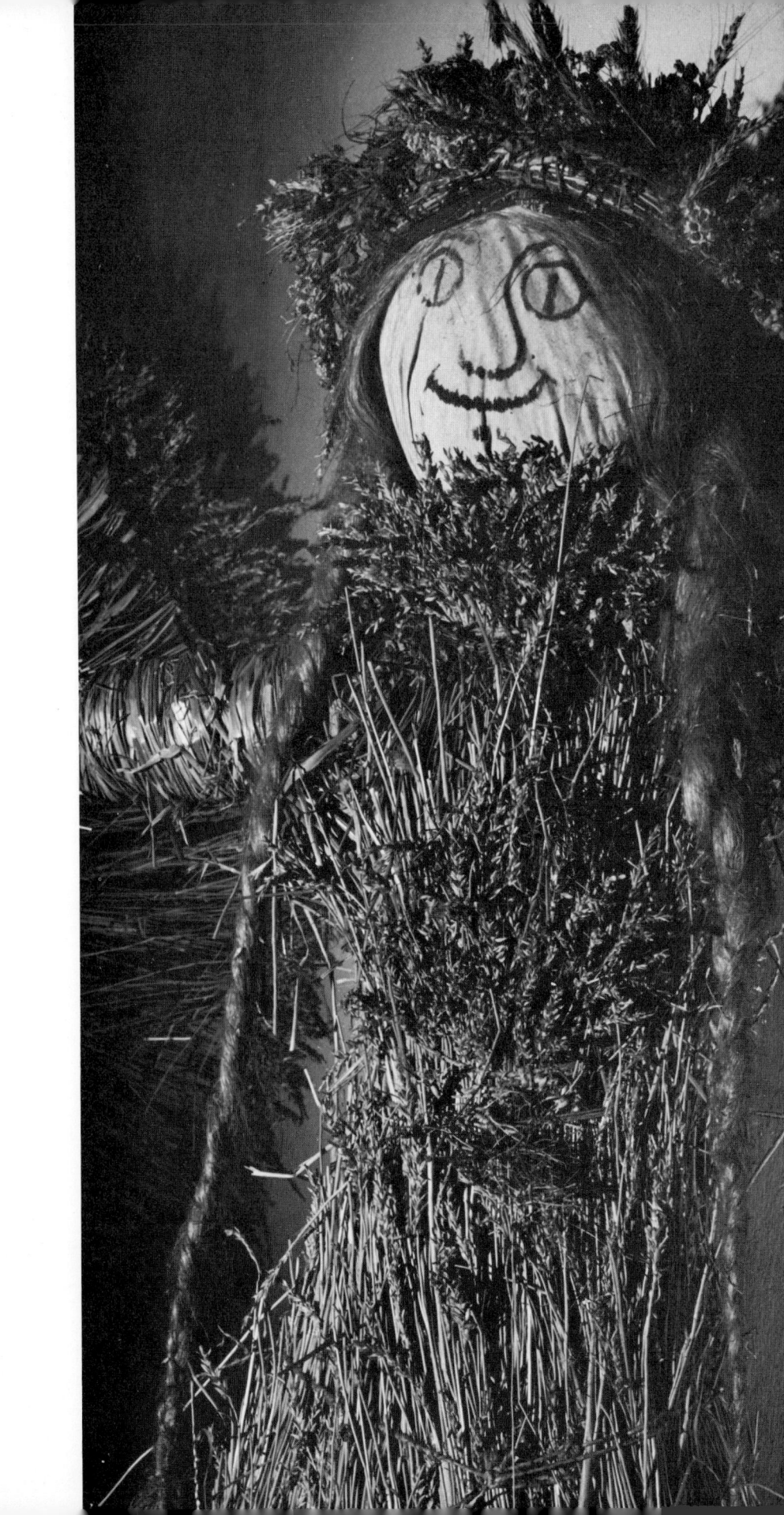

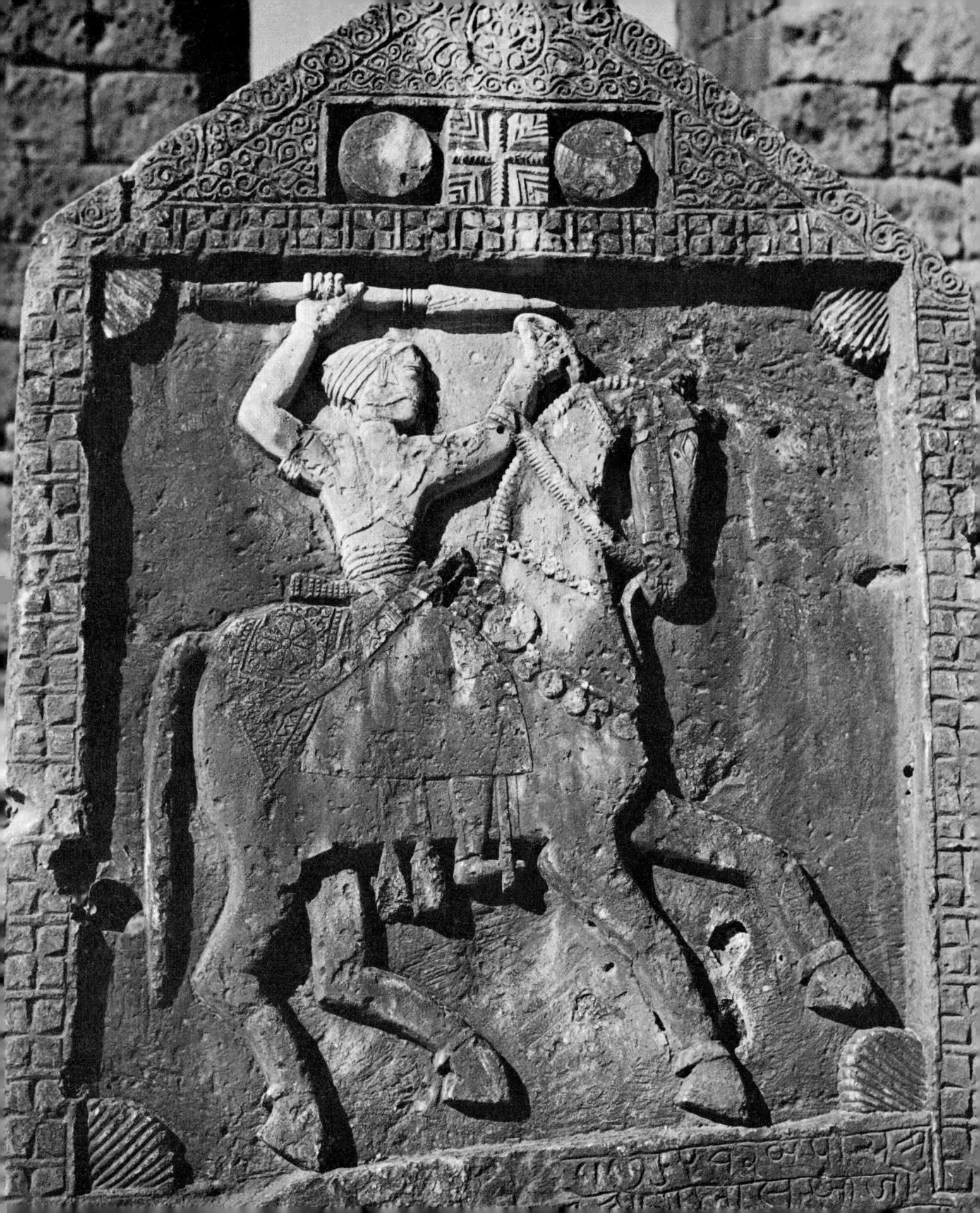

111 MEMORIAL STONE FOR A WARRIOR
India, seventeenth or eighteenth
century
(Vikram Dalal)

112 Photograph:
SIGN OUTSIDE FOREST
LAWN MEMORIAL PARK
(Picturepoint, London)

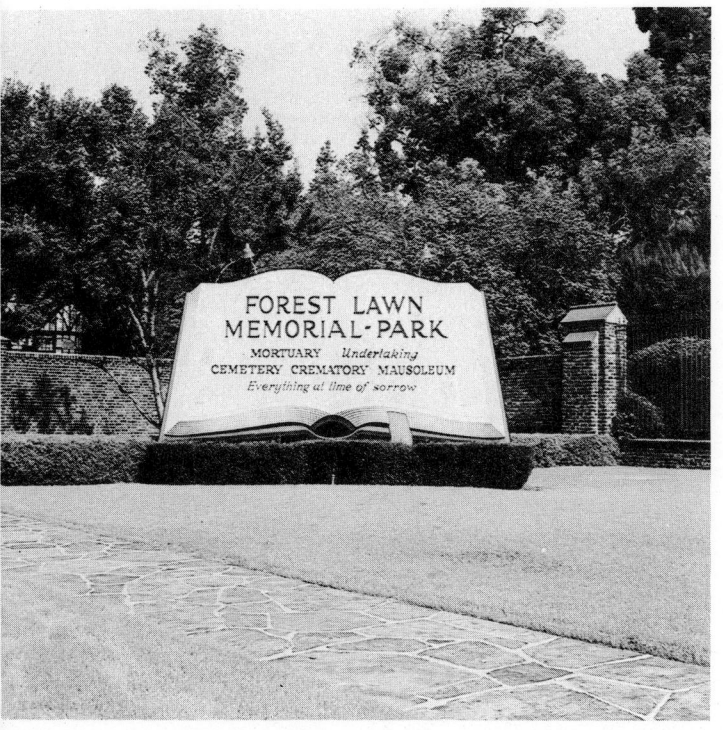

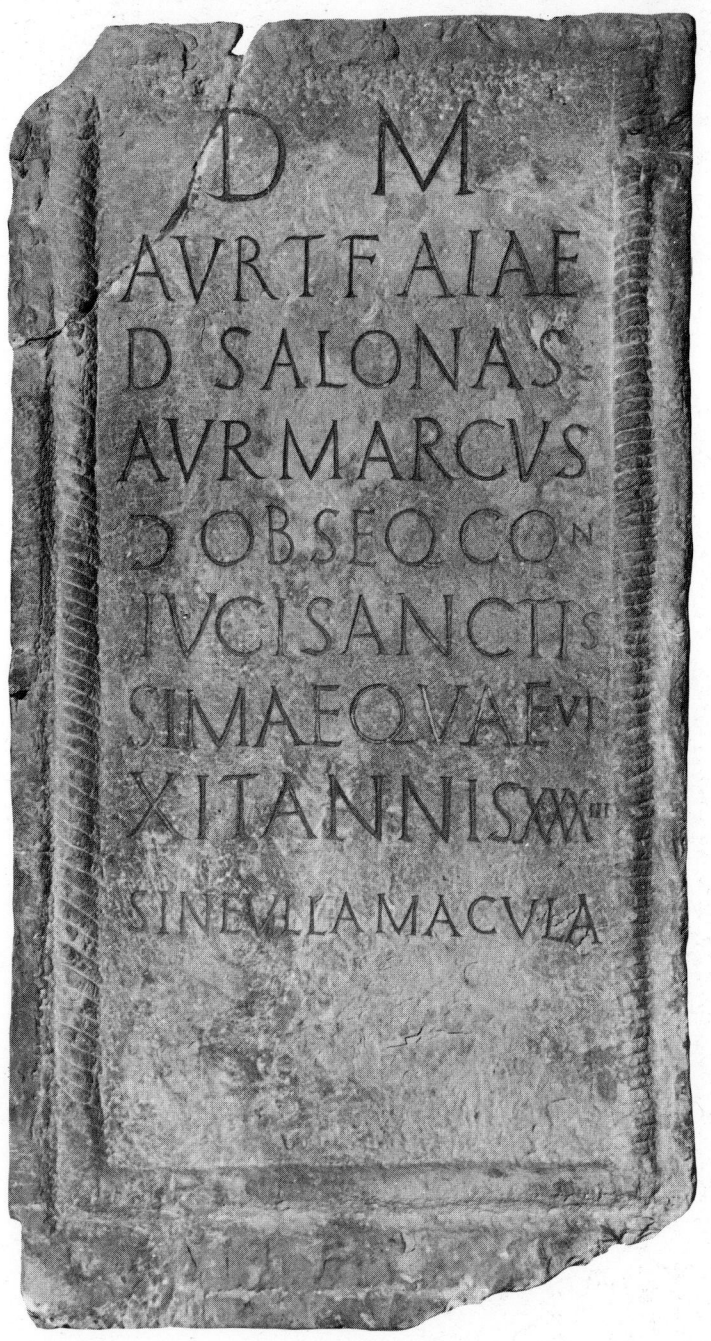

113 TOMBSTONE
Roman Britain, third century
(Museum of Antiquities, University of Newcastle
and Society of Antiquaries, Newcastle upon Tyne)

The stone bears the inscription: 'To
the deified souls of the dead [and to
the deified soul of] Aurelia Aia,
daughter of Titus, born at Solona [in
Yugoslavia]. Aurelius Marcus [soldier]
of the Century of Obsequens [erected
this] to his most holy wife who lived
33 years without any stain'.

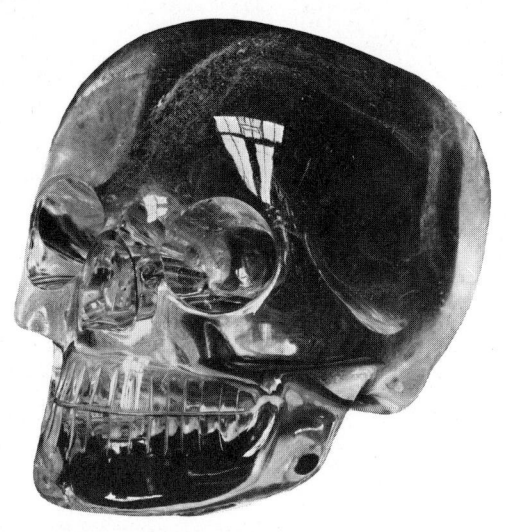

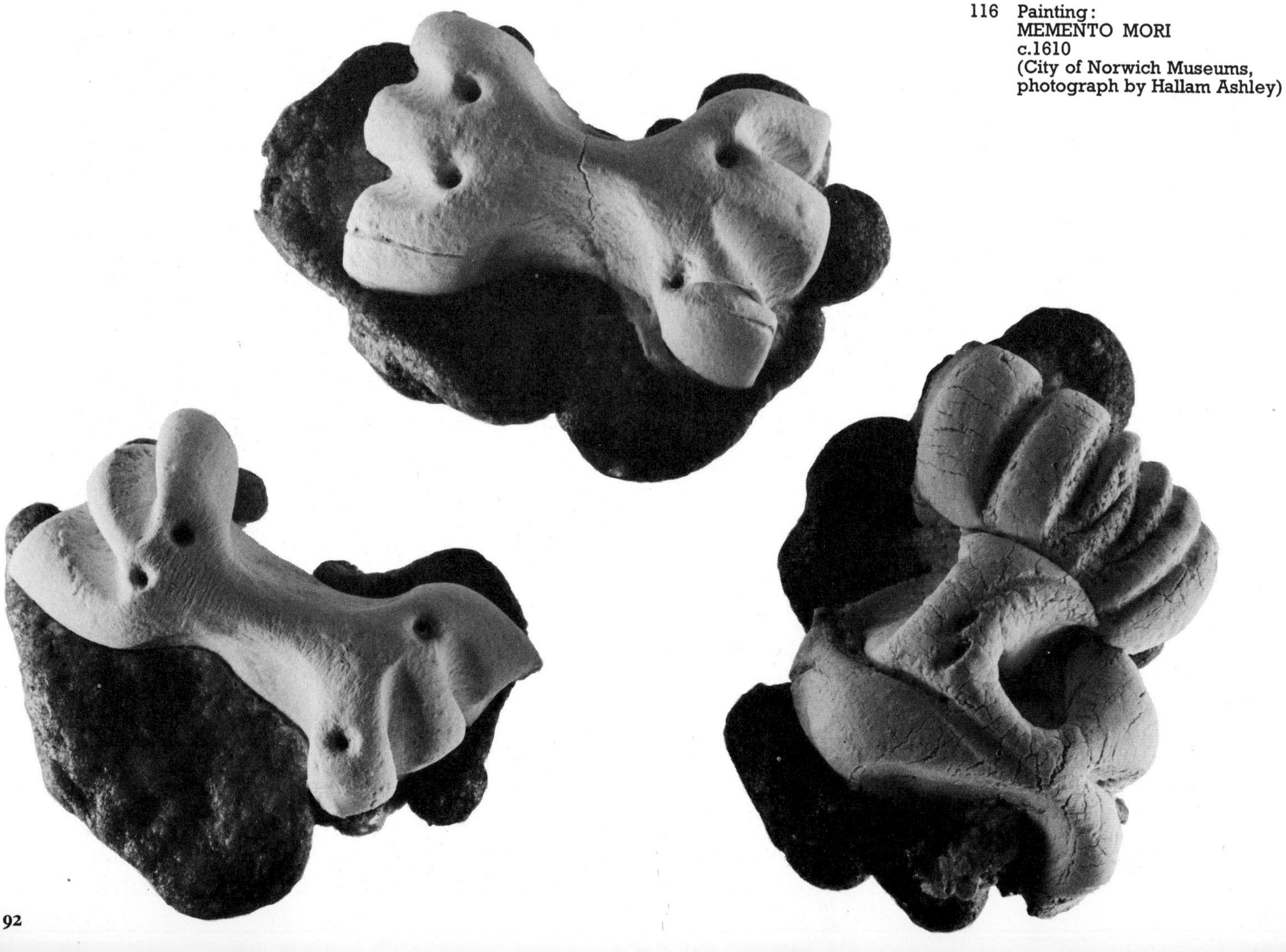

'**We shall die in these bodies.** I see
you living before me, with my mind's
eye, bretheren, I see your corpses:
those same bodies that sit there
before me are rows of corpses that
will be. And I that speak to you, you
hear and see me, you see me breathe
and move, this breathing body is my
corpse and I am living in my tomb.
This is one thing certain of your place
of death; you are there now, you sit
within your corpses; look no farther:
there where you are you will die.' –
Gerard Manley Hopkins, from **The
Sermons and Devotional Writings
of G.M.H.,** edited by Christopher
Devlin S.J. and published by the
Oxford University Press.

114   Sculpture:
       SKULL
       Aztec, Mexico
       (British Museum)

115   Cakes:
       OSSO DI MORTI (BONES OF
       THE DEAD)
       Sicily
       (from **Cookies and Breads:
       The Baker's Art,** Museum of
       Contemporary Crafts, New
       York: photograph by Ferdinand
       Boesch)

116   Painting:
       MEMENTO MORI
       c.1610
       (City of Norwich Museums,
       photograph by Hallam Ashley)

Lorde thow haste a poynted owte my lyfe
In length lyke as a span
Myne age is nothynge vnto thee
So vayne a thyng is Man

This myrrour meete for all mankynde
To viewe & still to beare in mynde
And do not mys

Man walketh lyke a shade and dothe
In vayne hym selffe annoy
In gettyng goods and cannot tell
Who shall the same enioye

For tyme brynges youthfull youthes to age
And age brings Deathe our herytage
When gods will ys

Consyder man howe tyme doth passe
And lykewyse knowe all flshe is grasse
For tyme consumes the strongeste oke
So deathe at laste shall stryke the stroke
Thoughe lustye youthe dothe bewtye beare
Yet youthe to age in tyme doth weare
And age at length a death will brynge
To Ryche, to Poore, Emprour, & Kynge
Therfore still lyue as thow sholdst Dye
Thy Soule to saue from Ieopardye
And as thow woldst be done vnto
So to thy neyghbour alwayes doo
The heauenlye Ioyes at lenghe to see
Lett fayth in Chryste thyne Ancor bee

The Lorde that made us knoweth our shape
Our moulde and fashion iuste
Howe weake and frayle our nature is
And howe webe but duste

And howe the tyme of mortall men
Is lyke the wytheringe haye
Or lyke the flower righte fayer in seilde
That vadethe soone away

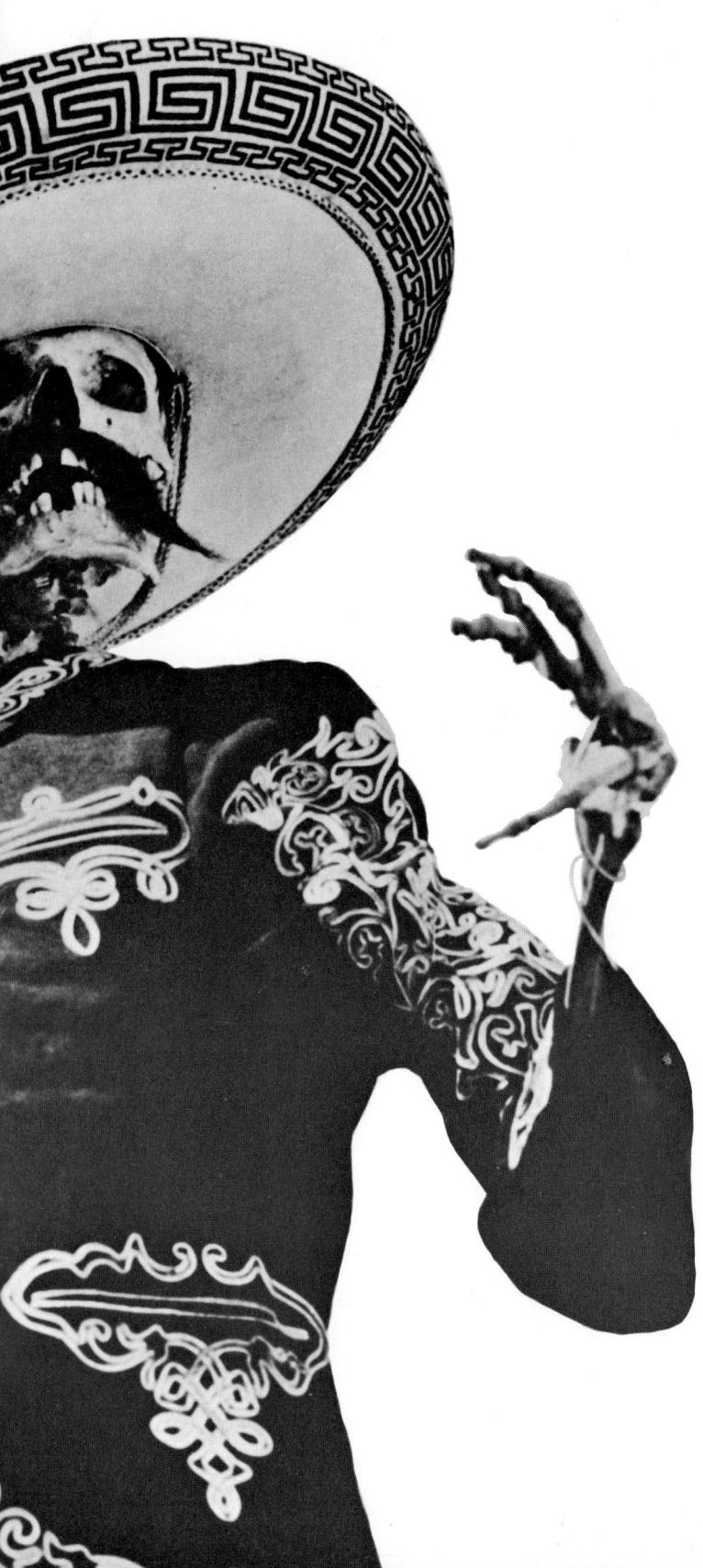

117   Detail from a film still:
from QUE VIVA MEXICO
Directed by Sergei Eisenstein,
1931
(National Film Archive)

118   Illustration:
SCENE FROM THE
APOCALYPSE (ANGELS
HARVESTING MEN)
from a seventeenth-century
manuscript
(British Museum)

119   Sculpture:
FIGURE OF DEATH WITH
DEATH CART
New Mexico, nineteenth century
(The American Museum in
Britain, Bath)

This figure was used by the
underground, and penitential,
Morada sect in New Mexico. B de L
Carey writes of the ceremonies of the
sect: 'The Brothers would have
chanted their way through the
Prophecies and Lamentations, each
of which is represented by a candle,
while the yucca scourges rose and
fell in the dim light, and as the final
candle at the apex, the one
representing Christ, was finally
extinguished as a symbol of His
death, so the matracas – the
noisemakers – rolled and thundered
in the darkness as the earthquake did
when He died. The Death Cart would
emerge with the Procession, filled
with stones and its axle fixed so that
it must be pulled by force – a good
penance over a rough road, and **La
Muerte** grinned from her perch as
she was drawn by. This figure of
death, clutching her bow and arrow,
was one of the most common features
of the old mystery plays adapted to
the Penitente Rite.'

120   Hat:
HOTO-KAMAPAH
Nicobar Islands
(Pitt Rivers Museum, University
of Oxford)

Decorative hats such as this were
placed on the skull of a disinterred
woman on the night of a final feast
held in her memory.

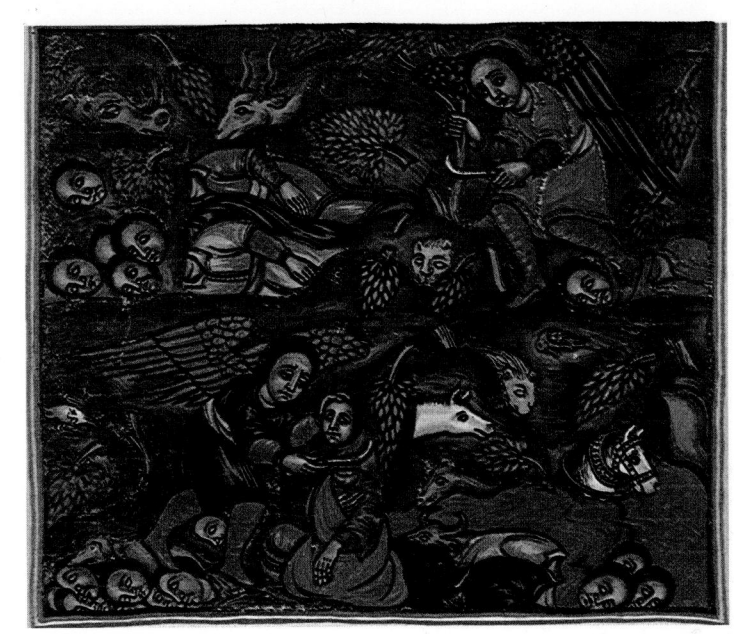

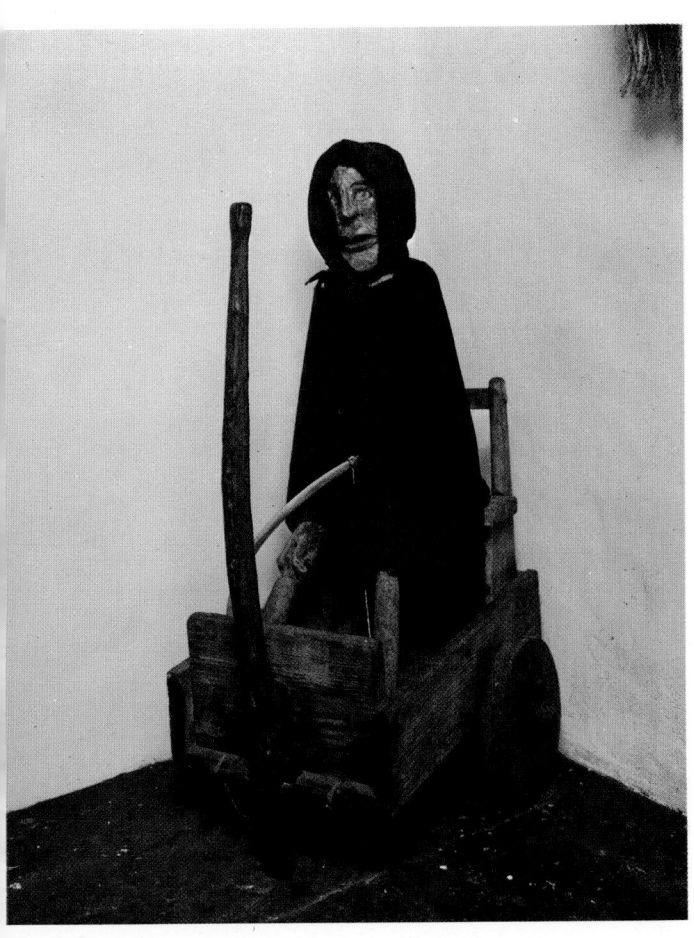

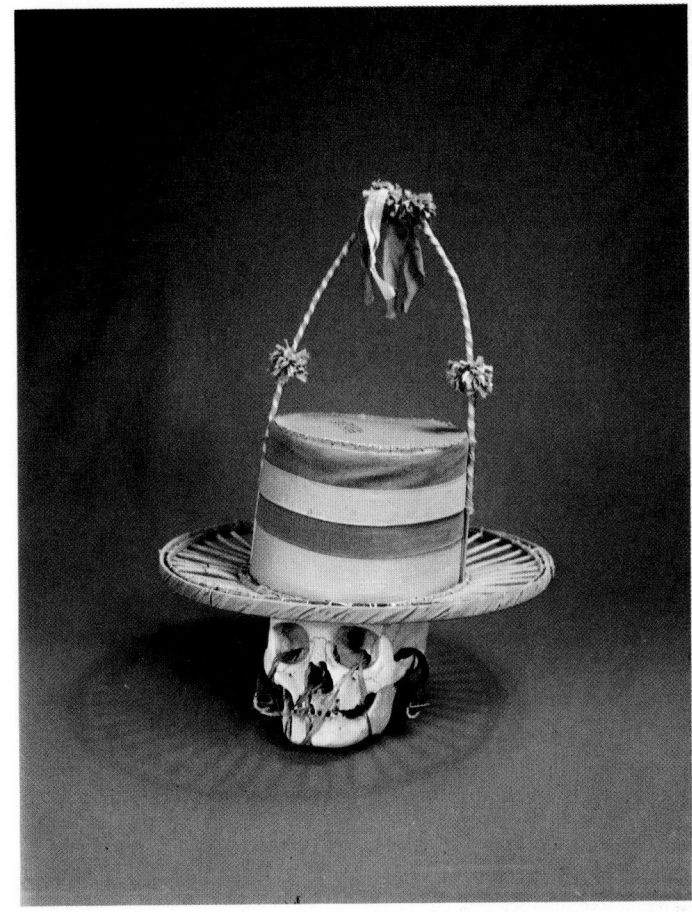

121   Embroidered text:
       GOD IS LOVE
       Wales, nineteenth century
       (Peter Jones)

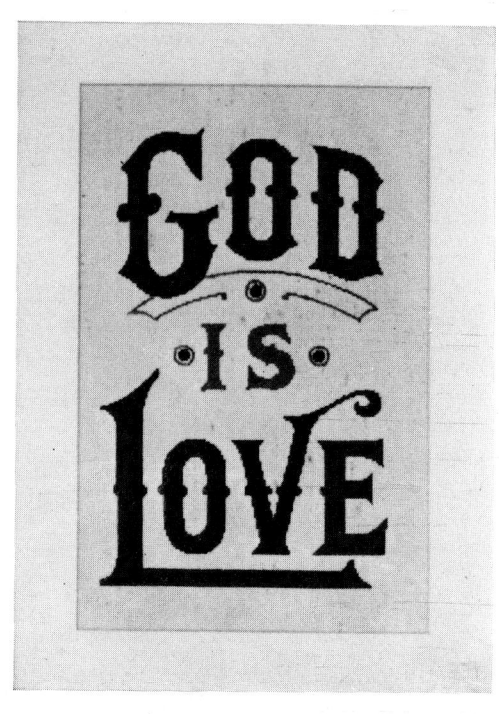